Performative Language Teaching in Early Education

Also available from Bloomsbury

Children's Literature and Learner Empowerment Children and Teenagers in English Language Education, Janice Bland
Essentials for Successful English Language Teaching, Thomas S. C. Farrell and George M. Jacobs
Language Education in the School Curriculum: Issues of Access and Equity, Ken Cruickshank, Stephen Black, Honglin Chen, Linda Tsung and Jan Wright
Process Drama for Second Language Teaching and Learning: A Toolkit for Developing Language and Life Skills, Patrice Baldwin and Alicja Galazka
Teaching English to Young Learners: Critical Issues in Language Teaching with 3–12 Year Olds, edited by Janice Bland
Using Graphic Novels in the English Language Arts Classroom, William Boerman-Cornell and Jung Kim
Using Literature in English Language Education: Challenging Reading for 8–18 Year Olds, edited by Janice Bland
Transforming the Teaching of Shakespeare with the Royal Shakespeare Company, Joe Winston

Performative Language Teaching in Early Education

Language Learning through Drama and the Arts for Children 3–7

Joe Winston

BLOOMSBURY ACADEMIC
LONDON • NEW YORK • OXFORD • NEW DELHI • SYDNEY

BLOOMSBURY ACADEMIC
Bloomsbury Publishing Plc
50 Bedford Square, London, WC1B 3DP, UK
1385 Broadway, New York, NY 10018, USA
29 Earlsfort Terrace, Dublin 2, Ireland

BLOOMSBURY, BLOOMSBURY ACADEMIC and the Diana logo are
trademarks of Bloomsbury Publishing Plc

First published in Great Britain 2022

Cover design: Toby Way
Cover image: © FatCamera/iStock

A catalogue record for this book is available from the British Library.

A catalog record for this book is available from the Library of Congress.

ISBN: HB: 978-1-3501-9916-3
PB: 978-1-3501-9915-6
ePDF: 978-1-3501-9918-7
eBook: 978-1-3501-9917-0

Typeset by Newgen KnowledgeWorks Pvt. Ltd., Chennai, India

To find out more about our authors and books visit www.bloomsbury.com
and sign up for our newsletters.

For Meri, Phoenix and Milo,

three early years language learners who love stories, each in

their own way a natural performer

CONTENTS

FIGURES

ACKNOWLEDGEMENTS

I am especially grateful to Didi 王美懿 Mei Yi Wang for inviting me to work with the teachers in her school, and for her advocacy of and passionate interest in drama education.

My gratitude extends to Eric 黄旭升 Yuk Sing Wong, Cherry 唐文婷 Wen Ting Tang, Jenny 刘嘉 Jia Liu, Christine 黄莉 Li Huang, William 叶逊谦 Yip and all the teachers at MEIYI RKEC.

I would also like to thank Gill Winston and Sally-Anne Taylor for their valuable feedback and comments; Professor Mei Chun Lin of National University Tainan; and Chenchen, Cleo, Ding Li, Donna, Echo and Marphy for their support and interest in my work with young children in China. I am grateful, too, to National Drama for first airing some of the material in this book in the Drama Magazine, Summer 2020, 26.2.

The photographs are the property of MEIYI RKEC and have been published with their permission, apart from Figures 6, 7, 10 and 14, which were taken during teachers' workshops and belong to the author.

The teachers who feature in the photos are Felicity MacLean, James Scott and Karina Semenenko.

Finally, I would like to express my gratitude to Maria Giovanna Brauzzi, Evangeline Stanford and Kalyani Kanekal at Bloomsbury for their help and advice during the writing of this book.

谢谢大家

ABBREVIATIONS

AO	age of onset
CEFR	Common European Framework of Reference for Languages
CLIL	Content and Language Integrated Learning
CLT	communicative language teaching
CPH	critical period hypothesis
EAL	English as an additional language
ECEC	early childhood education and care
EFL	English as a foreign language
ELA	English learning area
ELL	English language learning
ELP	European language portfolio
EMI	English as the Medium of Instruction
ESL	English as a second language
EYL	English for young learners
MEIYI RKEC	MEIYI Royal Kindergarten Education Centre
OECD	Organization for Economic Co-operation and Development
TESOL	Teaching English to Speakers of Other Languages
TEYL	Teaching English for Young Learners
TPR	Total Physical Response
UNDESA	United Nations Department of Economic and Social Affairs
UNESCO	United Nations Educational, Scientific and Cultural Organization

INTRODUCTION

This book has emerged from practical work with teachers in East Asia that I have been involved in since my retirement at the end of 2015 from full-time teaching and research at the University of Warwick. Most of this work has been in mainland China, where drama education has been going through a period of expansion, particularly in private and state-run kindergarten settings, attended by children in the age group of 3–6, where its use in support of the teaching of English is an area of keen and growing interest.

In my early teaching career I was a specialist in French as well as drama, but, although I practised a range of active, oral-based approaches, I never integrated the two fields in any systematic way. My subsequent work at the university provided me with the chance to develop expertise as a teacher trainer and researcher in primary and early years drama. The connection between drama, first language acquisition and the development of literacy has long been an area of attention, with many publications devoted to it.[1] Many of my own writings were also in this area before I began to consider seriously the relationship between drama and second language learning and this as editor of two broad-ranging volumes in the field rather than through my own projects.[2]

In 2018, I was invited by the Royal Kindergarten Education Centre (now renamed MEIYI Royal Kindergarten Education Centre, or MEIYI RKEC for short) to help devise a curriculum for drama that would support the teaching of English. The school was set up in 2007 by Mei Yi Wang and is situated in the city of Shenzhen, on the border with Hong Kong. It already had a Chinese drama curriculum in place, developed in partnership with Professor Mei Chun Lin, director of the Department of Arts in the National University, Tainan, in Taiwan. It is a very well-resourced school, where children are taught across the curriculum in English in the morning and in Chinese in the afternoon. It thus follows models known as Content and Language Integrated Learning (CLIL) and English as the Medium of

Instruction (EMI), and it includes as part of this lessons devoted specifically to learning English through drama. This complements the strong performance culture of the school, where shows have been staged annually and with very high production values for children of such a young age.

The practical work at the heart of this book has emerged from my work with MEIYI RKEC and is presented here as a guide for all teachers interested in using drama and other art forms as core pedagogies in the teaching of English, more specifically English as a foreign language (EFL), to very young learners. At its heart are a series of strategies used to craft schemes with both children's and teachers' needs in mind.

MEIYI RKEC follows a specific model of *immersion education*, where 50 per cent of the school day is taught in the second language. In such a model, language, culture and content are integrated and the languages employed for instruction – in this case Mandarin Chinese and English – are used by teachers fully proficient in them.[3] This approach to the teaching of English to very young learners is influential in East Asia, in countries such as Japan, South Korea and China and even in Hong Kong, where nearly all privately run kindergartens offer some form of immersion in English.[4] Murphy presents a global overview of these immersion programmes and points to their success in promoting 'bilingual proficiency, intercultural sensitivity and good academic outcomes'.[5] However, many young children learning English as a second language will be doing so in very different settings. If the children in MEIYI RKEC can be described as *majority language learners* – children who share a common, culturally dominant first language other than English – other majority language learners will not be in immersion programmes and will be receiving just one or two sessions of English a week. Still others can be categorized as *minority language learners*, children who are being taught in countries where English is the principal language but who speak a different language at home. In the United States, this language is commonly Spanish, in the UK it might be Urdu or Hindi or one of an increasing number of global languages spoken by economic migrants or other recent arrivals fleeing warfare and human rights abuses.

Although this book had its genesis in an immersive programme, I have attempted to take account of the diverse ways in which very young children are taught English by presenting strategies and adapting the schemes to be broadly applicable to very different settings. Informed as it is by the pattern in MEIYI RKEC of regularly making use of drama pedagogy, I see this as a model that can be informative for other, less privileged schools. As Murphy implies, the need to identify effective pedagogical techniques is important notwithstanding whether English is being taught in immersive programmes or otherwise.[6] This is particularly the case, perhaps, for those very young learners who are barely or not at all ready for reading, writing and the teaching of grammar, yet who nonetheless need some form of structured learning programme. Zhou and Ng point to the prevalence throughout East Asia of inappropriate methodologies that focus on copying and memorization, which fail to make learning English enjoyable, communicative and meaningful for children so young.[7] Similarly, Wong has pointed to an over-reliance on market forces in the same region, where English teaching often deploys such inappropriate processes as they tend to be those most recognizable and hence valued by parents as constituting visible signs of learning.[8] On the other hand, we might also recognize the inadequacy of a curriculum that focuses solely on language games, songs and colouring activities in an unstructured and repetitive manner. The schemes at the heart of this book, and the rationale that underpins them, are intended to help provide a sound alternative to such inappropriate pedagogies that fail to interest and motivate young learners or fail to offer them an adequate learning challenge.

Like many educationalists, those who write in the field of drama education are rightly concerned with issues of social justice and intercultural awareness. As such they may feel that the detailed schemes I outline are somewhat limited in range. The schemes are drawn from well-known children's texts, mostly picturebooks, which often illustrate Western and, in particular, British settings. In the context of an immersive programme offered by a Chinese kindergarten, this constituted the kind of intercultural programme they were seeking, but this would not be the case in the UK or the United States, where a more diverse set of stories and picturebooks will be seen as desirable. For this reason, in Chapter 3, I draw upon a more diverse range of stories and sources to illustrate specific performative strategies and also provide reasons for regarding cultural relevance and diversity as not solely dependent upon the settings and illustrations of specific stories. I also reference a number of websites that list a range of picturebooks specifically addressing different aspects of diversity. As I point out, not all of these books will lend themselves readily to the performative potential we find in the detailed schemes of work, but all can contribute to a balanced curriculum by being read and displayed and by perhaps making use of just a few of the approaches presented in Chapter 3.

The English teachers at MEIYI RKEC are young and outgoing, and many come from countries such as the UK, the United States or Australia, thus having English as a first language. Others come from European countries but demonstrate a high competence in English. They all, however, face different challenges on being asked to incorporate drama into their English teaching. Not all have been trained in early years settings or to teach English as a second language, and some have had no real experience of drama or the performing arts, either as a personal interest or as a teaching methodology. The school therefore employed me to provide a series of training workshops to accompany and inform the development and implementation of these schemes and to observe and support actual classroom practice.

Research globally shows that the levels of expertise and training needs of EFL teachers in pre-primary and early primary settings are not dissimilar to that of the staff in MEIYI RKEC. Zhou and Ng point to a persistent view in

East Asia, where native speakers of English, including those with no teaching qualifications, are more likely to be employed than well-qualified, local, non-native English speakers. They also cite research conducted in 2008 in Taiwan showing that only 27 per cent of primary school English teachers had a qualification in the teaching of English and that 25 per cent held neither an English nor a general primary school teaching qualification.[9] In Europe, Murphy points to extensive research carried out in 2006 by the European Commission, in which 35 per cent of respondents were found to have no qualification to teach young children and 21 per cent were unqualified to teach a foreign language. However, 79 per cent did express a desire for further professional development courses.[10] More recent research in the UK, published by the Sutton Trust, has shown that the number of qualified staff in early childhood education and care (ECEC) has been declining significantly.[11]

Training may well be needed, but its success is never guaranteed. Zhou and Ng write of the resistance of many pre-primary and primary teachers of English in East Asia when faced with the introduction of communicative or task-based approaches to teaching English. This, they point out, has often been underpinned by values, by their being unconvinced of the worth of such methods, by the demands they place on classroom and time management and by their lack of confidence in being able to implement them successfully. If professional development is to be successful, teachers need to be adaptive and receptive to change, have a desire to improve their professional expertise and have positive attitudes towards teaching in general.[12] Not all teachers will be fortunate enough to be offered the kind of in-house input teachers in MEIYI RKEC have received from experienced teacher trainers. However, if you are a teacher or teacher educator and are sufficiently interested to be reading this now, it is perhaps enough of an indication that you are open to the kind of pedagogy the book promotes. This is perhaps the most important first step and is why, in the chapters that focus directly on practice, I assume no prior knowledge of performative approaches to teaching on the part of the reader and provide step-by-step guidance and advice throughout, intended to address common concerns to do with classroom and time management, sequencing learning and adapting material to specific contexts. It is my experience that once teachers see how well children engage with and respond to performative language pedagogy, many are quickly won over and want to make it part of their overall skill set.

Finding correct terminologies to define the contours of this book has not been straightforward. English as a second language (ESL) is generally applied to children learning English in countries where it is not the national language and who share one majority language, as in MEIYI RKEC. English as an additional language (EAL) applies more specifically to those children who speak minority languages at home while receiving their education in English in countries such as the UK and Australia. In the United States the most common acronym is ELL (English language learning). Although I make use of these specific terms, I have tended to prefer two drawn from recent publications, though they are not themselves new:[13] English as a foreign language, which does not assume that children have only one other language at home and therefore has a broader application; and English for young learners (EYL). The latter is used to refer to children in the age group of 3–12, whereas this book clearly limits it to the age range of 3–7, but I am nonetheless drawn to the term's inclusivity, embracing as it does not only young EFL learners but also those other children who, for different reasons, may need systematic attention with their vocabulary development and structural language use. In fact, one of my intentions while writing the book has been to make it generally relevant to the social and linguistic development of all children, including those with English as a first language. And as the book's focus is pedagogy, I make some use of the acronym TEYL (Teaching English for Young Learners) in preference to the less specific TESOL (Teaching English to Speakers of Other Languages).

'Early childhood education' is a fluid term. It is used by UNESCO to refer to education from birth to the start of formal schooling and has more recently been superseded by the term 'early childhood education and care'.[14] 'Pre-primary education' is used more specifically to describe programmes for children from the age of 3 to the start of their primary schooling. In the UK, however, this begins at 4 years of age; in China and other East Asian countries at the age of 6, while in the Nordic countries it is 7. The term 'kindergarten' in the East Asian context is less problematic as it caters to children specifically between the ages of 3 and 6. 'Young children' and 'young learners' are rather vague terms. Three important books I draw upon use them to embrace the years of pre-primary and primary education up to puberty, from 3 to 11 or 12 years of age, and refer to 'the early school years' to include the same period.[15] At times I use phrases such as 'very young children' or 'very young learners' to refer specifically to those in pre-primary settings. Including projects targeted at children up to the age of 7, rather than stopping at the age of 6, has also allowed me to make use of work developed for slightly older children in the early years of primary education and is intended to signal the relevance of the book beyond kindergarten, embracing as it does all of Key Stage 1 in the UK.

This introduction has sketched out the scope and specific intentions of the book. These are essentially practical, aimed at providing approaches and detailed schemes of learning for teachers and teacher educators to trial and adapt for themselves. However, no teaching is devoid of theoretical underpinnings, and the first two chapters are intended to provide a rationale sufficiently robust to justify and explain the efficacy of what I am calling 'performative language teaching'. This is not a term I have coined, but, once again, it is its inclusivity that I am drawn to, embracing as it does a range of strategies that include the dramatic but also make use of music, art, movement, games, storytelling and other established early years practices that go under the broad heading of play.

Chapter 1, then, draws on studies that have specifically concentrated on issues that inform how young children learn English as a second language in pre-primary and early primary settings. In order to narrow down the focus here, I have concentrated on a small range of studies that provide robust empirical evidence that can be used to support the kind of performative approaches I will later promote. These are drawn from educators who have researched TEYL in settings that include both majority and minority language learners. The importance they place on social learning and on the role of play and playfulness for such children are key unifying factors that will point to the relevance of the performative strategies at the heart of the book.

In Chapter 2 I present a theoretical rationale for performative language teaching that draws directly from the fields of drama and performance studies, relating them to the concerns of teachers of young children. Terminologies such as performativity, embodiment and aesthetics can be off-putting to many non-specialists in the field, so I have tried to keep the concepts as straightforward as possible and the language accessible, while making clear their relevance and significance to actual early years practice.

The following three chapters form the practical core of the book. Chapter 3 describes the teaching strategies that constitute the building blocks of performative language pedagogy for young children. These include songs, rhymes, games, drama strategies, storytelling and music activities, all clearly described and exemplified with commentaries as to how they can be adapted to fit within a range of fictional frameworks. As previously stated, I am assuming on the part of the reader neither any prior knowledge of drama teaching nor acquaintance with the strategies being promoted. Knowing how intimidated teachers sometimes are by the classroom management of such active approaches, I also provide substantial commentaries on how they can be organized efficiently.

A similar amount of detail and explanation is included in Chapters 4 and 5, which outline schemes of work, nine in all, five aimed at children between the ages of 3 and 5, and four at the older age range. Three key ideas here are the centrality of good stories to appeal to children's imaginations, hold their attention and engage them both cognitively and emotionally with the learning; the importance of shaping the narrative rhythm of the lesson to do the same; and the careful use of performative activities to bring the fictional world to life in the classroom. Language learning is always in the foreground but is never in my approach de-contextualized from these three central pedagogic concerns.

There is no such thing as a typical class of children, of course. The schemes will need to be adapted into specific settings and should not be seen as recipes to be blindly adhered to without due attention being paid to the specific language and social needs of the children being taught. In the form presented, they are best suited to children working in immersive settings, as either majority or minority language learners. For children with less exposure to English, some adaptation and translanguaging may well be necessary. That said, my experience of teaching in many different countries and cultures reassures me that there is much broadly in common in what interests, motivates and makes very young learners feel secure enough to use and practise new language. The schemes, as presented here, have been scrutinized by experienced teachers from pre-primary and early primary settings in different countries, so I remain confident in what they have to offer.

Chapter 6 addresses the important, though often vexed issue of assessment. I use the term 'assessment for learning' in the title to indicate the thrust of my argument – that assessment will be of little use unless it feeds directly into and improves the learning process. For this purpose, I propose a straightforward and manageable model for assessing these schemes of work, one that teachers should not see as time consuming and burdensome but rather as a serviceable way to sharpen their practice and make their teaching more effective.

How I address the reader varies somewhat between the chapters. While covering more theoretical issues, as I do in Chapters 1 and 2 and in parts of Chapter 6, I generally use a more indirect form of address, referring to 'the teacher' or 'teachers'. This changes in Chapters 3–5, where I address the reader more directly, as 'you', this being more appropriate to the direct, practical and friendly advice I am offering.

Books advocating the use of drama and other performative approaches are sometimes evangelical in their enthusiasm, making very broad and insistent claims about the wonderful results they can generate. This can be irritating for educators outside the immediate field who are often mistrustful of such evangelism, and it can serve to deepen rather than alleviate their scepticism. I am anxious to resist any claims that this approach to teaching EFL is the best, or the only valid one, or is in any way a panacea for early years teachers. It is demanding, requires thought and preparation, the gathering or making of different resources, and commitment and belief on the part of teachers. But as part of a structured learning programme I believe it has much to offer TEYL. For teachers, it can invigorate their pedagogy, develop their creative energies and foster their capacity for play. For children, it can tap into their natural enthusiasm and provide them with a sense of fulfilment and collaborative enjoyment. It can generate a classroom atmosphere that is both productive and a joy to be part of, for teachers and young learners alike. This is my sincere belief but it takes commitment, time and energy to make it work. If you are ready for the challenge, I am confident that you will find the journey worthwhile.

CHAPTER ONE

Young Children Learning English as a Foreign Language

A Growing Global Trend

The widespread provision of ECEC has increased internationally over recent years as, globally, more and more women join the workforce and education continues to be seen as key to prosperity. In 2019, for example, 87 per cent of 3- to 5-year-olds in forty-two OECD countries were enrolled in pre-primary education in establishments that met internationally recognized standards, which include an adequate level of intentional educational properties; at least two hours of educational activities each day; a relevant and recognized curriculum; and trained or accredited staff.[1]

As this overall provision of ECEC has been growing, so too has the teaching of EFL in pre-primary and early primary settings. While English is currently only the fourth most spoken language in the world by native speakers (after Mandarin Chinese, Hindi and Spanish), when non-native speakers are included, it has over 1,500 million speakers, far more than any other language.[2] Effectively, English has become the language of globalization, and this has sparked a trend to teach it at ever earlier ages, driven not only by governmental policy decisions but also by parental pressure as it is seen as the main international language of trade, commerce and culture. In the words of Shelagh Rixon, 'Increasing the grasp within a nation of a politically and economically important subject such as English sounds to many politicians and their public to be an uncontroversially desirable proposition.'[3] As countries become more international in their outlook, being competent in English is seen as increasingly important in furthering business and commercial opportunities in the eyes of politicians, and in promising opportunities for their children to study abroad and attain better job prospects in the eyes of many parents. In East Asia, the urge parents have shown in recent years for their children to learn English from a very young age has become so notable that words such as 'craze', 'frenzy' and 'fever' have been used to describe it.[4]

Another undeniable factor impacting on the numbers of very young EFL learners has emanated from the increasing flow across borders of migrants and international refugees. The United Nations Department of Economic and Social Affairs (UNDESA) estimated the number of migrants globally at 272 million in 2019, up 40 million over the previous six-year period. Many arrive from non-English speaking countries to those where English is the language of instruction. For example, 58.6 million of this total is located in North America.[5]

In China, English was introduced in cities and suburban areas as a compulsory subject from the age of 6 upwards in 2001 and rolled out into rural areas a year later.[6] For many native English speakers, 6 would seem to be a very young age to begin to learn a foreign language, but in China, Japan and South Korea, for many ambitious parents, it is not seen as early enough. Consequently, the provision of English teaching in kindergarten classes for children between the ages of 3 and 6 has become increasingly common in urban areas and is now seen as a feature of overall first-rate educational provision.[7] This reflects not only the perception of the high stakes of English learning but also a commonly held belief that, indeed, the earlier one starts to learn a foreign language, the easier it is and the more competent one will become in its use. And the phenomenon is not simply noticeable in East Asia. In research conducted in 2012, which involved 2,500 kindergarten teachers in forty-nine non-English speaking countries, over half of the respondents stated that children began to learn English at the age of 6 or earlier.[8]

The social and cultural pressures that young migrant children face while attempting to learn English will, of course, be very different from those faced by the relatively privileged children whose parents are pushing them to learn English, but one fundamental question remains the same: when learning a foreign language, is starting younger a benefit in and of itself?

English for Young Learners: Does 'Younger' Equate with 'Better'?

'Everyone knows that with languages the earlier you start, the easier they are.'[9] This statement from 1999, by the then UK prime minister Tony Blair, reflects a generally held 'common-sense' view based on the ease with which children appear naturally to acquire remarkable competence in their first language compared with the difficulty many older children and adults seem to face when trying to learn a second. This assumption has driven both parental pressure and policy decision-making in East Asia and has received theoretical support through the concept of a 'critical period hypothesis' (CPH), first developed in 1967 by Lenneberg. He proposed that the crucial age for picking up and processing a new language lies between the ages of 2 and 12, after which the human brain finds it more difficult.[10] Subsequent proponents of CPH narrowed its boundaries by suggesting that the age of onset (AO) begins at birth, with the offset at around the ages of 5 or 6 years. Still more studies, focused on the neurology of the brain, have proposed that the optimal period is later, from 6 to pre-puberty, due to the 'furious growth' in the language area of the brain that characterizes these years.[11] Rather than argue about the existence or otherwise of rigidly determined, onset and offset boundaries, other educators have come to prefer the idea of a 'sensitive' rather than a 'critical' period of acquisition, whose age-related boundaries are more fluid.[12] This theory still suggests that the young brain is hardwired to facilitate second language acquisition in ways that become less effective after the child reaches maturity.

However, more recently, Singleton and Pfenninger have questioned the validity of theories that stress 'hard-wired' maturation as the major determinant to learning a foreign language successfully. They point to numerous examples of research worldwide that show how many students who start at secondary school level perform equally as well as those who start much earlier, commenting that 'there is much more to age than maturation, and that age-related social, psychological and contextual factors may play as significant a role as maturational factors'.[13] Referring to a range of research projects, they conclude:

> in an educational context, age of onset (AO) has been found to interact with school effects or treatment variables (e.g. type of instruction) as well as micro-contextual variables such as classroom and clustering effects.[14]

In other words, although young children may well have a propensity for acquiring language, their learning environment, social skills and how well they are taught can be of equal significance.

A recent example that illustrates this can be seen in a study that focused on minority language speaking children in Australian preschool settings. Here, Oliver and Nguyen support the concept of a sensitive period of language acquisition, observing that younger learners can learn grammatical rules intuitively given the right kind of exposure to the target language.[15] But they also point to features in children's interactions with one another, such as the way they will play with and repeat language patterns in their talk, particularly when working on content-specific tasks together, as key features in the effectiveness of their learning of a new language. This kind of group interactivity and social learning they see as particularly advantageous to preschool learners. They emphasize the importance of social interaction, of using the language for meaningful communication and of specific contexts for learning that make it enjoyable as well as meaningful, such as learning through play in structured classroom settings.

We might reasonably postulate that any learning in an educational setting, linguistic or otherwise, will result from a combination of innate and social influences, supported by structured opportunities for language use; and this would appear to be reflected internationally in the ways most ECEC settings are organized. Here, Murao has pointed to the two philosophical traditions at either end of a continuum, the one showing a teacher-led focus on preparing children for 'school-readiness skills' such as literacy and numeracy, the other more child-centred, emphasizing broad educational goals learned through play and interactivity with adults and peers. If the former emphasizes the attainment of cognitive skills, the latter encourages the child's social and cognitive well-being. She then makes the important point that, in practice, most fall somewhere between the two extremes.[16] This is certainly the case with settings such as MEIYI RKEC, in which teacher-led activities and structured, interactive play characterize the progression of the school day.

Second Language Learning in the Early Years of Education: A Cognitive and Social Process

Patton O. Tabors is a Harvard scholar who has conducted long-term research with minority language learners in a pre-primary setting in the United States, all of whom were recent arrivals in the country.[17] In her account she provides clear and detailed examples of such learning in action. In doing so, she emphasizes the need for these children to receive the kind of support that will help them become socially effective communicators. Indeed, her study suggests that communicative competence and social competence are so closely related as to be of equal importance in a child's learning a new language and she looks in detail not only at those outgoing, confident children who make the kind of rapid progress in communicating in a target language that commentators such as Tony Blair have been so impressed by, but also attends to those children who are much slower to do so. Her study points to the need for teachers to embrace the twin aims of cultivating a willingness in the child to take risks with the target language and of helping them become motivated to want to learn it. Exposure to the target language may not be sufficient in and of itself; and this, I would argue, is applicable to majority language children learning English in immersive environments such as RKEC as well as for minority language children in English speaking countries. The teacher's job of care, Tabors emphasizes, is to help all her children achieve their potential while recognizing that there will always be differences in their levels of attainment; and this is, of course, true of all teachers in all settings.

We have seen so far, then, that the rapid spread of ECEC, and EFL as part of that provision, is an internationally recognizable phenomenon; and that, although there is evidence to support the commonly held view that early childhood is a good age for learning a second language, this should not be regarded as a natural and inevitable process, dependent solely upon exposure. We have seen, too, that most preschool settings and kindergartens are set up to provide a balance between structured learning and freer, social opportunities for playful interaction, a combination of which can be deployed to enable foreign language learning. If children's attainment is not simply to rely on innate aptitude or personality traits, then teachers must structure learning opportunities that cultivate a willingness to use the language and motivation to learn it. Instrumental motivation, relying on the parental idea that English is an important examination subject and can advance career prospects, is signally inappropriate for inspiring young children, of course. What matters is that their experience of English feels enjoyable and rewarding in itself as well as a learning process; hence the need for models of good practice in the early years of education.

When considering such examples, Murao points to several studies that advocate a range of activities, most of which I will later embrace as aspects of my own performative pedagogy – 'songs, rhymes, riddles and chants, craft activities, games and Total Physical Response activities, stories, project work, puppets and drama activities.' Importantly, she sees such practices as shared characteristics of good educational practice worldwide 'though interpreted by different cultural groups according to their own cultural meaning'. She quotes UNESCO guidance that stresses the need for programmes that should be holistic, supporting 'children's early cognitive, physical, social and emotional development'. A key characteristic of such practice will be 'interaction with peers and educators, through which children improve their use of language and social skills.' The UNESCO guidance also points to the importance of play-based activities, which, she says 'thus far is rarely discussed in relation to pre-primary language learning.'[18]

Murao's subsequent discussion of what such playful activities might consist of will be looked at in more detail later, but at this point I would like to highlight how, in this guidance, language and social development are twinned together. This will form a key part of the rationale for my own pedagogy, but by attending first of all to research that has looked specifically at the processes of foreign language learning and the specific pedagogies that have been promoted for its furtherance with young children, we will see evidence of how, in particular, the twin aspects of language learning and developing social skills are intimately connected; and how traditional ways of teaching grammar and vocabulary need to be rethought in their more formal teaching contexts. This is intended to provide a firm foundation upon which to build a rationale for performative pedagogy that will not only help justify its approaches as a whole but also elucidate specific aspects of its practice.

How Young Children Learn a New Language

Progressive Stages in Speaking a Second Language

Very usefully, Tabors describes a language system as a puzzle with five inter-locking pieces, 'all of which must fit together for the puzzle to be complete':[19]

1. *Phonology*, or the sounds of the language
2. *Vocabulary*, or the words of the language
3. *Grammar*, or how the words are put together to make sentences in the language
4. *Discourse*, or how sentences are put together to, for example, tell stories, make an argument, or explain how something works
5. *Pragmatics*, or the rules of how to use language

She points out that even very young second language learners have already mastered all these aspects of their first language; but, she argues, they may well be hampered in their learning of this new language if they lack social competence, for, she suggests, *communicative* competence, which includes gestural as well as verbal skills, is so closely related to *social* competence that it is impossible to separate them. In fact, the tactics she observes the children using in her study in order successfully to integrate themselves socially into groups where they can hear, understand and then begin to use their new language are not only pertinent to minority language speakers but also highly informative to TEYL in majority language settings, as they illuminate how all young children can get started in a new language.

Firstly, she notes a non-verbal but communicative gestural phase, which she observed children using in order to gain attention, make requests, pro-test and joke, persistently if not always successfully. She then notes two fur-ther non-verbal stages in which they 'gather data' about the new language which she calls spectating and rehearsing. In the spectating stage children are quiet but not uninvolved in what is happening linguistically around them as they watch, listen and gather data intensely. This is followed by a rehears-ing stage in which they often repeat what they have just heard, developing their receptive abilities, understanding the sound and meanings of the new language before attempting to communicate in it. The next phase she calls 'sound experimentation', as children begin to mimic the sounds of the new language in a variety of ways, rather like baby talk but evidently displaying enjoyment in the process. Interestingly, she refers to one young Korean boy experimenting in this way and likens it to 'practicing the tune – the sounds and intonation patterns of English – before learning all the words of the new song'.[20] In this preverbal phase, then, it is noticeable how she makes a strik-ing use of language associated with performance – gestural communication, spectating, rehearsing and musical experimentation with the sounds, tones and rhythms of the new language.

When children begin to speak the new language, she notes further stages of development as they attempt to communicate in it. Firstly, she draws a distinction between *telegraphic* and *formulaic* speech. Speech is telegraphic when children use 'a few content words as an entire utterance'. Colours, numbers and simple naming words such as 'car' or 'chair', accompanied by a physical gesture that indicates whether it is an inquiry or a confirmatory statement, are the basic skills children are rehearsing here. With formulaic speech, they use 'unanalysed chunks of formulaic phrases' in situations they have observed them being used in. Phrases such as 'My turn!', 'Me first', 'Not fair' and 'Be careful' allow children to be expressive in their communication before moving on to what she calls 'productive language use' when they begin to generate 'creatively constructed phrases'.[21] These make use of formulaic phrases and simple verbs that may be grammatically wrong but enable children nonetheless to communicate clearly expressions of pleasure, want or need.

This developmental process she describes as cumulative, meaning that the stages are not neatly compartmentalized, one ceasing as the next begins. Instead, children add skills to the previous techniques in order to bring 'a range of communicative possibilities to any situation, giving them the best possible chance of getting their meaning across'.[22] It is also worth noting here that, although only in simple terms, all five aspects of language use have been in play during this process. Play with the phonology of the language is at times distinct from attempts to communicate with it; vocabulary use is combined with other communicative processes, which include gesture and use of objects; grammar may be faulty, discourse may be simple but children's pragmatic use of the language is appropriate in the way they question or express themselves affectively.

The Interaction between Social and Linguistic Goals in Young Children

In moving on to consider how children combine cognitive and social strategies in order to learn a second language, an important study by Wong Fillmore reported how five Spanish speaking children made different levels of progress in the same English speaking setting, concluding that 'the individual differences found among the five learners ... had to do with the way in which cognitive and social factors of language acquisition interact together'.[23] As a result she proposed a list of successful strategies, listed as maxims, as though the children had written them themselves. Notably, she lists cognitive and social strategies separately but in ways that work together.[24] The cognitive strategies include maxims such as 'Get some expressions you understand and start talking', 'Make the most of what you've got' and 'Work on big things, save the details for later'. The three key social strategies she defines thus:

- Join a group and act as if you understand what's going on, even if you don't.

- Give the impression with a few chosen words you speak the language.

- Count on your friends for help.

If we were to reinterpret these maxims as advice for teaching English to young learners, we might suggest the following:

- Make sure that children have every opportunity to feel secure in the language class and are not given individual exposure before they are ready.

- Ensure children are provided with scenarios for successful communicative language use at all stages.

- Provide a secure atmosphere in the class and give children plenty of opportunities to learn together and feel positive about belonging to a group.

This list will be of particular significance to performative language teaching, as we shall see in more detail later.

Philip and Duschene cite Wong Fillmore in their study, which focuses on the interaction between social and linguistic goals in young children's second language learning.[25] They, too, see linguistic, social and cognitive growth as interconnected and stress the importance of two key social goals that involve language use, namely affiliation and social positioning. They emphasize the importance of peer acceptance for children both in developing their social skills and in providing opportunities for them to further their language competence. In their study, based in a primary school classroom, of a 6-year-old Ethiopian girl Yessara, recently adopted by an Australian family, they note three ways in which both her teachers and peer group help her linguistically through their social interactions. The first of these is 'scaffolding', a process by which a more experienced user of the language was able to help her perform a task that was otherwise still beyond her linguistic means; the second was 'recasting', by which Yessara's interlocutor would reformulate her speech in a way that retained its meaning while correcting its linguistic form; and the third was 'negotiated interaction', by which the speaker would make conversational adjustments – perhaps paraphrasing or repeating segments to clarify meaning in ways that were accepted by Yessara.

Their study noted how playful uses of repetition and mimicry between Yessara and her peers were applied to cement friendships and as a mark of solidarity between them. Significantly, this worked both ways, with both Yessara and her English speaking peers enjoying imitating one another and trying to make the same sounds as each other, such as the way that Yessara would roll her /r/ in the word 'rubber'. What is interesting here is how the children enjoyed the aesthetics of making, sharing and copying verbal sounds independent of meaning, as small pieces of music, and the positive communal effects such playful sharing brought. Such performative uses of rhymes, chants and singing can constitute patterns of play that incorporate second language use and patterns of affiliation, reciprocity and mutuality that bolster the desire to communicate.[26]

Young Children Learning Grammar and Vocabulary in a Second Language

The examples of language learning above indicate how young minority language speakers can successfully learn English through incidental learning, in surroundings where English is spoken as the prime language of communication. This naturalistic approach would appear to reflect Krashen's emphasis on language *acquisition* rather than language learning, acquired through what he termed 'comprehensible input', focusing on meaning rather than grammatical structures. As we saw in the examples above, comprehensible input needs to be nurtured socially and can be seen to have its own processes of progression. Key to the child making progress in the language are emotional states: fear and nervousness of making errors will be detrimental, positive feelings about being able to understand and communicate in the language will accelerate their level of communicative capability which, over time, will become increasingly accurate.

Although a young child learning a foreign language in a majority speaking classroom, for maybe just an hour a week or less, faces very different challenges, the notion that input should be largely comprehensible to young learners is now generally accepted as crucial. Young children below the age of 10 do not yet have the cognitive analytical capabilities to learn a language through the teaching of its grammatical rules and are unable to think about language in abstract or explicit terms.[27] This means that any attempt to teach grammar to them must be dealt with in very different ways.

The emphasis on comprehensible input has had a major impact on the teaching of foreign languages in recent years, with the development of communicative competence in learners replacing a more grammar-oriented approach. Communicative language teaching (CLT) conceives a second language as best taught 'not primarily through memorization but through meaningful tasks involving real communication'.[28] The influence of CLT, which has thankfully impacted on the teaching of young learners, has not, however, brought with it any solid agreement about the place of the teaching of grammar. Puchta suggests that there are still two opinions – that grammar needs to be taught formally versus grammar cannot be taught and will take care of itself so long as the teaching is enjoyable and the language focused on meaning – and various points in between, influenced by individual teachers' beliefs, knowledge, the resources at their disposal and their own experience of language learning.[29]

Tatiana Gordon is very much in the first camp, believing that grammar is best learned incidentally. In support of her position, she points to research that suggests that corrective feedback of all kinds has a minimal effect on children's grammatical use; and that classroom drills and practice do not seem to impact on their subsequent, spontaneous use of speech.[30] She points to several studies that have concluded that cognitive developmental constraints in young children prevent them from making judgements on whether a phrase or sentence is grammatically correct or not.[31] Puchta, however, promotes a more nuanced approach. He proposes that grammar needs to be understood more as a process, something that grows and emerges over time, rather than as something taken in through teacher explanation; but that some intentional, focused instruction by teachers that orientates children explicitly to different language features can lead to larger gains than teaching that simply hopes that these gains will arrive incidentally. He uses the term 'noticing', suggesting that teachers should consciously help children notice certain salient grammatical forms when they occur; that they should be exposed to input that focuses on them and have opportunities to practise their use.[32] Concentrating on fun alone in TEYL is insufficient, he argues; children need to be progressively challenged to notice and think about language.

This need not be dull and reminiscent of old-fashioned grammar-oriented instruction, however, as his examples indicate. He is keen to signal that short, practical activities and language play can work in tandem with noticing tasks. So a brief shopping game can help children distinguish between and practise the correct usage of 'How much is ...?' and 'How much are ...?' by displaying cards which show one pullover, say, or shirt, and two of the same item. If the teacher asks 'How much is ...?' the children must point to the correct card, with the teacher responding, 'That's right, How much is the pullover?' This leads on to an activity in which the children must ask the right question as the teacher holds up the card.[33] There is nothing earth-shattering in this example, but it points to the kind of playful, game-like activity a teacher might develop with grammar as a conscious focus.

Turning to the learning of vocabulary, Gordon draws attention to studies that once again promote incidental learning rather than instruction, through having children hear and use words in context rather than learn them through memorizing word lists. She points to a number of studies, which suggest that 'young learners learn more words when they read exciting, interesting books than when they perform vocabulary exercises'.[34] Learning straightforward words such as elephant, door, chair and so on may not need a lot of contextualization to understand them, she explains, but this is not the case with more expressive vocabulary. She uses the simple adjective 'sneaky' as an example. A teacher may give a definition as 'clever' and 'not honest', but that does not capture all the shades of meaning.

> If on the other hand, children first hear the word sneaky when they listen to a well-illustrated fairy-tale about a sneaky fox that tricked every animal in the forest, and if the shenanigans of the sneaky fox are described in great detail, children have little difficulty understanding the entire complexity of the word's meaning.[35]

Offering a translation of the word in a first language, or *translanguaging* as it is sometimes called, can be a perfectly valid option for a teacher, of course, but it will not provide the same memorable, contextual richness that the appeal of a good story can provide. Stories can thus 'help words themselves do a marvellous job of teaching what they mean'.[36]

Hestetraeet, like Puchta, while not denying the validity of the significance of such incidental learning, argues that, following more recent research, a more balanced approach to vocabulary learning is necessary, with *explicit* learning complementing the *implicit* kind children might gather from reading or listening to stories.[37] She sees vocabulary rather than grammar as the core component of language skills and views its focused teaching to be of critical importance for TEYL. Drawing on research by Nation, she proposes four strands to guide the process of teaching and learning vocabulary – namely, 'meaning-focused input', to be gained from listening to stories, watching films or reading suitably graded texts; 'meaning-focused output', through spoken interaction or the making up of stories; 'language-focused learning', in particular focusing on the explicit study of high frequency words; and 'fluency development', focusing on the recycling and consolidation of vocabulary that children have previously come across.[38] She stresses the incremental nature of vocabulary learning, which she usefully divides into the integral relationship between the form, meaning and use of words.

> It takes many encounters to develop word knowledge of form, meaning and use, and for this knowledge to be consolidated and enhanced. At the beginning stages of learning a word ... explicit study is to be recommended whereas later in the process learning from context, implicitly, can improve word knowledge.[39]

One major problem that Hestetraeet points to, however, is the fact that many teachers of EYL use only a limited variety of instructional practices when teaching vocabulary. She points to research both in East Asia and in Europe that shows a strong bias towards practices focusing on word recognition and memorization and on de-contextualized vocabulary lists chosen by the teacher. These studies point to a general need for more balanced vocabulary teaching, she suggests, which should also include contextualized vocabulary, 'such as in storytelling and reading and meaning-focused output, such as in spontaneous interaction'.[40]

Implications for Teachers and Models of Pedagogy

In this section I will begin by examining the strategies for teachers that both Tabors and Gordon provide as a result of their considerations of how young children learn a second language. The former concentrates on preschool settings, the latter on the primary school, and, as such, they provide complementary advice that, between them, is highly relevant for performative language pedagogy for children aged 3–7.

Listening and Speaking

Tabors provides detailed guidance on three interlocking aspects of working with very young ESL learners – namely, how to communicate with them, how to organize the classroom to assist them and how to structure a curriculum that can support the development of their oral language and literacy. Her advice is highly practical and significant, and I summarize some key aspects of it below.[41]

- Start with what children will know and keep the communication simple and straightforward.

- Be prepared to *buttress the communication* or *double the message* by using clear gestures, actions or facial expressions to emphasize the meaning.

- Make use of repetition, emphasizing key words.

- Ground your communication in what is happening here and now.

- Look for opportunities to expand and extend second language skills, still starting from what the children already know.

- 'Up the ante', challenging children to use language more extensively when they are ready for it.

- Be prepared always to 'fine tune' your own language so that your questioning or statements are clearer than they might initially have been.

Although the examples she provides to illustrate these points are with individual children, experienced teachers will surely note that this is equally good advice for working with very young children as a whole class, whether in their first or second language, and whether they are majority or minority second language learners.

Tabors points to the organization of space and the need for *safe havens* in which children can play safely, with materials such as Lego and building blocks; and to the need for clear routines which children can quickly get used to, whatever their language level. Such routines help them acquire a set of activity structures that allow them to act like members of the group, thus enabling a sense of inclusion as well as an understanding of specific uses of language. As she puts it:

> Minimising confusion and maximising structure will help the second-language learners tune in to the classroom and feel more secure sooner. Allowing children to participate in activities in easily understood ways will help them join the social group and be exposed to more language.[42]

'Minimising confusion and maximising structure' is also something that teachers need to attend to in individual lessons, particularly when movement and group play are involved. The sooner children understand the rules involved in a playful activity and the language patterns it uses, the more they will be able to join in with confidence and focus on the learning.

One particularly successful technique that Tabors observes in teachers is what she calls providing a 'running commentary', what has also been called 'event casting' or 'talking while doing'.[43] Here, teachers perform an activity or guide children through one, while explaining what they are doing as they perform it. This combination provides children with vocabulary and syntactic structures in English that are readily comprehensible, as the actions simultaneously perform the meaning. In addition, she points to the importance of providing children with opportunities to hear *context-embedded language*, or 'language related to the immediate situation', particularly in the course of socio-dramatic play.[44] This kind of play, in which children improvise in role, usually as adults in a specific, imagined social setting, such as a doctor's surgery, will often involve children providing their own running commentary alongside their actions. In performative language teaching, we shall see that the teacher, too, can combine the two strategies in a range of activities that buttress the language learning opportunities.

Tabors provides guidance on two additional oral activities of particular relevance to our concerns, namely, book-reading time and circle time. Once again, her advice is particularly apt for TEYL in both pre-primary and early primary settings, and below I summarize some of her key points, starting with her guidance on book reading.[45]

1. *Keep it short.* This does not preclude the use of longer stories, but it does mean that teachers must be prepared to take a break if necessary, asking children what might happen next and carrying on with the story at a future time. The key thing is that children stay tuned in and that their attention spans are not overstretched.

2. *Choose books carefully* – for content, length, vocabulary and cultural sensitivity. She advises teachers to spend some time thinking in advance about how best to present the books and specifically recommends what she calls 'predictable books', those that combine engaging stories with a repetitive use of language patterns.

3. *Talk the story through, rather than read it.* This is a useful way of introducing children to good stories in well-illustrated picturebooks, where the language of the text may be too advanced or difficult for them.

4. *Read books more than once.* Children enjoy listening to their favourite stories many times, but often teachers feel pressurized to move on and cover more content at the expense of rich immersion in a text; and repeated readings are bound to re-enforce vocabulary.

For circle time she offers similar detailed guidance, emphasizing the importance of keeping to a routine, for example, by starting with the children's names and moving on to discuss the day's weather. Songs and movements with 'highly predictable components' should be included, and she emphasizes how young learners often find their voice or 'go public' in their new language for the first time when joining in with such songs. Themed material in circle time should be short, simple, visual and make use of clearly explicit vocabulary; and children should be encouraged to respond to teachers' questions either in unison or on a voluntary basis, as 'by calling out to a second language learner to respond in front of the entire class, teachers may render even the most confident child speechless'.[46]

Performative language teaching, as I practise it, both builds on this advice and deepens its argument, as we shall see in later chapters.

In concentrating on the more formal language learning young children will face once they start primary school, Tatiana Gordon begins by emphasizing the need for teachers to create a learning environment that is 'unthreatening, comfortable and stress-free'.[47] Unless young children are made to feel relaxed and uninhibited, she argues, negative emotions will greatly impede their ability to understand and produce their new language. Referring to Stephen Krashen's theory of an *affective filter* that can present an emotional barrier to second language learning, she comments that 'a classroom with a low affective filter provides an optimal language-teaching environment'.[48] Recognizing children's cultural backgrounds visually within the classroom and ensuring that their names are known and pronounced correctly are key strategies in making the environment comfortable and secure for young language learners. She emphasizes the need for peer bonding but also the crucial importance of teacher–pupil bonding. In this, teachers have to be aware of the signals they give off non-verbally, through body language, while making sure their use of language is 'not only clear, simple and accessible but also unstilted, rich and personally meaningful'.[49] The tone of teacher talk as well as the content is therefore very important, conversational rather than plainly instructional, and allowing young EFL learners time to decide when they are ready to speak individually rather than demanding that they do so.

She then pays particular attention to comprehension-based activities, beginning by providing teachers with advice on how to make their own language input comprehensible. Much of this we have covered already: the need for clarity, for teachers to speak slowly and use repetition, to use language embedded in an immediate and comprehensible context, such as in games and movement activities, to keep their sentences short. Some of her advice is clearly performative, however. She advocates the use of gesture and also mime to help convey various shades of meaning and also to use the voice dramatically, with intonation to suggest character when reading, for example, or volume adjustment to evoke atmosphere. She is emphatic that first instructional activities should focus on comprehension rather than production of language, something that will be built systematically into the schemes at the heart of this book.

Equally performative is her detailed advocacy of an established instructional approach called Total Physical Response (TPR), first developed by James Asher. This involves the children remaining silent but responding physically to the teacher's directions, or to actions narrated in a story, or to movements suggested in a song. In concentrating on word–action connections, Gordon argues, the neurological effect is to make the words more memorable as TPR involves *procedural kinaesthetic memory* as well as *factual declarative memory*, in effect pairing up motion and language learning in a way that leaves 'more durable and profound imprints on learner memories'. She adds:

> When children connect word and action, foreign words cease to be sound shells that contain some tentative meaning. Rather they are filled with full-bodied, real life meaning.[50]

She lists a variety of action songs and games, many of which are commonly known, such as the song 'Head, Shoulders, Knees and Toes' and the game Simon Says. Others are less well known, and all are very helpful. Games such as Preposition Gymnastics, in which children are given a toy or a ball and have to place it either on, under, behind or in front of a chair, will find an echo later in this book, as will *directed drawing* activities, in which children create pictures according to directions they are given; and the TPR Tour of the City, in which pictures are spread around the room and children have to form a specific action according to the instruction ('Run to the bus'; 'look at the tree'; 'get into the car!' and so on).

Gordon next looks at strategies intended to encourage speech and points to the importance of *choral singing* as a way of lowering the affective filter, as it shelters children from fear or embarrassment and provides an opportunity for them to form an emotional bond with peers. This claim has been supported by a number of researchers,[51] while Kirkgoz has commented on how song-based activities are particularly good at 'fostering listening skills, understanding of basic nouns, aiding pronunciation and learning and retention of vocabulary and structures'.[52] Gordon advises that the songs that work best are those with 'a repetitive structure, simple wording and an easy-to-follow rhythmical pattern and pace'.[53] She also sees what she calls the 'gesture approach' as highly effective, in particular those gestures which make use of the hands in ways that are integrated with a use of language. She argues that such gestures clarify meaning and make language easier to understand and remember because they indicate meaning in ways that are independent of verbal language. Step-by-step guidance is given on how to implement this approach effectively, as illustrated by the exercise below, involving a short poem entitled 'Good Night'.

Time for children to go to bed	*Finger points at an imaginary wrist watch*
On the pillow put your head	*Head rests on two hands put together*
Mommy and daddy turn off the light	*Gesture of a hand turning off the light*
Close your eyes	*hands are placed on the eyes*
and say, 'Good night!'	*Children lie down and lie still while the teacher counts one to five*
Good morning!	*Children 'wake up'*[54]

She suggests that first of all the teacher speak the poem aloud; then repeat it with the hand gestures; then lead the students through a choral recitation; finally inviting the children to read it while silently conducting the recitation (apart from the counting), using only hand gestures to do so.

First Steps in Developing Literacy

Given this book's focus on very young learners, developing oracy rather than literacy is its key focus. However, in the schemes for the older learners, some attention will be paid to how literacy activities can emerge from and relate to the performative practices. In this, they not only attend to the principles of learning vocabulary and grammar examined earlier but also chime with further guidance provided by Tabors and Gordon, as outlined below.

Tabors identifies five types of activities that are used to prepare young children for the challenges of learning to read and write, namely: those that target letter recognition; those that emphasize phonologicial awareness, or the sounds that make up words; those that demonstrate how books and other print materials work; those that emphasize words and their meaning; and those that encourage discourse skills, such as telling stories or providing explanations.[55] For second language learners, the needs and approaches will be similar to those used with first language learners, though with more emphasis on their particular need to get used to the sounds of the language. To help with this, she advises teachers to demonstrate clearly how they make the sounds of English with mouth, tongue and teeth, encouraging children to watch them closely as they do so. She also stresses how playful rhyming texts in song and poetry help children connect sound with meaning and see how changing one sound in a word can change its meaning entirely. She stresses, too, how teachers should intentionally present new words to children in their activities by using, explaining, reading and generally helping them understand their meanings, suggesting that children in EAL settings should be learning six to ten new words a day.

Discourse skills she describes as developing the ability to use language 'in structured ways that go beyond the basics of conversation',[56] storytelling and explaining being particularly apt for very young children. Here teachers should be skilful and expansive in their questioning, ensuring that their questions develop their verbal interactions with children and avoid closing them down with simple yes/no responses.

Gordon, in concentrating on slightly older children in the primary years, provides more specific advice on how to develop reading and writing in TEYL. She points to how research has shown that de-contextualized vocabulary lists in the target language are singularly unhelpful to young learners, who need authentic literacy approaches that concentrate on communication first and foremost. Basing her advice on referenced research, she writes:

> Language learners benefit most from reading and writing stories and fairy tales, letters, newspapers, recipes, prescriptions, travel pamphlets, advertisements, song lyrics, and poems, as well as other authentic literacy pieces.[57]

These 'literacy pieces' can be very short and repetitive but benefit from being the kinds of text children will see around them outside of the classroom. The classroom itself should be a literacy-rich environment, she suggests, with attractive displays of words and images on display and evidence of the children's own writing alongside photographs they have taken, pictures they have drawn or models they have made.

Gordon sees *pattern texts* as particularly useful, those texts, whether stories, fairy tales, poems or songs, 'that contain a recurring pattern of words, phrases or sentences'.[58] She emphasizes the pleasure that children can derive from anticipating and chanting words that are becoming increasingly familiar as the text progresses, so long as the language is simple and relevant to their interests. Such texts can also provide what she calls 'literacy scaffolds', which she regards as the most important instructional strategy to foster literacy and advocates the use of *literacy blocks* as particularly useful. Literacy blocks, 'like lego, assemble writing out of ready pieces' and ensure that the child can construct syntactically well-formed writing by providing a common sentence starter and a word bank for children to choose from in order to complete the sentence.[59] An example she provides is drawn from the song 'The wheels on the bus', reimagined as a new song entitled 'All around the school'. Taking the verse 'The driver on the bus says ...' as the pattern, children are invited to write their own verses for what different people in the school say – 'The teachers in the school say ___ ', 'The children in the school say ___ ' and so on – after suggesting a number of possibilities to choose from. *Fixed form verse*, such as the nursery rhyme 'One, two / Buckle my shoe' and 'Entering the Text' activities, in which children imagine themselves in a situation described in a story, are just two more examples she provides of good literacy scaffolds that teachers can make effective use of to encourage young children in their reading and writing of the new language.[60]

Towards a Performative Language Pedagogy

As we have seen, then, a number of specialists in TEYL have propagated teaching practices that loosely relate to performance – singing, chanting, games, physical response and fictional scenarios. Some of these also place performative demands on the teacher, such as the use of gesture and double messaging in order to buttress meaning and the need to adapt the voice expressively when reading stories and to show an awareness of body language when communicating to young learners. Notably, all of these practices have been based on research within the field rather than suggested by or adapted from the arts. More recently, however, some leading practitioners of TEYL have consciously made use of educational drama and associated disciplines, such as oral storytelling, and the structured, playful activities it has long promoted.

Yasemin Kirkgoz, in paying specific attention to the development of speaking and listening in a range of settings, notes that many researchers have commented on the suitability and effectiveness of games, puppets, stories, drama, role play and singing in motivating young learners to repeat, memorize, internalize and use English creatively. She notes, too, how songs can make repetition and the internalizing of vocabulary enjoyable rather than boring for young children; how role playing imaginary characters can be both entertaining and motivating for them; and how puppets can make dialogues come alive for young learners, stirring them emotionally into wanting to communicate.[61]

Sandie Murao has concentrated on how play-based activities in the pre-primary classroom can re-enforce English second language learning by providing a 'powerful scaffold' to learning.[62] She advocates the kind of playful, teacher-led circle time activities that we have already come across, including games, stories and songs, all in English, and particularly emphasizes playful routines that integrate mime activities with repetition and formulaic language. As an example, she describes a Listen and Do game, in which the teacher leads a chant of 'Brr, it's cold, put on your hat! Brr it's cold, put on your scarf!' all of which children would mime, while repeating the instruction.[63] Drawing upon the wonderful work of the US-based teacher educator Carolyn Graham, this and exercises like it could readily be adapted into a jazz chant, using a four-beat rhythm for each line.[64] What particularly interests her is how children naturally enjoy the activities and will take the opportunity to mimic and repeat the games on their own if they are provided with a suitable space and teacher-initiated opportunities for doing so. She gives examples from her own observations of how children have made use of English in their own play in what she calls an English learning area (ELA). She notes that while the younger 4- to 5-year-old children could master the form of the playful English activities, the older 5- to 6-year-olds were also able to master what she calls the 'script-like exchange', the formulaic language of the games. These they emulated creatively, while also helping with and correcting one another's English. 'All pre-primary educators I have worked with over the years,' she comments, 'describe their children showing an enormous amount of motivation to play in English.'[65]

Murao is also a strong advocate of the use of picturebooks, and she provides a detailed definition of just what the picturebook as an art form is, and what its many values are that stretch beyond the utilitarian into realms that are both aesthetic and ethical.[66] The term 'picturebook' – as a single-word, compound noun – denotes the individual identity it has been given by academics as an art form in itself, one in which the visual language of the pictures and the verbal language of the text are interdependent, relating to one another in different ways. At the simple end, very useful for very young learners, the pictures will reflect the meaning, whereas at the more complex end, they may interact with the written language in more complex, ironic ways. In either case, she points out, the very act of turning a page in a picturebook can have a dramatic quality to it. This potential for visual signs to either contradict or complement verbal signs is, of course, a central concern for drama and theatre practitioners and is key to the depth and complexity of meanings dramatic performances can convey. It is a potential I will make much of in many of the schemes presented in the later chapters.

The two examples Murao provides for children within the age range of this book are demonstrative not only of an inclusive curriculum for intercultural awareness but also of how performative activities can be built naturally into a TEYL pedagogy that makes use of picturebooks. For example, the book *Head, Shoulders, Knees and Toes* by Annie Kubler uses the well-known song to depict images of young children of all ethnicities. When the book is read to them, not only are children singing along to the song, but the images 'act as mirror, enabling children to see themselves in the pictures, and as windows, so they can see what others are like, too'.[67]

More complex and for slightly older children is the picturebook *Yo! Yes?* which, too, relates to diversity and tolerance with the theme of a developing friendship between two young boys, one Black American and the other white Caucasian. She traces how the images demonstrate far more complex feelings than the words denote, tracing how the white boy's initial confusion and hesitation moves to a gleeful acceptance of the Black boy's offer of friendship. This quite naturally leads into activities in which the class is divided into two, each half taking a character's words and the whole class thus participating in a choral reading. She stresses that they should be encouraged 'to say their lines with as much emotion as possible, using voice, facial expression and body language'.[68] She suggests the learners can then make their own similar dialogues based upon other informal greetings, both in their own language and in English such as 'Hiya!', 'Hey!' and 'Wotcha!' Focusing on one's own culture as well as looking at others, she suggests, 'produces an intercultural awareness based on "Knowledge, awareness and understanding of the relation (similarities and distinctive differences) between the world of origin and the world of the target community"'.[69]

Particularly worthy of attention here is the work of Janice Bland, a specialist in the teaching of English to young children, who is based in Norway and has written extensively on the subject. Learning English through literature, oral storytelling and drama and theatre approaches have long been a central interest of hers, and much of her practice will find an echo in my own work, not only in her advocacy of drama but also in her understanding of the importance of literature, including oral storytelling, as integral to a good curriculum for TEYL.

Bland considers a range of authentic literary texts, seeing their advantage in language terms in the way that they 'sensitise young learners to grammatical relations and the semantic associations of words as well as formulaic sequences'.[70] The earlier these are introduced to young learners, the better as they match their implicit learning mechanisms and tolerance of ambiguity. Very importantly, in addition to their potential for language learning, is the aesthetic pleasure that they offer. In fact, as part of her literary categories, she uses the term 'performative formats', which includes oral storytelling, plays and also playground and nursery rhymes. These latter, she points out, can provide a wealth of rhythmic, participatory material for TEYL 'to satisfy children's need for rhythm and pleasure in rhyme', often suggesting strong and bizarre visual images that can contribute greatly to their memorability.[71]

The playful language of poetry, Bland argues, can help children internalize grammar templates that, when they are older, will provide a basis for a more analytical understanding of grammar. Although not advocating the kind of conscious focus on grammar that Puchta advocates, she nonetheless

sees it as something teachers need to be aware of, to help children internalize specific grammatical constructions through repetition and performance.
She advocates the use of poems that present children with 'mini storyworlds'
as particularly well suited for children to act out. One engaging example
she offers is of a short, four-lined poem by Anholt and Anholt, about a
busy mummy 'buzzing home to me', in which children sit in a circle, some
performing a buzzing *ostinato* chorus, while others recite the poem, and
one child takes on the role of mummy, miming various busy tasks that have
been agreed beforehand.[72] When the mummy 'buzzes home', she does so
to another child who then takes on the role and the game is repeated. This
combination of anticipation and repetition she sees as an aspect of the com-
pulsiveness of games that supports learning through 'overlearning actions
and language'.[73] This concept of *overlearning* denotes the way doing and
saying something playfully again and again gives time for body and mind to
reconfigure themselves 'to a new level of control and flexibility'. However,
Bland is careful to point out that playful repetition of this sort, enjoyable
and meaningful as it is to young children, is very different from the kind
of pattern drilling associated with the more conventional, audio-lingual
method that still characterizes many second language classrooms.[74]

Oral storytelling, Bland notes, is an important skill that practitioners
of TEYL ought to develop. Unlike picturebooks and other fixed texts, it
is flexible and easily adaptable for different audiences. However, in words
that would strongly support the argument offered earlier by Gordon, she
emphasizes that 'the standard story patterns and formulaic language (such
as: "Once upon a time, little cottage, wicked wolf, deep dark woods …")
must remain unchanged'.[75] Like Gordon, she sees these patterns of story and
language as reassuring and comforting for young learners, with repetition as
a source of enjoyment, as well as a crucial support:

> Additive language … avoidance of complex sentences, familiar stock
> characters, iconic settings with few details and recurrent themes and tri-
> ples (such as three brothers or sisters, three wishes, three attempts). This
> characteristic helps young learners to predict, and it activates their prior
> knowledge of the creatures of tales, such as witches, monsters and trolls.[76]

The structural advantages afforded by traditional tales need to be complemented, however, by the telling, what she calls 'creative teacher talk'. This
talk is described in a way that emphasizes the performative qualities that a
good telling should consist of, including 'expressive prosodic features (pitch,
tempo, volume, rhythm – including dramatic pauses), exuberant intonation,
gasps and, where suitable, even sighs'.[77] The younger the audience, the more
exaggerated the gesture and facial expressions are likely to be and the more
repetitive the speech.

When considering the use of plays, as well as improvised dramatic
activities, Bland draws very important connections, both theoretical and

practical, between second language teaching and drama practices recognizable to any drama specialist, whether in the form of scripted plays or nonscripted improvisation. In both forms of drama, she draws attention to their complex combination of semiotic systems and how they resemble the sociocultural forms of interactive language play of children. These sign systems she lists as linguistic and verbal, whether in the form of improvised dialogue or written scripts; as visual, such as pictures to inspire role play or theatrical items such as costume and scenery; as touch related, whether through physical human contact or through a use of puppets; as gesture, consisting of facial expressions, body language, movement and stillness; as the audio system – vocal intonation, volume and sound effects; and as the use of space, between interlocutors or characters and audience.[78] Thus drama is defined as a holistic method, involving the whole person and a whole language system in context.

Such language learning in an improvisational context that manages successfully to engage children will involve them in using language in all its major dimensions. They will exercise *cognitive* levels of suitable language choice, practising language they have already learned, and explore *sociological* dimensions, through social interaction with partners or in groups; the *affective* dimension, taking pleasure in speaking as a different character; and the *physiological* dimension, as they move in space and use actions and gestures to communicate.[79] Bland sees its multidimensional approaches mirrored in more formal scripted drama, which she promotes as an excellent example of task-based learning that can be particularly good at creating a motivating classroom environment. Citing Dornyei, she notes that characteristics of such an environment are typically found in drama activities, including 'proximity, contact and interaction; (and) the rewarding nature of group activities'.[80]

If drama is good at creating opportunities for such holistic language learning, Bland sees it as particularly apt for younger second language learners as it is congruent with what Saville-Troike has listed as a set of advantages they enjoy.

These advantages include brain plasticity (helpful for the acquisition of target phonology), non-analytical processing mode (helpful for the acquisition of language chunks holistically), fewer inhibitions (helpful for taking risks) and weaker group identity (helpful for acquiring intercultural competence).[81]

Despite these evident advantages, and despite its widespread advocacy among early years practitioners in many countries, she notes that, in the field of EYL, drama is 'often given little systematic, focused attention by teacher educators, and suitable material to promote drama is sparse'.[82] Much of her chapter is then given over to addressing this lack, providing detailed examples of approaches that can be adopted and illustrated by examples from her own practice.

These examples highlight the specific language learning that particular approaches can encourage, together with very practical advice for anyone who might want to make use of them. So the short example of scripted drama Bland presents clearly demonstrates how such work can help young learners acquire target phonology through using formulaic sequences of multiword units such as 'I hope so!' and 'Let's have a go!' arranged in a way that makes helpful use of rhythm and rhyme.[83] With regard to unscripted drama, she provides a range of TPR activities, demonstrating how the teacher can use salience and repetition to re-enforce particular language patterns ('Who is taller, you or your partner? ... Jump higher than your partner ... Run faster than your partner ...'); or rehearse specific themes, such as transport ('Steer a ship ... the sea is wild ... Ride on a camel ... Gallop on a horse'); or simply to create positive feelings of fun and togetherness with a partner ('Shake hands with your partner ... Show your right hand ... Give five'). She also provides commentary for and examples of a number of well-known drama conventions, again showing clearly how they can be adapted for specific language activities. Many of these are more applicable to children older than 7 years of age, but her description of an activity called *Whoosh!* in which she makes use of the story of the *Three Billy Goats Gruff* is particularly well conceived and exemplified.[84] This involves children in a multisensory, highly playful enactment of stories and is a strategy that I myself am credited for inventing, one I will return to in more detail in Chapter 3.[85]

Conclusion

We can see from the examples provided in this chapter that many of the implications of theory and practice in TEYL are supportive of what I am calling a 'performative pedagogy'; and that aspects of this pedagogy have been developed by specialists within the field of early years language education. Concepts such as scaffolding through TPR and the gesture approach, buttressing communication and doubling the message, providing running commentaries and event casting feed directly into performative approaches advocated by these specialists. These have included the use of games, puppets, stories, picturebooks, movement, drama, role play, action poems, nursery rhymes and singing to encourage young learners to repeat, memorize, internalize and begin to use English in creative ways. Such activities have been demonstrated as effective tools for learning and as enjoyable for young children, matching as they do their developmental needs in both cognitive and social terms. At their best, they incorporate conscious, focused instruction with opportunities for incidental learning. They thus constitute the foundation for a rationale for performative language pedagogy in the early years, one that recognizes both the need for structure and focus in its teaching and, given the demands it makes on teachers, the need to offer them clear guidance and models of practice. The next chapter is intended to build upon this foundation and complement it by addressing theory and practice in second language learning that has emanated from educators who position themselves as drama and arts specialists. As part of this, I will offer a rationale for my own practice that I position firmly within this developing field. A series of new concepts and ideas will be added to those explored in this chapter, even though many of the practices will re-emerge in various forms. Central to these will be the immersion of children within fictional worlds for sustained periods of learning; and the use of the aesthetic to help children feel as well as speak the language, to find its use sensual and enjoyable as well as meaningful.

CHAPTER TWO

Performative Language Teaching in the Early Years: Key Concepts

One of the most delightful performances by young schoolchildren I have witnessed was in a primary school in Romania several years ago. The school was near the border with Hungary, so the children's mother tongue was Hungarian; but the performance incorporated elements of English, which made it very easy for me to follow. The setting was very informal. There was no stage as such, just a simple but clearly marked out performance space in a small school hall. The class teacher shared this space with the children, occasionally joining in but by no means dominating the storytelling. The atmosphere was informal, but the audience appeared to be as delighted as I was throughout. There were no costumes, and the props in use were simple. What mainly characterized the performance was the playful interaction, spoken and physical, between the children, all of whom were more or less equally involved. True, one little girl shone with her natural grace and charm, but she had been given no special star status as such. In fact she spent much of the time holding the hand of a boy with special needs and guiding him with ease and care through the performance space, quietly helping him feel as fully engaged as possible, encouraging him to join in with the choric actions and the chanting that constituted a key feature of the storytelling. The entire show lasted no more than twenty minutes. I did not feel that the teacher had spent an inordinate amount of time rehearsing it; rather, it was apparent that drama was an integral part of her pedagogy and that these children were used to playing dramatically together. The performance conveyed a sense of natural energy, of children at ease with one another; it was also evident that they very much enjoyed being watched and appreciated by the audience.

At a conference I attended in China a few years ago, I had a very different experience when a primary school teacher showed a video of a play in English that she had directed and in which a group of children from her class had participated. Very few of them appeared to be actively involved, and those who were spoke in an English that was for the most part incomprehensible. Indeed, it was hard to see whether they had any understanding at all of what they were saying. Costumes and staging were lavish, but the educational value was highly dubious. This was tactfully pointed out by a young Chinese professor, who expressed doubt about his own students' involvement in drama projects such as this in higher education. In his experience, they consumed considerable amounts of time and energy whilst often producing very poor results, whether these were evaluated in terms of language learning or the dramatic qualities of the production. I silently concurred with him. We judged the performance we had watched as weak, as a demonstration of poor professional judgement and as an inefficient use of both the teachers' and the children's time. As a professional educator and experienced teacher trainer, I gained no pleasure from it of the kind I had from watching the class of young Romanian children or, indeed, the kind I derive from witnessing a well-structured lesson taught effectively.

Many readers will have been similarly delighted or disappointed by dramatic performances they have seen in educational settings. I am doubtless not alone in suggesting that it is always an error for costumes, lighting and painted sets to take priority over the linguistic and dramatic qualities of any production, doubly so when it is performed in a foreign language.

In the previous chapter, I introduced performative language teaching as a flexible pedagogy that does not confine itself to narrow and possibly misconceived ideas of performance in the target language, such as the one described above. Instead, I proposed that it makes use of various practices connected directly to performance – singing, physical movement, role playing, for example – in conjunction with playful activities, such as games, and with stories, both in the form of oral storytelling and picturebooks. I wish to hold on to this idea of it as a pedagogy that embraces a range of forms and activities that teachers can choose from and make use of in their daily classroom practice, rather than confining it to the more usual idea of a rehearsed performance in front of an audience of parents. However, a more complex theoretical explanation is needed to act as a rationale for the specific practice that will be illustrated later in this book. This chapter will attempt to provide such a rationale, one that is conceptually thorough whilst remaining accessible to readers who are not necessarily conversant with theories relating to drama and performance studies.

Performance and Performatives

The term 'performative language teaching' was first used by Manfred Schewe as 'an umbrella term to describe … forms of foreign language teaching that derive from the performing arts'.[1] In order to examine the rich and unique potential for learning that this connection makes possible, and to appreciate this potential as far more than a bag of practical activities, we need to look more closely at the words 'performative' and 'performance' and examine some related concepts that are generally associated with them. There has in recent years been an enormous amount of academic research in this field, but for our purposes we can begin with the work of Erika Piazzoli.

Piazzoli has provided the most comprehensive and thoroughly researched study to date of drama, performance and second language learning.[2] In it she draws upon the seminal work of Richard Schechner, who did much to establish performance studies as an interdisciplinary field of inquiry, encompassing the concept of performance as something that happens in social life as well as in the imaginary world of the theatre. Rather than see these as binary opposites, he suggested that we envisage performance as a continuum that encompasses performances on stage, in ceremonies and rituals and in everyday life. Piazzoli makes special reference to a particularly useful distinction proposed by Schechner, between performance as 'make believe' and performance as 'make belief'. If the former maintains a clear boundary between what is real and what is imagined, the latter blurs that boundary in order to 'create the very social realities they enact'.[3]

This latter idea draws upon John Austin's speech act theory and in particular his definition of the 'performative'. Performative speech acts, as defined by Austin, are not only statements but also utterances that, in effect, perform an action. For example, to say 'I do' in a wedding ceremony, to make a marriage vow, is to cement a relationship in a particularly powerful and socially approved way. The purpose of a performative is to make something happen; so a wedding vow, and the ceremony that surrounds it, creates the social reality of a marriage and is a clear example of performance as 'make-belief'. If we extend this idea to the professional context of the classroom, we can see that teachers use various performative speech acts to 'make-belief' in their pupils – issuing commands, requests, instructions and so on – to establish and maintain their authority as they perform the social role of teacher. Importantly, Austin suggests that we do not judge performatives by assessing whether they are true or not but rather evaluate their effectiveness in succeeding in what they set out to achieve. The professional role of the teacher embodies two types of performative proposed by Austin: those that carry a certain conventional force with them, such as the marriage vow, that 'seek to call into being, order and promise'; and those that intend to bring about a specific effect on the hearer – 'convincing, persuading, deterring, even surprising or misleading'.[4] In this sense, then, we can say that the teacher and children work effectively together when the teacher's performance is convincing enough for the children to agree to go along with the established rituals of the classroom; and that her persuasive use of language will be integral to this success.

This concept of the teacher's use of performance to 'make-belief' in the classroom is not antithetical to the idea of the teacher making use of performance to get the children to join in activities in which they 'make-*believe*' and agree to play with language in imaginary worlds and fictional contexts. What matters, as Austin pointed out, is not whether the imagined reality is true or not but whether the teacher is effective in the way she gets the children to play along with her. The challenge for teachers is that this calls for subtler and different performative activities than they may be used to, for to encourage children to behave in ways that will assist their language learning in a world of make-believe requires a pedagogy in which the teacher herself will need to perform her role differently. She will need successfully to mediate between the social world of the classroom and the imaginary world of a fiction in ways that, rather than confusing children or disrupting their learning, actually grab their attention and sharpen their involvement.

Piazzoli, in referring to the word 'performative', breaks it down into its constituent parts. *Per* (from the Latin) means 'through'; 'formative' relates to educating, as in the phrase 'her formative years'; and the root word – 'form' – is at its heart. In this sense, Piazzoli suggests, the word 'performative' means educating through form.[5] But the word 'form' itself carries different, related meanings, both as a noun and as a verb, as highlighted in Schewe's original definition, quoted below:

> The goal of performative foreign language didactics is to create a new approach to teaching and learning, whereby emphasis is placed on forms of aesthetic expression. This means that special attention is given to 'language form' and to the pleasure and even desire to play with words, sentences and expressions. 'Form' also implies the ways in which the body speaks and how sound, word sentence and movement all interact with each other.[6]

How the body can *form* meaning through language and how aesthetic *forms* can be harnessed purposefully by teachers find twin expression here. As Piazzoli puts it, a performative approach to language is 'an embodied approach, with particular attention to the aesthetic domain'.[7] Before we look at the aesthetic domain, then, we must first attend to what is meant by an 'embodied approach' and why it is important.

Embodiment

It is not uncommon for teachers to see the body as an impediment to learning. To make this point, I have sometimes joked in training sessions that somewhere in a secret laboratory, scientists commissioned by government officials have been tasked with finding a way for children to leave their bodies in the cloakrooms along with their coats. In the classroom of the future, so they hope, children's brains will be plugged directly into personal computers without the interface of the body. Gone will be the fiddling, the giggling, the restlessness, the need to go to the toilet. Teachers' lives will be so much simpler and children will learn so much more easily, removed from bodily distractions. Some teachers laugh in response to this, of course. They understand the perverse appeal of such a dark idea, but it also ironically parodies an idea of human learning that has deep cultural roots in educational practices in schools across the globe.

The tendency to draw a sharp distinction between mind and body is commonly referred to as 'mind-body dualism'. As a concept, it is based upon a belief that the rational, intellectual processes of our minds are distinctive from, and superior to, emotions and passions, understood, by contrast, as bodily impulses. In educational terms, it has led to an emphasis on disciplining the body to stay still and inactive in the classroom so that the brain, undisturbed, can attend to its tasks. When the body is called into action, it is solely to carry out those tasks necessary to process and give account of what has been learned. The value of the affective life is radically reduced in such a view of teaching and learning.

The terms 'embodied' and 'embodiment', currently very common in the discourses of drama education and performance studies, offer a different, more holistic idea of how we learn.[8] Rather than seeing the mind as an autonomous, meaning-making machine, it locates our capacity to make meaning as primarily dependent upon how the whole body, including the mind, engages with its environment. As the philosopher Mark Johnson puts it, an embodied view of meaning 'sees meanings growing out of and shaped by our abilities to perceive things, manipulate objects, move our bodies in space'. If we 'reduce meanings to words or sentences', he adds, 'we miss out where meaning really comes from'.[9] To understand knowledge as *embodied* is to see it not as located in or belonging to a disembodied mind but to appreciate that without the senses, without feelings, without the body, the mind would know nothing.

Johnson illustrates his point by referring to a poem by the American poet Billy Collins entitled 'Purity', which, when I first read it, immediately called to mind my own joke about the disembodied pupil in the classroom. Here the poet imagines himself taking off not only his clothes but also all of his flesh and organs, becoming 'entirely pure: nothing but a skeleton at a typewriter'.[10] The problem is that when he comes to compose a poem, he can only imagine and write about death. Our embodiment, the poem wittily reminds us, is the very condition through which we relate to and make sense of the world. Thus the concept 'embodied cognition', wherein learning is understood as a holistic process, working at once through mind and body, through the senses and the environment in which the learning takes place.

None of this should surprise preschool teachers, where practices such as sand and water play, play with Lego and building blocks, socio-dramatic play and other physical activities are common and seen as core to how very young children learn. We have also seen in the previous chapter how many specialists in TEYL use physical gesture, voice intonation, facial expression and active movement to amplify the meaning of words. Strategies such as 'double messaging' or 'buttressing meaning' as well as the full range of TPR activities make use of the body to re-enforce the meaning of words and can thus be seen as incorporating embodied approaches to teaching. 'Through the body, a language learner may communicate well before mastering the words to speak a sentence, feeling or idea aloud.'[11] This observation is from Claire Coleman in reference to the relevance of drama to language learning, but it might well have been written by Tabors in her study of working with individual children learning English in a preschool setting.

Performative language teaching goes further than this, however, in con-sciously incorporating emotions into the language learning process as it sees thought and feeling as intimately connected and always colouring one another when we communicate in the social sphere. Piazzoli provides an example of this in a warm-up exercise carried out with mature students, the Emotional Palette routine, in which they are asked to greet one another with the Italian word *benvenuto* (welcome) colouring their greeting with differ-ent emotions, such as jealousy, euphoria, horror, suspicion. Gradually this extends not only from how they use their voice but also their eyes, hands and whole body posture. She then takes it into more abstract territory, experimenting with what she calls a 'basic form of embodiment', asking participants to experiment with how they move through the space and to play with rhythm, action and stillness, 'interpreting key words, coloured by key emotions (in the target language) as they connect to their body aware-ness'.[12] To conclude, they gather and talk in small groups to reflect upon their collective experience.

This exercise is too sophisticated for young children, of course, but it nonetheless illustrates how performative pedagogy uses the communicative potential of the body not only to make language comprehensible but also to express and respond to meaning, and to provoke talk that describes, specu-lates and reflects upon shared experience. It clearly relates to the kind of communicative teaching processes referred to by Gordon in the previous chapter, whose intention is to fill words with full-bodied, real-life meaning. This form of embodiment is central to how I plan for TEYL.

Like the adult participants in the exercise above, the vast majority of young children are skilful readers of body language. They know what sad-ness, anger, joyfulness, fear, friendliness, hostility and other key emotions sound like through tone of voice and what they look like in terms of facial expression, gesture, posture and gait.[13] Some gestures may be culturally determined but many – smiles, tears, the body slumped over in sadness, the body stiff, upright and aggressively waving a clenched fist – are fundamental to our shared humanity. These children will respond readily to how they read the emotions of characters in well-illustrated picturebooks. Presented with a cartoon illustration from *Max the Brave* of a kitten wearing a superman cape and looking defiant, they will identify that he is trying to look brave. When examining a picture from *Peter Rabbit*, in which Peter has his back turned while his three sisters listen carefully to their mother giving them instructions, young children can tell that he isn't listening to his mother's advice, whatever that might be.[14] Many young children will make use of body language such as this spontaneously in their pretend play, but such pictures can be physically reconstructed by children in the classroom to introduce new language and to draw out language that children already know. However, if these images fail to trigger an emotional response in the children, neither will they trigger any desire in them to use language or learn new language.

Piazzoli's exercise illustrates how movement and sound are integral to how the body can both generate and express emotion simultaneously. This is very evident in children, albeit in less subtle ways. They will often laugh when they run collectively through space, feeling the joy and exuberance of a shared release of energy at the same time as they create it. A teacher's skilful use of the voice when telling a story can result in children sitting absolutely still, listening in hushed silence, followed by a collective burst of laughter when the tension is broken. Singing together can help young children feel emotion as well as express it, as can moving through space while responding to music under the guidance of the teacher's narration. Perhaps the teacher is narrating in hushed tones as the children imagine they are moving fearfully through a forest; perhaps the music is lively as they imagine themselves bravely leaping from rooftop to rooftop, like a powerful cat.

The key point for the foreign language classroom is that embodiment as a concept signals how a range of feelings can be experienced and communicated physically, in ways that add depth and emotional resonance to the words and hence make them more memorable. Krashen's affective filter is important as it helps us recognize how emotions will influence language acquisition, with fear, shyness and boredom hindering learners while enthusiasm, curiosity and self-confidence will assist them. A narrow range of emotions is here identified as either helpful or a hindrance. Performative language teaching, however, sees emotional engagement as central and brings a greater range of emotions into the classroom, albeit through playful, imaginative activities presented within the protective shelter of fictional scenarios. It seeks to rid the classroom of the negative emotions identified by Krashen whilst striving to develop and harness those that bring with them more positive energies. How it strives to achieve this brings us to that other key term used by Piazzoli, namely, the aesthetic domain, and to the key roles of play and playfulness, to the kind of stories we play with and the dramatic processes we use to do so.

The Aesthetic

Aesthetic theory is yet another field of study with volumes written that could fill a whole library. Since the days of the enlightenment, philosophers, many of whom have been greatly influential, such as Kant, Hegel and Schopenhauer, have debated its nature and disputed what it consists of. For the sake of this study I will limit my attention to two areas associated with aesthetic experience and learning, drawing from the work of the highly influential American philosopher John Dewey and a very recent contribution to the field from Matthew DeCoursey, a Canadian educator who has worked in Hong Kong.

Dewey lamented the experience of education that many young people suffer in traditional schooling, where the ends of learning are seen as what matter rather than the means by which they are taught. He feared for the many young people who consequently come to associate the learning process with feelings of ennui, boredom, dullness and drudgery.[15] In his educational writings, he proposed that teachers should consider the quality and nature of children's learning experiences as their key concern. In this sense, he was promoting an idea of education as something that should be *intrinsically* motivating to children, seen and felt as worthwhile in itself, rather than reliant on arguments focused on its potential future usefulness. Hence he is seen as a key figure in what it is commonly known as child-centred or progressive education.

It is in his book *Art as Experience*, however, that we find a definition of experience that connects the process of learning directly with aesthetic concerns.[16] He makes this connection through what he saw as the ways in which humans interact directly with the natural world, in ways that we have earlier called 'embodied experience', in which the body and the mind work together through the senses to create meaning through emotion. In making this argument, he distinguished between ongoing, formless experience and the sense of having *an* experience, the latter being dependent upon certain aesthetic qualities that provide it with form, completion, relevance and emotional power that define it as something memorable in and of itself. That is why he concentrated in his writing on the aesthetic *experience* of art rather than the aesthetic objects that art produces. What matters, he argued, is the effect of art, what it produces in the person who is gripped or moved by the experience of listening to a piece of music, looking at a painting, watching a piece of theatre, reading a work of literature. During this process, their attention is sharpened, their focus is intense; he writes that art 'quickens us from the slackness of routine and enables us to forget ourselves in finding ourselves in the delight of experiencing the world about us in its varied qualities and forms'.[17]

Importantly, Dewey saw this kind of aesthetic experience afforded by art as characteristic of *any* experience that is similarly marked out from the ordinary stream of life. The qualities of unity and coherence, the sense of consummation rather than mere cessation when the experience ends, these are temporal qualities that, mingled, with a sense of delight, absorption and purpose, could characterize scientific inquiry as much as looking at a painting or, indeed, a beautiful landscape in natural surroundings. And I will argue that it something we can strive for when teaching English to young learners.

Just how the aesthetic can motivate learners has been examined by Matthew DeCoursey in relation to Kant's argument that an experience of art is essentially one of 'disinterested contemplation'. Very briefly, Kant meant by this that such contemplation removes us from any utilitarian considerations; we value such an experience for its own sake, not for any instrumental purpose. In this sense, at least, the idea of disinterestedness can be seen to relate to Dewey's idea of 'forgetting ourselves to find ourselves'. DeCoursey distinguishes the Kantian idea of *dis*interest from any confusion with the very different idea of *un*interest by using the term 'disinterested interest'; as a learner, I am interested in what I am being taught for the pleasures of the moment that the process of learning is providing. This kind of aesthetic engagement DeCoursey defines as 'a fixed, sustained attention of a non-instrumental sort to appearances in the here and now'.[18] In this sense, aesthetic experience and intrinsic motivation in the classroom become intimately related.

It may at first appear rather daunting to recommend that teachers of EYL should consider their pedagogy in aesthetic as well as instrumental terms, but that is what the lessons outlined later in this volume attempt, and it is not a far cry from what many good teachers do already. We might begin by considering how words themselves are not simply instrumental conveyors of meaning but also consist of the prosodic qualities of sound, rhythm, tonality and musicality, those attributes that poets make use of and that we readily find in children's enjoyment of nonsense rhymes, playground chants and song. Janice Bland, as we have seen, has commented on children's need for rhythm and pleasure in rhyme. Her examples are clearly indicative of an awareness of the power of aesthetic pleasure that can be harnessed from language itself and of the learning potential they afford to TEYL. She also identifies the pleasure potential in other performative formats, the intrinsic motivation that engagement in activities such as storytelling and drama can bring.

Dewey's argument, however, also leads us to consider how we, as teachers, might attempt to organize our lessons on aesthetic principles, as aesthetic experiences in themselves. Once again, many good teachers are more or less doing this already. In attempting to grab children's attention and harness it through a range of focused activities that they sequence in a manner aimed at introducing, re-enforcing and reflecting upon learning, teachers may well be seeking instrumental outcomes, but they are approaching the aesthetic if they aspire to create a rhythmic balance between movement and stillness, sound and silence as a means to help sustain children's attention. What may well be different is the way in which I propose, in a later section, that the entire lesson can be more or less framed within a unifying, fictional, *aesthetic* construct, namely a story, that will be shared and explored collectively. Here I will liken the whole lesson to the unfolding of a drama and will consider its structure in dramaturgical as well as instrumental terms; in other words, how to sequence learning activities purposefully in ways that sustain intrinsic engagement within a coherent and appealing imaginative framework. As DeCoursey puts it, such a use of drama 'can create a virtuous circle', instigating and maintaining aesthetic engagement and therefore sustaining intrinsic motivation.[19]

Play, Playfulness and Games

In the previous chapter, I stressed the importance of seeing young children's social learning and their language learning as interdependent, drawing attention to existing research and inferring that the classroom needed to provide a secure atmosphere, with plenty of opportunities for children to learn together and feel positive about belonging to their group. One of the best ways to get them to learn together is to get them to play together.

Writings on play in the early years are extensive and refer to many forms of play, but in this section it is the social forms of play I wish to concentrate on, those that drama makes ready use of. In particular, I will stress the importance of games to social and language learning and show how, as performative forms of learning in themselves, they can both prepare for and relate directly to drama activities framed within an ongoing story world.

In her study on play and co-operative learning in the early years, Pat Broadhead concentrates on the value of free play and socio-dramatic play but is careful not to argue that play in itself will foster co-operative behaviour and positive social learning.[20] Indeed, she emphasizes that children need to learn how to play together and that the teacher needs to foster their ability to do so. Games and playful rituals are very good at this for a number of reasons as can be illustrated with explicit reference to just one or two below.

In introducing her English class, one teacher calls the children into a circle time activity in which they all sing hello to three different children in a short song, clapping their hands together in a simultaneous rhythm. In each lesson the names of the children will change, so that all children will be welcomed in this way over a short period of time. There is a clear and visible rota so that children can see whose turn it is this lesson. The teacher always concludes with a fourth verse in which the class sings 'Hello everyone!'

In a very different playful activity, a game called Sharks and Fishes, the teacher spreads a number of hoops or gym mats around the outside of the space. These, she explains, are caves in which the fish can hide from the shark. She also explains how many can hide inside each cave. Children take on the role of the fishes, swimming up and down the centre of the space until they hear the teacher call out 'The shark is coming!' At this, they must run to hide in one of the caves while the teacher, as the shark, chases them, moving her arms stiffly together mimicking the jaws of a shark. If she touches one of the children with one of her hands before they escape into a cave, they have been eaten. She can then go round and count that no more than the agreed number of fishes is hiding inside each cave. If there are more, then all the fishes in that cave are counted as eaten by the shark. The game is played three times. There is no need for the children eaten in one round to be left out of the next, however; they just join in and try their best not to be eaten again!

In the first activity, inclusivity and co-operation are emphasized. The singing and clapping are acts of togetherness, dependent upon the need to listen and respond to one another. There is also turn taking. It may not be my turn to be welcomed personally in this lesson, but I know it will be soon. Hence there is a regulatory system behind this ritual, one the individual child can quickly learn to trust. This regulatory system both establishes and fosters such feelings of trust through creating a sense of fairness as well as community.

The second activity is also based upon rules, though these are more complex and need to be understood and agreed to; otherwise, the game will not work. However, the thrill of the game (children love being chased) makes the game intrinsically appealing. Hence it helps to re-enforce the idea that rules are necessary and socially enabling rather than inhibiting. In classroom settings, teachers often enforce rules as negative commands: 'don't shout', 'don't run', 'don't all speak at once' and so on. The rules of games, on the other hand, generally take the form of positive statements: 'do this', 'do that' and 'we will all enjoy ourselves!' In this way, games can activate two forms of social learning whose importance is emphasized by Broadhead, namely, a sense of common purpose and the exercise of self-control.[21] They can be an important means for children to understand that there are greater benefits in being in control than out of control, and in working with others, so as to maintain the momentum of the game rather than to undermine it.

Games in sport are very clearly competitive, but team games depend upon co-operation as well as competition. Two key differences between games in a sporting context and those in a drama context are that, in the latter, success is far less dependent upon physical strength or technical ability; and any sense of winning a game is a lot less important. As a result, errors in sport are regarded more seriously than in a drama game, where they are often sources of communal amusement. If a child gets chased and eaten by a shark, it is a cause for laughter, not for recrimination; if the teacher as shark flails about hopelessly unable to catch any fishes, it may cause even more laughter.

Games in drama strive to be inclusive. Teams or groups will, as a result, often form and reform very quickly. In Sharks and Fishes, children are encouraged to welcome a certain number of others into their cave. If a child cannot enter a cave, it is because the rules say she can't, not because the other children don't want her there. If a shy child has a problem with this, an adult helper can encourage her by pointing to where there is a place, and the teacher (as shark) can chase her clumsily, making sure she doesn't catch her.

In sporting games as in drama games, there are rules that tell us how to use space and how to relate to one another, and these are different from the norms and conventions that usually govern our behaviour. But there is never any fictional frame in sport. Drama games, on the other hand, are often framed within a fictional context, and these fictions can deepen children's imaginative engagement with the tensions they bring into play. Being chased by a shark is infinitely more dangerous in real life – and so infinitely more fun in a game – than being chased by a teacher! This kind of thrill can enhance children's natural desire to help one another. The game actively encourages them to do this, not only save themselves. The teacher can emphasize the importance of this each time the game is played. Furthermore, the fictional context of the game can be changed to adapt to different story worlds. Maybe it is a giant chasing children in a forest; or a tiger chasing monkeys; or a cat chasing birds; or a shark chasing children who are swimming, in which case the hoops or mats become islands rather than caves. With young children, the strong regulatory framework of a game may often be the best way for teachers to help them experience dramatic suspense and to play with strong tensions and emotions such as fear and anticipation, present in many good stories, in ways that are secure, controlled and thrilling rather than messy and frightening.

Guy Cook has provided a fascinating perspective on the relationship between play, games and second language learning. He proposes that language play works at three interlocking levels, namely the formal, the semantic and the pragmatic. The *formal* level refers to rhythm, rhyme, the kinds of patterned repetition that young children find pleasure in and that we have mentioned in previous sections, such as nursery rhymes, songs and playground chants. The *semantic* level refers to our enjoyment of fiction and fantasies in which novel or strange uses of language can appeal to us, as can the story worlds they bring into being, releasing us temporarily as they do from the normal conventions and predictable patterns of our daily lives. The *pragmatic* relates to the value we find in playful uses of language, in how they create solidarity and a sense of community as well as tap into and channel any natural, competitive instincts in a safe and enjoyable way. Prayers and hymns, football chants and playful, witty banter are common cultural practices that reflect how such uses of language are far from trivial; indeed, Cook proposes that they are essential for our learning, creativity and intellectual development and that second language teachers ought to recognize this and shape their pedagogy accordingly.[22]

Teachers of EYL are well placed to take advantage of the appeal of such language play for young children, and we have seen many examples of this already. If we look again at the game described by Bland in the previous chapter, in which the mummy is likened to a busy bee, all of this language appeal is present: the rhythm and rhyme of the chant, the mini story world it suggests, the sense of communal relationships it enacts. What I am particularly interested in is how these performative formats can interlock in ways that bring ever closer together the formal appeal of language, the imaginative appeal of stories and the pragmatic appeal of communal play for the length of a whole lesson. Here, I am much taken by the metaphors for the teacher that Cook offers to those who might wish to activate language learning in this way. He identifies three figures, all drawn from different forms of cultural play, namely the referee, the storyteller and the magician.[23] What unites, them, he suggests, is that all three are authority figures that children naturally respond to in the promise of enjoyment they afford. The teacher as referee we have seen in this section, as the figure who establishes the rules of the game and monitors it to ensure that it is played fairly. The teacher as storyteller we shall consider in more detail in the next section; the teacher as magician, I will argue, is closely related to this, particularly in the way she can magic up stories and bring them to life in the classroom through performative strategies. To bring this about she must be playful in her pedagogy and not see such playfulness as being frivolous or contrary to her work and hence to the children's learning. On the contrary, it is a deep and purposeful performative skill to work on and develop.

Stories

No teacher needs telling that children enjoy stories, or reminding that they can be used for teaching purposes. When teaching EYL, we know that stories can provide a clear context and thus comprehensibility for introducing and recycling vocabulary and chunks of formulaic language, often accompanied by illustrations that complement and clarify meanings. Stories can be chosen to introduce vocabulary reflective of children's own experiences whilst taking place in the cultural context of the target language. However, none of this is sufficient for a story to be viable for performative language pedagogy.

In the *Backpack* series, for example, there are numerous illustrated short stories written by the authors in order to introduce or recycle language being taught in specific units. One featured in *Backpack 2* is called 'Moving Day' and features a smiling young girl with blond hair and pigtails called Sophie. The story starts with her saying goodbye to her old bedroom. On arrival at her new home she takes her teddy on a tour, introducing him to the different rooms in the house, but when her mother shows her her new bedroom, she is upset, as it is bare and empty. 'I want my old bedroom,' she exclaims. Once her old bed and furniture are in the room she is much happier. The story ends with her words, 'I'm so happy. I love my bedroom now.'

This story is meant for reading and not for adaptation into any kind of performance, of course. The authors suggest a range of activities, some of which are intended to encourage children to read the story aloud to a friend or to take it home and read it to members of their family. There is also a checklist intended to encourage critical thinking, in which children are asked to reply *Yes* or *No* to questions such as 'Moving Day is a good title for this book', 'This book is sad' and 'I want to read this book again'. One feels that if a child did respond positively to the last question, it would be because they felt some sense of achievement in being able to read it aloud, not because they felt it had any merit as a story, as it has evidently been written swiftly and entirely for instrumental reasons.[24]

Yet when I have worked with kindergarten teachers in Asia, this and other stories like it have occasionally been chosen by them as suitable for drama work. One teacher insisted that, as well as useful language practice, this story would teach little children that to listen to and trust their parents would make them happy. She wanted to encourage children to act out the story, demonstrate happiness and sadness in their faces and their voices and show that they could read out a prepared script and create other scenes illustrating how children should always listen to and obey their parents. In this way, not only was she meeting language objectives but she was also incorporating moral education into her drama work.

The problem is that this is an example of a story that meets a teacher's extrinsic objectives whilst offering no intrinsic interest at all for children. It may or may not work as a vehicle for language learning, but as a story it is boring, predictable and entirely conventional in its content, problems compounded in this example by the moral didacticism imposed on it by the teacher. Rather than starting from what the teacher thinks is good for children, we need to prioritize stories that will appeal to children's imaginations and satisfy their aesthetic preferences.

We saw in the first chapter arguments presented by leading practitioners of TEYL – strong, convincing and well researched – in favour of the use of stories and picturebooks in the classroom. Whilst nonetheless aware that aesthetic considerations are important, they naturally emphasized the linguistic case for their use. Janice Bland, for example, stresses the importance of the recurring structural patterns we find in fairy tales, for the ways they can activate what young learners already know and help them make predictions. She points to the appeal that nursery rhymes have for children, the memorable and bizarre images they stimulate in their imaginations, the anarchic humour that holds their attention, as ways that help them internalize and recall a verbal text. I entirely concur with these arguments and strive to make my own teaching reflect such reasoning. Here, however, I wish to consider some important characteristics of good stories for children independent of how they can be used for language learning so as not to confuse the intrinsic appeal of the story with the extrinsic language objectives of the teacher.

This appeal, I suggest, often incorporates and plays with the patterns that Bland points to in oral folk tales and fairy stories, in ways that repeat but with slight variation, satisfying children's need for surprise as well as predictability, dissonance and harmony, independent of any moral the story may superficially seem to be making.[25] There are, for example, variations on the tale that tells of the good girl who makes her way in the world, is kind to those she meets and is rewarded when they, in turn, help her to escape from a wicked witch in whose house she has found gold.[26] When her bad sister makes the same journey, things turn out differently; the good sister is kind to those who need her help, the bad sister is mean to them; the good sister returns with the witch's gold, the bad sister returns with a beating. The story does offer a reassuring moral agenda that children appreciate, namely, that small acts of kindness are a good in themselves and that, if you are nice to people who need your help, they are more likely to help you in return. However, it is the symmetry in this tale that holds aesthetic appeal for children, the pattern that repeats with different outcomes each time, rather than its simple moral message. In fact, in my experience, children enjoy the antics of the bad sister rather more than those of the good sister and find her transgressive behaviour amusing. They enjoy stories such as this not for their conventional morality but for the ways in which they play with their desire for autonomy as well as security, transgression as well as order, adventure as well as security, whether they are set in fantasy worlds where treasure is discovered in a robber's cave, in a forest where frogs can talk or in a bedroom from where a child can sail to an exotic island.

Three features will recur in the stories that form the core schemes of work in this volume, and they are characteristic of many classic stories for young children. The first is the absence or marginalization of parental authority figures. The second is the adventurous nature of a journey away from home followed by a safe return (often to bed, where many young children will be fortunate enough to have such stories read to them by their carers). On their return from such a journey, the protagonists will be, in some small way, wiser than they were before. The third feature is that courage, cunning, kindness and knowing who to listen to and who to ignore are signalled as key virtues that will help children survive, make their way in the world and triumph over bullying, bluster, brute force, arrogance and deceit. Each story will not necessarily contain all of these features, but they will nonetheless dance in and out of them in different ways.

A quick look at two favourites for very young children that do not feature in this book will demonstrate different ways that these characteristics are played out in classic stories for young children. While reading *Where the Wild Things Are*,[27] an adult may well appreciate that Max's journey to and from the land of the wild things, where he becomes their king, is all happening in Max's imagination as a means to purge himself of feelings of anger and frustration. The child, however, will be happy just to follow Max and experience vicariously the emotional trajectory of his journey, perhaps identifying with just how he feels, as they most probably know what it is like to have bad days like this and to be punished for it. If Max's mother remains downstairs in the kitchen throughout the story, the parents in *Not Now, Bernard*[28] are visibly and vocally present but mentally absent, refusing to give to their son the attention he needs, failing to see that this is turning him into a monster, despite the neat way they dress him, the toys and food they provide him with and the regular bedtime they make him keep to. Again, the adult reading this immensely clever, perceptive and amusing little tale may appreciate all of this, whereas the child will be happy to have it read to them again and again, enjoying the wonderfully evocative illustrations and the irony of the very silly parents who cannot see what is obvious to them. Max demonstrates courage and daring in his adventure with the wild things; kindness features in Bernard's story in its evident absence from his life.

For older children, the tale of *Baba Yaga* is a powerful one as it embodies all of the above principles in a vivid and thrilling way.[29] Tatia's father is absent, her mother is dead and her stepmother wants her dead. Her journey through the forest is terrifying, her return more so as she is being pursued by the cannibalistic Baba Yaga; but she survives her ordeal by knowing who to listen to (the voice of her doll, a present from her dead mother), by showing kindness to Baba Yaga's animal servants and by bravely and cunningly managing her escape.

These tales, then, do not treat children as intellectual and moral simpletons; instead, they respect their ability to appreciate subtle meanings, ironic humour and strong, often negative emotions. This respect for children's imaginative capabilities, together with a consideration of what appeals to them aesthetically, are what guide me first and foremost in my choice of stories to work with.

A good story, as I perceive it, can serve to grab and hold the attention of young learners, luring them into an imaginative world within whose boundaries they can be encouraged to spend time playing in structured and purposeful ways. In the EFL classroom, it will afford playful possibilities for language learning by providing a strong context within which are embedded patterns of language and vocabulary to be harnessed for receptive, formulaic and productive usage. It will stimulate emotional responses that we have seen as integral to children's cognitive development. It will also serve the more long-term aim of introducing children to a world of literature that, as Janice Bland has pointed out, can be considered as 'an opening to lifelong learning'.[30] And it will readily lend itself to being brought to life in the classroom through a range of performative practices that include games as well as drama activities and that may also include songs, chants, music, movement and art work woven together and sequenced in ways intended to make the learning experience feel coherent and purposeful as a whole.

The choice of stories in this volume has also been influenced by the preferences of the teachers in the kindergarten where they were developed. The protagonists in these stories are often male, even the anthropomorphic animals such as Max the kitten and Peter Rabbit. Nor are there any stories that explicitly feature Black or ethnic minority experiences. The stories were seen as providing desirable intercultural learning suitable for these classes of young Chinese children. To counter this bias, I have included stories in the next chapter that feature greater cultural, ethnic and gender diversity, applying them to exemplify the range of performative strategies used to structure the schemes featured in Chapters 4 and 5. I am also happy to point teachers towards sources where they can find a number of picturebooks that specifically promote diversity.[31] However, I do want to make three further related points before I move on.

The first is the fairly obvious one that not all good stories are suitable for the kind of pedagogy I am promoting in this book. As I said in the introduction, I see performative language pedagogy not as a replacement for but as a complement to other effective methodologies in TEYL. Many picturebooks are beautiful resources in themselves and are best used as that. The second point, which should be equally obvious, is that just because a story features male characters does not mean that it reflects a specifically masculine view of the world. Indeed, Peter Rabbit – surely one of the best children's stories ever written (and illustrated) in English – was authored by a woman who brings a particularly female, if delightfully ironic, perspective to bear on the exploits of this disobedient little bunny who so nearly gets his comeuppance. It is also pertinent to point to research by Enever that has shown how young boys, although enthusiastic when they begin to learn English, tend to lose motivation over the first four years of instruction.[32] Stories that amuse and engage them can be used to counter such a tendency. The third point is that when such stories are used in drama, the physical representation of these characters, whether male or female, becomes more complex depending upon the gender, ethnicity and physical characteristics of the person taking on their role, be it teacher, adult helper or child. Gender may well play a large part in determining which characters in a story children choose to identify with; in drama, however, we can inspire them to move further than this, encouraging them playfully to explore roles that cross beyond the boundaries of gender as well as culture. As Inglis and Aers put it:

It is surely important, as every teacher recognizes, to encourage children in what in any case comes naturally to them, and have them play out those fictional narratives in which they can experiment with being other people and try out the powerful notion of human difference before coming safely home to bed.[33]

Which leads us into the next section: the use, purposes and modes of drama in performative language teaching.

Classroom Drama

Drama education, like many of the terms in this chapter, has, particularly in the UK, been an area of debate, contentious argument and conflicting terminologies. It is unnecessary for me to engage with this history for the purposes of this book, but, for anyone wishing to know more within the context of second language education, Piazzoli has provided a brief and useful summary of the often stormy history of the field, as well as a clear introduction to the term 'process drama', which she uses to describe her own practice.[34] I, too, have adopted this term in the past, but it does not serve for the schemes in this book. There are commonalities. Many of the teaching strategies I make use of such as *still imaging, teacher in role* and *the whoosh* can be found in the lexicon of process drama. In my schemes, as in process drama, a story will unfold gradually in the classroom and children will participate actively in this unfolding in ways that blur the distinction between actor and audience. Very significantly, teachers and other adult helpers will be expected to join in, temporarily taking on roles that intentionally remove them, albeit temporarily, from being the ones who are supposed to come up with all the answers. These principles may already seem challenging enough to some teachers, but process drama as a pedagogy presents further challenges, particularly for teachers of young children who are not working in their first language. It requires a lot of negotiation and sustained concentration, and the language demands may well be too high for most of them.

My pedagogy for TEYL, as exemplified in this book, remains clearly within the umbrella of drama education, but I feel that the looser term 'performative language teaching' serves best to describe it. As a concept, Fleming believes that this term 'embodies a culture of learning that promotes engagement, joy, ownership and active participation'.[35] These have been fundamental principles and ever present considerations in the planning process.

The next chapter will move on to list and exemplify the range of performative strategies the schemes make use of, as well as offering variations to suit different classes and levels of competence in the target language. Many of these are current and well known, but some have been especially modified or reinvented to suit very young children and children with very little English. Others draw directly from music and sometimes link with practices more akin to dance and art. Even the process of reading a story and sharing a picturebook I present in ways that portray them as performative practices. This breadth, inclusivity and flexibility are intentional. It is notable that the term 'performative language teaching' itself was first coined by Schewe in a European context and defined in intercultural terms, to mark it out as more inclusive of a range of performance-related practices than are commonly included in the English speaking tradition of drama education. This has been particularly important in the context of the development of these schemes, as drama without some kind of performance in front of an audience is a particularly difficult idea for many Chinese teachers, school leaders and parents to accept.

Drama as performance is, of course, a natural integrator of other art forms. Set designs, lighting, costumes, theatrical properties, puppets, make-up all directly draw upon the visual arts. Opera and musical theatre are popular styles of performance that fuse drama with music. Such an integrated approach to the arts, centred around play, is also seen as a natural practice within many early years settings. As Julie Dunn and Susan Wright point out:

> Within early childhood education, strong links exist between play, play-fulness and the arts. These provide children with opportunities to portray their thoughts and emotions and to see the world in new ways by experimenting with symbols and meanings.[36]

Dunn and Wright go on to point to how children learn the symbol systems – in other words, the *languages* – of the arts in parallel and in ways that can interrelate one with the other. This interconnectedness, in which children 'playfully engage with drawing, storytelling, dancing, singing and other forms of artistic communication', they see as potentially providing a rich and multilayered learning environment that can be used as a springboard for learning across the curriculum, particularly in language and literacy.[37]

Conclusion

In presenting the schemes included in this book, I am assuming that many practitioners of TEYL require a pedagogy capable of engaging learners with limited or very limited English language resources. These young children will need a chance to engage receptively with vocabulary and lexical chunks before they can begin to use them in formulaic phrases, let alone productively in their own sentences. In this I view repetition, scripted performance and language play of various kinds as ways to make language memorable; and appreciate that improvisation activities may often need to be subtly provoked by a teacher in role, who knows what language she might expect the children to understand and begin to use creatively for a range of discursive purposes, whether to describe, narrate, persuade, argue, explain, inquire, praise or scold. Furthermore, I work on the basis that some activities can be used to deepen children's involvement in the story world through the symbol systems of art forms that do not necessarily make use of verbal language. Such activities should not, I believe, be viewed as superfluous or irrelevant to learning in the target language; rather they should, as Dunn and Wright point out, be seen as enriching the learning experience, as springboards to enter the language of the story world and as a desirable means to stimulate a particular culture of learning, the kind of joyful engagement and active participation that Fleming sees as core to performative language pedagogy.

CHAPTER THREE

Performative Strategies for Teaching English to Young Learners

In this chapter I will present various strategies, many of which have been used or adapted to provide the building blocks for the detailed schemes outlined in subsequent chapters. In different ways, they foster the social and language development that was detailed in Chapter 1 and embody the rationale for performative language teaching presented in Chapter 2. The strategies can be used as stand-alone exercises, as short, introductory activities within a conventional language lesson or in circle time, for example. I have, however, argued in the previous chapter for the desirability of integrating such activities within particular story worlds in order to bring imaginative coherence to the lesson and intrinsic motivation to children's learning. Teachers will, of course, have different levels of confidence and experience in planning their own lessons of this kind. You may wish to begin by bringing a song, a game and a story together in one session rather than attempting to design an entire scheme. Some suggestions are provided throughout to foster this kind of experimentation. Remember, all of these activities can be returned to again and again in different lessons to help children absorb the language they each contain.

Songs, Chants and Rhymes

Songs and rhymes have much to recommend them as formats for young children learning English, as we saw earlier. Their language is playful rather than transactional, suggestive of mini story worlds, and appeals to children through the prosodic and aesthetic qualities of the sound and feel of words. They help children concentrate pleasurably on the phonology of English, emphasizing its natural stresses and rhythms, making repetition fun rather than boring. As Sarah Hillyard has pointed out, their regular, articulatory patterns are easier to pronounce than irregular ones and provide a predictable framework that can enhance linguistic processing.[1] On the social side, they can be used to encourage a sense of communal well-being in the classroom and to develop children's receptiveness to others as they listen and chant or sing together.

Action Songs

Adding actions to songs and rhymes can take a number of forms. Sometimes clapping or tapping out a rhythm will emphasize the stress of the language and so help children keep time together. Sometimes there are actions that add a mimetic accompaniment to the meaning of the words or there is a group game that children play, in which the rhythm and meaning of the words work together in different ways. Always the spirit of play is foremost.

The following songs have been selected for their suitability for children of this age range, including some for the very youngest, and for the ways in which they can be used or readily adapted to fit within different story worlds. They are mostly well known, in the public domain and accessible on YouTube. For this reason I have not felt it necessary to include any music. However, if you need to access YouTube, please only do so to learn the tune so that you can sing it yourself. This is very important! The versions on YouTube are often sung at too fast a pace to perform any actions to. Besides, children are far more likely to join in if they hear you singing at a pace and volume they can follow. They won't expect you to be able to sing like a rock star, and you really must avoid thinking 'I can't sing'! Everyone can sing, and it is a very important pedagogic skill for those who work with young children.

With the youngest children, it may be enough for them initially to perform the actions to the songs and keep time together with their classmates, responding to the verbal cues. You should emphasize these cues, orchestrating their actions through physical gestures. There is no need at all for any musical accompaniment.

'Have You Seen the Rabbits Sleeping?'

Have you seen the rabbits sleeping till it's nearly noon?
Shall we wake them with a merry tune.
They're so still. Are they ill? Wake up soon.

Hop little rabbits, hop, hop hop
Hop little rabbits, hop, hop, hop
Hop little rabbits, hop and stop!

Actions

Children lie still on the floor pretending to be asleep as you sing the first three lines softly. As you sing 'Wake up soon!' they quietly stand up. When all are ready, sing the final three lines with more volume and energy, while they hop along to the words.

Variations

Both the animals and the action verb can change. If there is a monster in the story you are working with, for example, then it can be monsters rather than rabbits sleeping, and these monsters might jump rather than hop.

'Wind the Bobbin Up'

Wind the bobbin up, wind the bobbin up.
Pull, pull, clap, clap, clap!
Wind it back again, wind it back again.
Pull, pull, clap, clap, clap!
Point to the ceiling, point to the floor,
Point to the window, point to the door.
Clap your hands together, one, two, three
Put your hands upon your knee.

Actions

These are self-explanatory. Children should be standing in a circle, and it will help to show them a large cotton bobbin before you first sing it. You will need to teach the actions for winding it up, reversing the hand movements for winding it back.

Variations

- Different parts of the classroom can be pointed to, provided you keep the rhyme and rhythm the same; for example, 'Point to the whiteboard, point to the floor / Point to the teacher, point to the door.'
- The final two lines can change so children point to different parts of their own bodies; for example, 'Point to your ears and point to your nose / Point to your tummy and point to your toes.'

● In the scheme for 'The Opposite', later in the book, you will see how the lyrics have been adapted to fit with the ideas introduced in this story.

'Driving Along in My Little Red Tractor'

Driving along in my little red tractor
Driving along in my little red tractor
Driving along in my little red tractor,
Bringing in the hay.
HEY!

Actions

Children stand in a circle and mime driving, without moving from their space, by holding an imaginary steering wheel. You should model this for them. The final 'HEY!' should be called out loudly.

Variations

● The colours can change, of course, but so can the verb. Perhaps the green tractor is very old and you go *bumping* along in it; perhaps the blue tractor is new and you go *racing* along in it (i.e. singing the song slightly faster); perhaps the yellow tractor is old and you go *crawling* along in it (singing the song slowly).

● The song and the variations above can accompany a number of stories that feature farms and farming, such as Frann Preston-Gannon's *Dinosaur Farm*, which indeed features a farmer in a little red tractor on the cover![2]

Some songs can be accompanied by different gestures tailored to fit each line. The following is a good example and, as it stands, could be used as part of the scheme for *The Tale of Peter Rabbit*.

'In a Cabin in the Wood'

In a cabin in the wood,	*Hands over head in the shape of a roof*
A little boy by the window stood.	*Hands upright on either side of face*
He saw a rabbit hopping by	*Hands perform hopping movements*
Come knocking at his door.	*Mime knocking on door*

'Help me! Help me! Help!' he said	*Hands outstretched, pleading*
'The farmer wants to shoot me dead!'	*Mime farmer with rifle*
'Come little rabbit stay with me,	*Hand performs beckoning gestures*
Happy we will be!'	*Mime cuddling the rabbit*

Variations

The rabbit might be a squirrel, or a monkey, anything that a young child might like the idea of cuddling but seldom has the chance to. And the farmer might be a hunter.

'Tommy Thumb'

Tommy Thumb, Tommy Thumb, where are you?
Here I am, here I am, how do you do.
Peter Pointer, Peter Pointer, where are you?
Here I am, here I am, how do you do?

The song continues in this pattern with 'Toby Tall', 'Ruby Ring', 'Baby Small' and finally 'Fingers All'.

Actions

This involves children making gestures with their thumbs and each individual finger in turn, from thumb to little finger. For the first line of each couplet, children hold both hands in the shape of a fist, their fingers hidden. On the second line, they show the finger in question on each hand, and as they sing 'how do you do', they bring both together to mime shaking hands (in this case, fingers) to the rhythm of the song.

Variations

- In order to have more 'female' fingers, Toby Tall can be renamed Tina Tall.
- The song can be adapted to fit a story that involves a character carrying out a search, as exemplified in the scheme for *Max at Night* in Chapter 4.

The following two songs involve a game that is played out as the song is sung and are suitable for the older children in this age range.[3]

'Charlie over the Ocean'

Charlie over the ocean
Charlie over the sea
Charlie caught a big fish
You can't catch me.

Actions

Children sit in a circle, and one child is given a beanbag. She starts walking around the outside of the circle. She sings each of the first three lines as the children stay seated, clapping the rhythm and repeating each line after her. At the end of the fourth line – which is not repeated – she drops the beanbag behind a child, saying the child's name. She then runs round the circle, chased by the child she has chosen, and must sit down in the newly vacated place before being caught. The game then repeats with the new child taking the lead.

Variations

- Charlie need not catch a big fish. In fact, you might stipulate that each time he must catch something different. Children might help you make a list of the different things Charlie might catch – a blue whale, a fierce shark, an old shoe and so on – before playing the game.

- The song probably shouldn't be sung more than six or seven times each time you play this game. You can make a list of the children who were named, and, next time you play it, these can join in, of course, but simply be ruled out of being Charlie for this round.

- You will see in the scheme for *The Shopping Basket* in Chapter 5 that the song has two new adaptations to reflect the experience of the protagonist in the story.

'At the Bottom of the Sea'

At the bottom of the sea
All the fish are swimming
Here and there and everywhere
Come and join us, we love you.

Actions

The class sits spaced out on the floor, facing the teacher at the front. They sing together while one child 'swims' among them to the rhythm of the song.

At the end of the verse, she calls out the name of the child who happens to be nearest to her, who then joins in to form a line behind the first child. The verse is sung again, and this time the second child calls out the name of a new child and so the song continues. If the class is too big for all the children to eventually join the line, you can play the game again in a subsequent session, with the children who were chosen this time seated in a circle around those who weren't. They will still, of course, join in with the vocals.

Variations

- If you think the children need a simpler organization, you can play the game in a circle, with the children as fish swimming around the inside of the circle, with the help of the teacher or classroom assistant, if necessary.

- This singing game can fit readily with the reading of a story like *The Rainbow Fish*. The lyrics of the first two lines can also be adapted to fit different environments and different animals, for example, 'At the top of a mountain / all the birds are flying.' To accompany the picturebook *Mrs Mole, I'm Home!* by Jarvis, we might sing, 'In the ground under my feet / Mr Mole is digging.'[4] With older children, to accompany a story about pirates, the children could sing:

All across the deep, blue, sea
The pirate ship is sailing,
Seeking treasure everywhere,
Come and join our jolly crew.[5]

Action Rhymes

'Teddy Bear, Teddy Bear'

Teddy bear, teddy bear, touch the ground,	*Touch the ground*
Teddy bear, teddy bear, turn around,	*Turn around*
Teddy bear, teddy bear, climb upstairs,	*Raise hands and knees in turn*
Teddy bear, teddy bear, say your prayers.	*Put hands together*
Teddy bear, teddy bear, switch off the light,	*Mime this with index finger*
Teddy bear, teddy bear, say goodnight.	*Wave hand*

This is a very simple action rhyme, suitable for the younger age range. It is best introduced with an actual teddy bear that the children are going to copy. You can show it doing the actions, copying them yourself, inviting the children to copy them with you.

Variations

- Once the children know this well, invite a child to do the actions with the teddy bear.

- If you have other animal puppets or toys, change the rhyme accordingly. 'Pussy cat, pussy cat' or 'Puppy dog, puppy dog' are possible variations. 'Crocodile, crocodile' and 'Dinosaur, dinosaur' are both comic versions that children will enjoy.

- To introduce work with the story of *Goldilocks and the Three Bears*, you might have three different sized and costumed teddy bears for three different versions of the rhyme over the course of three lessons, one each with mummy bear, daddy bear and baby bear.

'Slowly, Slowly'

Slowly, slowly, very slowly
Creeps the garden snail,
Slowly, slowly, very slowly,
Up the garden rail.
Faster, faster, so much faster,
Runs the little mouse,
Faster, faster, so much faster,
Round my little house.

Actions

The first part of this is spoken slowly, the second part noticeably faster. Children can stand in a circle and crouch forward as they perform it. For the snail, they can have their hands flat in front of them and slide them slowly backward and forward; for the mouse, they can place their hands adjacent to their cheeks, wriggling their fingers like whiskers. For the last line, they can turn around on the spot.[6]

'Bananas, Bananas'

This jazz chant follows a regular four-beat line. I have marked out the pulse on the first line, and this is repeated for each of the others. Try it by clicking your fingers and vocally stressing the pulse until you have it. Older children will enjoy it if you give it quite a jazzy feel.

Bananas, bananas, **clap**, clap, **clap**
Bananas, bananas, snap, snap, snap
Bananas, Bananas, flick, flick, flick
Bananas, Bananas, kick, kick, kick

Continue with *tap, tap, tap*; *slap, slap, slap*; *say it soft, turn it off*.

Actions

The children stand in a circle. They are to perform a different gesture three times at the end of each line – clapping their hands, snapping their fingers, flicking their wrists, kicking out a leg, tapping an imaginary nail, slapping on paint with an imaginary paintbrush. For the penultimate line, there is no gesture, but children should crouch a little and say the line much more softly. The last line gradually gets louder, stopping suddenly on the word 'Off!' followed immediately by a stabbing gesture with their forefinger, pressing an imaginary on/off button a few inches in front of their noses.

Variations

Different vocabulary to replace the word 'bananas' can be introduced or recycled each time you use this as a warm-up exercise – pyjamas, for example, or sultanas and even piranhas!

Nursery Rhymes

Nursery rhymes are very good formats for rhythm and rhyme. Take the following, which can be used to play a simple circle game. I have marked out the regular beat that can be clapped out as the rhyme is spoken:

Old Miss **Rose**
Ne-ver **throws**
Crumbs to the **pi**-geons,
Only to the **crows**.

As with *Charlie over the Ocean*, a child is given a beanbag. The children all clap and recite the rhyme together. At the end of the rhyme the child with the beanbag calls out another child's name, throwing her the beanbag, and the game continues.

The following rhyme borrows the same rhythm to fit the story of *Goldilocks*. Older children can be taught it, sitting in a circle, clapping to a regular rhythm marked out below.

> **Gold**-i-**locks**
> **Wore** pink **socks**
> A **Yell**-ow **bonnet** and
> **Frill**-y frocks.
> She **wore** pink **socks**
> She **wore** pink **socks**
> A **Yell**-ow **bonnet** and
> **Frill**-y **frocks**.

This can be used to play a passing game, in which one or two yellow bonnets (or hats) are passed around the circle to the clapping rhythm. When the verse is completed, any child holding the bonnet at that moment is invited to put it on and wear it. If they don't wish to, they may say 'Pass', and it can be given to a volunteer. They can then be invited to enter the circle and show themselves as Goldilocks, either portraying her manner or miming something she does in the story. The children watching are then invited to say what they can see: that she is very bad-tempered, perhaps, or that she is eating the porridge that is too hot. The children wearing the bonnets then sit back in the circle and the game continues.

This rhyme is deliberately parodying what stereotypical little girls might wear, undermining and making fun of such stereotypes by inviting boys as well as girls to wear the bonnet and pretend to be Goldilocks. It also hints that, just because girls may be dressed conventionally by their parents, they may not behave so, something emphasized in the following, also adapted from a nursery rhyme, that could be applied to Goldilocks.

> **My** mother **said** I ne-ver **should**
> **Play** with the **an**-imals **in** the **wood**
> **If** I **did** then **she** would **say**
> '**Naugh**-ty **girl** to **dis**-o-**bey**!
> **Dis**-o-**bey**, **dis**-o-**bey**,
> **Naugh**-ty **girl** to **dis**-o-**bey**!'

This could be taught to children at the upper end of this age range, sitting in a circle together. In a later session, once children know it well, each child can sit opposite a partner and work out a way to clap the rhythm together on their own and their partner's hands as they recite it.

The rhyme, using the same rhythm, can also be adapted to fit as a gloss to the story of *Red Riding Hood*, as below:

> A little girl had a bright, red hood.
> She wore it walking through the wood.

She wore her hood,
She wore her hood,
Her bright red hood in the deep, dark wood.

Her mother said she never should
Talk with the animals in the wood
If she did her mom would say,
'Naughty girl to disobey!
Disobey! Disobey!
Naughty girl to disobey!'

Games

Apart from providing children with enjoyment, games can be used to hold attention and hence bolster learning in a number of ways:

- as warm-ups to bring children playfully together;

- to refocus children's energies by changing the dynamic of the lesson;

- to mix children up socially so that they become used to being close to and working with different members of their class;

- in particular, when framed within the fictional context of a story, games can be used to introduce characters or situations and adapted to help capture and manage particular dramatic tensions.

Circle Games

Cross the Circle and Greet

Children stand. Child A calls out the name of Child B across the circle from them and says 'Hi, (name)!' to which they receive the same greeting in reply. They both cross the circle and meet in the middle, where they give each other a high five and say, 'Let's have fun!' Once across the circle, Child B calls out the name of another child – Child C – and the game continues. If girls choose only girls and boys only boys, then you can stipulate that a girl must choose a boy and vice versa to make things fair.

Variation

You can ask children to vary the greeting. Today we may pretend to be ladies and gentlemen and say 'Hello' rather than 'Hi' or 'Good morning'. In the middle we may bow or shake hands and say, 'Have a nice day.'

Roll the Ball and Greet

Child A has the ball and calls out a greeting to Child B, as above. They then say 'Catch the ball!' before rolling it to them. Children need to know that they should try their best to aim it straight at Child B who says, 'Thank you, (Child A)' once they pick it up. They then do the same for Child C and the game continues.

Variation

You can add suitable chunks of formulaic language to the game, such as 'Catch the ball! Be careful!'

Salt and Pepper

Standing in the circle, begin by turning to the child on your right, smiling and clapping your hands together as you look at them, saying the word 'Salt'. This child must do the same to the child on their right till the clap and the word return to you, whereupon you send the clap back in the opposite direction with the word 'Pepper'. With older children, you can time how long this takes, keeping a record to see if they can complete the round more swiftly the next time they play it.

Variations

- There need not be any language in this game when you first play it, as it encourages children to listen, respond and await their turn.

- Very young children will find even this hard! You might play this as 'Clap with me!' saying a child's name first. 'Graziella, clap with me! Pawel, clap with me!' and so on.

- Different commonly paired words may be used; 'sweet and sour', 'bread and butter', 'bread and honey' or 'cheese and crackers', for example. Make sure children practise saying the words and know what they mean before you play it, of course.

I Went to the Market

Begin with the sentence 'I **went** to the **mar**-ket and **bought** ...' Clap out the marked rhythm and have children repeat it with you a few times. The child on your right is then invited to complete the sentence, adding 'an orange' perhaps. In which case the whole class claps the rhythm together again and says, 'I went to the market and bought an orange.' It then passes on to the next child who must add a new item: 'a chicken', for example. The class then claps and speaks together, 'I went to the market and bought a chicken; I went to the market and bought an orange.' This carries on until the last child.

Variations

- This might be too difficult for some young children or too boring if the circle is too big. So be prepared to vary the game. Perhaps you are going to buy just five items for a delicious meal – what might they be? In this case we ask for volunteers rather than go round the circle.

- Children can always be invited to say 'pass' if they can't think of anything.

- You don't have to be going to the market, of course: it might be a pet shop or a clothes shop. It could be a zoo, in which case you didn't buy anything but saw lots of different animals. Perhaps you went to somewhere far away and travelled there: 'I travelled to Paris and went by … car/plane/boat/submarine/bicycle.' In this case, the logic of the journey is not important, just the vocabulary and the formulaic phrase.

- You may hand out cards with items pictured on them, or toy animals, and children are to say what they have been given when it is their turn.

Pass the Tambourine

A child is called to the centre of the circle and blindfolded. The other children all sit with their hands behind their backs. You give one of them a tambourine, which must be passed as quietly as possible around the circle, always behind the children's backs. When you call out 'Stop!' the child in the centre removes the blindfold, looks around the circle and points to the one they think is holding the tambourine, saying '(Name) has the tambourine!' If this is true, the child says, 'Yes, here it is!' If not, they shake their head and say, 'No, I haven't got it!' The child in the centre can have up to three attempts.

Point to Consider

Very young children often make it obvious that they are hiding it. If this is the case, ask the child in the centre how they knew. Try to encourage children not to give themselves away through their body language (an elementary acting lesson!).

Variations

- The language demands can be made simpler, if necessary. A simple use of 'There!' and 'Yes/No' is enough.

- This game can be used in a fictional context to reflect the tension of a character hiding and being searched for; for example, when Peter Rabbit hides in the shed from Mr McGregor, or Jack hides from the Giant in his kitchen. You can add an appropriate narration, as a puppet representing the character is passed behind the backs of the children. 'Hmm, thinks Mr McGregor, I wonder where that rabbit is hiding? Maybe it's behind one of those pots by the wall … And STOP! Well, take off the blindfold now, Mr McGregor. And where do you think Peter might be hiding then? Behind this pot? Well let's see …'

Pass the Puppet round the Ring

A number of small puppets are distributed round the circle (between three and five). These may well relate to a particular story you are working on. With the teacher, the children keep passing them round to the child on their left to the rhythm of the following, which is sung to the tune of 'London Bridge is falling down':

> Pass the puppet round the ring
> Round the ring
> Round the ring
> Pass the puppet round the ring
> Pass and stop.

Now the teacher calls or sings out: 'Who's got the princess?' The child who has the princess puppet holds it up and calls or sings back: 'I've got the princess!' This is done for the other puppets, whereupon the teacher counts in 'One, two, three, four' for another round of the game.

Variations

We have already seen a similar passing game to this with the rhyme about Goldilocks. A different variation will be seen later in the scheme for *The Emperor's New Clothes* as a way to introduce vocabulary for different materials.

Paint Box

Children sit on chairs in a circle while you go round giving every child the name of one of three colours in turn 'blue, green, red; blue, green, red', for example. You then stand in the centre of the circle and call out each of the colours in turn, at which children are to raise their hand if it is theirs. Once you are sure that each child knows which colour they are, children are told that if you call out the word 'blue' all of the blues are to leave their chair and find another one in the circle; in other words, they will be changing places. Play this a few times with just one colour, and then tell them you may call out two colours at once; for example, 'blue and red'.

Variations

- This may be enough for the youngest children, but it is more fun if you tell them that you will not be staying in the centre of the circle but trying to get on to a chair yourself. This means one child will fail to find a chair and will have to come into the centre of the circle and call out a colour, or more than one colour, to try to get back in. And so the game continues.

- You can then introduce the rule that if you call out 'paint box', *everyone* has to change places! One final rule, if necessary, is that you cannot move into a chair directly next to you.

- Colours can change each time you play the game but so can the language context. For example, it can be called 'Fruit Bowl', with different fruits being used; or 'Treasure Chest', with gold, silver, ruby as the named words and so on.

Rub Your Tummy If …

Children stand with you in a circle, and you invite them to rub their tummies if they agree with what you say. So if you rub your tummy looking very happy and say, 'I like chocolate', presumably you will have a lot of children join you, whereas if you say 'I like cabbage', maybe you will have a few less.

Variations

- Not only food and drink but animals or activities, such as reading, swimming, walking, running, playing football and so on, can be used. Avoid anything with proper names – people, TV series and so on – and certainly the names of children in the class.

- You can use different gestures, such as: 'Stretch your arms up!' or 'Scratch your head!' or 'Shake your hands' instead of 'Rub your tummy'.

- It need not be confined to likes and dislikes. Birthdays (months of the year) can be a theme. 'Shake your hands if your birthday is in April', for example.

The Sun Shines On ...

This brings aspects of both of the above games together and is best played according to what is visible, such as clothing or hairstyle. A child stands in the centre and the whole group says together, 'The sun shines on anyone who ...' whereupon the child in the centre has to complete the sentence: 'is wearing grey socks', 'is wearing blue' or 'has short hair', for example. If this applies to any child in the circle, they have to run and find a different chair, as in 'Paint Box', while the child in the centre tries to get back into the circle.

The Farmer and the Rabbit

Children are seated in a circle. One child has a farmer's hat placed on her head and another is chosen to be the rabbit. They both step back, and on your word the farmer chases the rabbit around the outside of the circle. The rabbit has to get back to her place and sit down before being tagged by the farmer. As they run, the children seated in the circle are given a chant and clapping rhythm to perform together, such as 'Run, rabbit, run, rabbit, run, run, run!'

Variations

- If the circle is rather small, then perhaps the rabbit has to run twice around the outside before getting home.

- The names of the roles can change. It could be the robber chief chasing Ali Baba, with the chant being 'Ali Baba, run away, find a place to hide today', for example.

Master and Servants

Place a hoop in the middle of the circle and put two each of three or four items inside it – two hats, two gloves, two shoes, two scarves, for example. This, you tell the children, is their master's wardrobe. Stand some way outside of the circle and take on the pose of an impatient master. You call out two names: 'Servant Nori and servant Li, stand up.' Then call out a command: 'Bring me my shoes!' whereupon they are to race to the hoop, grab a shoe each and bring them to you as fast as they can. Thank them but not too nicely – you are the master! Then decide you have changed your mind. Ask them to put the shoes back and choose another two servants to bring you different items from your wardrobe – or maybe even the shoes again. They must listen carefully and get it right! Once this has been played a few times you can see if any child would like to take on the role of the Master. This is an excellent game to adapt for a story such as *The Emperor's New Clothes*.

What Are You Doing?

Go into the centre of the circle and start miming an activity that the children can say already, for example, driving a car, eating a banana. When you stop, one of them is to ask you what you are doing, whereupon you give an answer that is wildly wrong, 'I'm watching TV', for example. They will say, 'No, you're not!' Provide wrong answers three times, before asking, 'Well what AM I doing!' whereupon at least one child will tell you, and everyone can repeat it together.

Variation

As soon as children are ready, this can be played with a child rather than yourself in the middle of the circle and you can encourage children to play it by themselves in the English learning area (ELA).

Games to Play in Space

Circle games are good to get children used to playing together in space, but you will also need to encourage them to use a larger drama space more flexibly and fluidly. The following games do that, while also encouraging listening and responding but also the speaking of new vocabulary.

Go/Stop/Jump/Clap

Children are asked to find their own space and stand still. You may need to help them with this, so they are not too close to anyone else and are not leaning against a wall. When you say 'Go!' they are to walk around that space keeping the same distance from others. When you say 'Stop!' they are to stop immediately, at which point you will walk around and congratulate those children who have more or less managed to keep their own social distance from others. If necessary, children are asked to find space again before you repeat the exercise. Praise those children who stop as soon as you say the word and who remain still and silent once they have. Offer this as a challenge to the other children. After a few tries, introduce the idea that sometimes, after asking them to stop, you will ask them to jump or clap. Say that the game here is to see if they can manage to do this all at the same time. To help with the younger children, you may need to count them in: 'With me, ready, one, two three … Jump!' Again, praise lavishly those children who are evidently really trying to clap or jump at the same time as you.

Points to Consider

- Moving in space, sharing it sensibly with others while listening to the teacher – this is a lot to ask of very young children. Such a simple exercise may well need to be introduced gradually, but it is important in performative language teaching. The more used children become to working in this way, the smoother your lessons will run.

- Begin by modelling carefully with the children to set the pace of the movement. Change direction a lot, however, as you don't want children following and crowding around you!

Go/Stop/Show Me

As above, but asking children to freeze and show you a particular emotion – happy, sad, angry, frightened, brave, fierce are emotions young children understand and recognize. Try to encourage them to make these very clear, using their whole bodies and their faces. Praise particular children who are doing this well, perhaps asking the other children to look carefully and see if they can mirror what this child is doing.

Points to Consider

It is important that these images remain still and silent. Children are being asked not only to be expressive but also to exercise self-control.

Variations

- This exercise is best done when related to a specific story. In *Red Riding Hood* we have a happy girl and a fierce wolf, for example.

FIGURE 1 'Show me a surprised face.'

Once children are well acquainted with a story, you can ask them to show you particular characters. 'Show me Red Riding Hood', 'Show me the Wolf.' Again, you may pick on one or two very good examples and ask questions. 'What is Red Riding Hood doing here? How is she feeling?' Do make sure, however, that you vary the children you single out in this way and seek every opportunity to use different children for this kind of attention.

- With very young children, you may prepare more slowly for this kind of work, initially keeping them in the circle and asking them to show and copy faces. By doing this, some children may naturally alter their body language, in which case you can point this out and ask others to copy.

Knights, Dogs and Trees

Children are asked to find a space and to freeze in turn as knights, dogs or trees. Agree on shapes beforehand so that each is recognizably different. Then one child is selected to come to the front and face the wall. On the

FIGURE 2 'Show me the Wolf!'

word 'Go!' the rest of the class then walks through the space until you call 'Stop!' at which point the children can choose which of the three shapes they are to freeze into. Once you can see that they have all managed this, ask the child facing the wall to call out one of the three. If she calls out 'Trees', then the game continues, but all of the trees have to stay frozen as trees until you call out 'Stop' again, at which point all of the children have to freeze again and the trees can adopt a new shape if they wish. The child facing the wall calls out again when you give the signal and the game continues in this way for a few more rounds.

Variations

As above, this is best played within the context of a particular story. So, with *Red Riding Hood*, it could become 'Hunters, Wolves and Trees'; for *The Frog Prince* it could be 'Princesses, Frogs and Trees'.

Huggy

This game is good for getting children to mix easily with one another and, with lower primary children, for getting them into groups that are not based on friendships. Children move in space, as in the games above, but instead of calling 'Stop!' you call out 'Huggy' plus a number – 'Huggy four' or 'Huggy five', for example. At this children are to immediately form groups of this number with the children nearest to them. Try to encourage them to form 'group hugs', if possible, but if this is culturally insensitive, then just ask them to get into the groups and stand closely together. Check the number in each group before breaking them up and continuing again. In this way, if any children do not make it into a group, it is not seen as too serious.

Points to Consider

- Tell children that they must not wait for the group to come to them but must quickly get into a group with any children near them. One of the rules is that groups must accept *any* child if they have room and not just wait for friends to arrive.

- If some children are trying to stick closely with their friends as they walk through the space, put yourself physically in between them to split them up. As the groups stay together only for a very short period of time, this should cease to be a problem, and you can point this out to children, if necessary.

Variation

Go around and have children count out loud with you the number in each group if you wish to re-enforce counting skills with them.

Sharks and Fishes

This has been described in detail, with possible variations, in Chapter 2 (see pages 42–3).

Chase and Tag

Ask children to spread out in the space, and then give one or two of them a hat to wear. They are to tag as many of the other children in the class as they can. Once tagged, a child must remain still until they are set free by another child who is not one of the chasers. They are freed with a touch and also a short, three-word phrase, which can differ each time you play the game. 'Quick, quick, run!' for example, or 'Run, you're free!'

Variations

- This is another game that can be played within the context of many children's stories. Mr McGregor chasing Peter Rabbit; the wolf chasing Red Riding Hood; Baba Yaga chasing Tatia, for example. The phrase can change accordingly. 'Run back home!', 'Run to Grandma's!' and so on.

- Older children can be asked to freeze into a shape each time they are tagged – a tree in the forest, for example, in the stories of Red Riding Hood and Baba Yaga, or a bird in Mr McGregor's garden. Each time they are tagged, they should make their tree or bird different.

- Children are given two explicit tasks: to stay away from the chaser and to set other children free. Ask them to count how many they set free and take a tally at the end, praising the generosity of those who do well.

Grandmother's Footsteps

You will need a classroom assistant or adult helper to play this game. Have the class and your assistant group together at one end of the room while you stand with your back to them at the other. The aim of the game is for the children to get to you by moving soundlessly while you have your back turned but freezing and remaining still and silent whenever you turn around. If you spot anyone moving, you offer the class a verbal challenge. If they cannot reply with the previously agreed response, or if anyone keeps moving or starts giggling while you are challenging them, they must all return to the wall and start again. Your challenge might be: 'Is anybody there?' and their response: 'No, no it's just the wind!'

Variations

This works best within the fictional context of a story, with the challenge and response changed accordingly. In *Handa's Surprise*, for example, the teacher could be Handa and the children all of the animals trying to steal her fruit. 'Are you animals trying to steal my fruit?' you might ask, whereupon the reply might be, 'No, no, we're not hungry!'

FIGURE 3 Playing Grandmother's Footsteps.

Simon Says

Everyone knows this game! You give instructions but children only do what you say when you begin the instruction with the words 'Simon Says'.

Variations

It need not be Simon, of course, but any authority figure in a story, and you can playfully pretend to be that character as you give the instructions, which might involve mimed activities. Agree with the children what these activities will be and how they need to be mimed before playing the game. 'Baba Yaga says sweep the floor/clean the windows/polish the glasses', for example. Keep up the character throughout the game but never be too scary! So if you only say 'Clean the Glasses!' and some children do so, you might point and look cross, saying, 'You are cleaning the glasses but Baba Yaga didn't tell you to! Hmm.'

Do What I Say, Not What I Do

As above, you will give instructions, but you may well perform the wrong action. In which case children must ignore what you are doing and obey the instruction. So if you call out 'Clap your hands' but jump up and down, they must clap their hands. As with the above, it can be played with mimed activities you have agreed to in advance.

Point to Consider

With young children, this might be best played with just three options. Make sure these are properly understood before playing a game such as this, which deliberately tests children by sowing confusion.

Variation

You can play 'Show Me What I Say, Not What I Show'. Again, these representations need to be understood and rehearsed in advance. In the story of *Goldilocks*, you might say 'Show me Goldilocks' but take the shape of baby bear; in the story of *Tiddalick: The Frog Who Caused a Flood* (which we will look at shortly), you might say 'Show me Tiddalick drinking all the water from the lake' but instead show him asleep and so on.[7]

Drama Strategies

Imaging a Character

This relates closely to games such as Go/Stop/Show Me, in which children are asked to show a character from a story. There are a number of ways you can do this. You may take a picture from the story and have children copy it, talking them through key features first. You may ask them to help you make an image of the character. If the children do not have the language for this yet, you can talk them through what you are doing and have them mirror you, perhaps doing only one or two features at a time. For Beatrix Potter's fierce bad rabbit, for example, you can work on the savage whiskers, the fierce claws and the turned-up tail separately and in turn. You can then move on to play 'Show Me What I Say, Not What I Do'.

Sculpting Your Partner

Older children can work in pairs here, one of them sculpting the other into a character from a particular moment of a story. They do this by gently pressing the part of the body they wish to move and then applying slight pressure to stop it. For the face, they show an expression on their own face that their partner then mirrors. Goldilocks is a good choice here as she does a number of expressive things – spits out porridge, falls off a chair, goes to sleep on a bed, runs out of the cave. Once the statues are made, children can look at them a few at a time, and you can draw out the vocabulary from what they can see.

Point to Consider

When children are showing their statues, don't try to make them stay still for too long. Maybe count to five and then let them rest and sit down. We can always ask to see their statue again if necessary.

Variations

- You can encourage children to make their statues more expressive by ostensibly copying from what they are doing but actually adding expression to it without saying as much. Instead, you can add a commentary. 'I like this one very much! Look, I can really tell that the porridge tastes horrible! I'll make my face show that with a big frown. Yuk!!!'

- You can ask the children to sequence the statues in the order they would appear as illustrations in a picturebook.

- You can ask children to add a caption to their image, perhaps photographing, printing out and adding the written caption later as part of a display.

Character Raps

This is a direct development from the activity above. Taking Goldilocks as an example again, you would look at the statues that represent the same moment in the story together and ask for words to describe her. Write these on a whiteboard. So for the image where Goldilocks is spitting out the porridge, you might be given words such as 'bad, sad, hungry, greedy, naughty, angry, upset'. You might also offer one or two of your own, of course, or encourage children to remember words they have learned in the past by saying only the first phoneme or mouthing the word silently. Have a child volunteer to show Goldilocks spitting out her porridge again and ask them to hold the image while you describe her. Do so rhythmically, drawing from the word list, choosing from those words that best suit this particular image. Have children repeat you each time, as in the example below, clapping your hands on the marked beat and invite children to do the same. Make your face and voice expressive as you do so, reflecting the meaning of the lines.

Bad, naugh-ty Gold-i-locks
Hung-ry, greed-y, Gold-i-locks
Naugh-ty, ang-ry Gold-i-locks.

You can do this with the other statues now and begin to invite children to choose two words from the word lists you create from each. You can then model how to say the lines children offer you, having children repeat them after you, as in the example above.

Imaging a Scene

Still imaging is a very popular drama strategy, but very young children cannot work independently in groups to produce something as disciplined and expressive as the exercise demands. Below I offer some ways in which this might be tackled with younger children, each step being progressively more demanding.

- Look at a scene from a picturebook together and work with a group of volunteers to create it with their bodies.

- Do the same exercise, only without the picture stimulus – for example, the scene in which the three bears discover Goldilocks asleep. Start with Goldilocks, then ask 'Where will Daddy Bear be? What will he be doing? How will his face look?' Don't make this too demanding or the exercise too long, but encourage the volunteers to be expressive.

- Let us suppose you are working on *The Frog Prince*. Show an image of one of the characters, telling the children that this needs a volunteer to help complete the picture. You might represent the princess opening the door of the castle, for example, and looking down with a look of horror at the (so far invisible) frog. You then relax out of the image and talk to children about who you were and what is missing from the image. Then a volunteer can come up and complete the image by showing the frog looking pleased with itself. Alternatively, you can ask for a volunteer to complete the image before you have any discussion about it.

- With all three of the above, you can ask children to help you write a sentence to describe what is happening; or to suggest two sentences of possible dialogue; or to voice the thoughts of any of the characters in the image.

The Whoosh!

This is an extremely playful activity, in which children sit in a circle and are invited to act out a scene or scenes from a story spontaneously, following the lead of the teacher. It is best done with a colourful story wand in your hand, suggesting as it does that you are going to magic the story to life together. Here I will use Robert Roennfeldt's *Tiddalick* as an example of how this might work. In this story, the frog Tiddalick was so thirsty that it drank all of the water from the rivers, billabongs and lakes, becoming so fat that it couldn't move. The other animals had no water to drink and had to find a way to make Tiddalick laugh so that the stolen water would gush out of his mouth. Eventually it was Eel who managed this through performing a mesmerizing but comic dance. As Tiddalick burst out laughing, the water spurted out from his mouth, filling the rivers and water holes. The animals were happy but Tiddalick shrank and hid away, not daring to come out again.

Begin by reading the story to the children, making sure they have time to look at and enjoy the pictures, then sit them in a circle. Now show the story wand to them and explain that you will tell the story again, only this time it will be different, as you need them to help you bring it to life. So if you say, 'Once upon a time there was a frog called Tiddalick,' any child who would like to be Tiddalick can raise their hand. If more than one child does this, you will choose by pointing the wand. No one will need to be upset if they are not chosen first time as there will be plenty of opportunities to join in later, whether as Tiddalick, as the other animals or as anything else we need to bring the story world to life, such as the river, lake and trees. Nor need they be worried about volunteering, as they will only have to do what you say; and, if there is any speech, you will tell them what they have to say – they will only have to repeat you. Explain, too, that when you wave the stick across the circle and make a mysterious sound – 'Whoooooossshh!' – they will need to return to their seats, as it will be time for other children to take on Tiddalick and the other roles. So the opening two 'scenes' might proceed like this:

Once there was a frog called Tiddalick	*Child enters the circle and adopts frog shape*
Tiddalick liked to jump around in the tall grass	*More children enter the circle, taking on the shape of the tall grass and Tiddalick jumps in between them*
Then he would take a rest	*Child stops jumping*
One day it was very windy	*Teacher invites the children still seated in the circle to blow or make the sound of the wind*
And this made the grass sway	*Children playing the tall grass sway*
But Tiddalick still jumped around in the tall grass	*Child jumps in and out again*
Then the wind began to blow very loudly	*Teacher invites children to blow harder*
And each blade of grass bent over	*Children as grass invited to bend their bodies right over*
And Tiddalick began to jump faster and faster and faster through the grass	*Teacher urges child through the pace of her voice to jump faster*

Then finally the wind stopped blowing	*Teacher indicates to the children in the circle to stop blowing*
And the grass was tall and still again	*Teacher indicates to children to straighten up and stop waving about*
Tiddalick stopped, too	*Child stops jumping*
And he said 'I am thirsty now!'	*Child repeats*
'I need a drink!'	*Child repeats*
WHOOSH!	*Children inside the circle all return to their places and sit back down*
Now nearby there was a river	*New children enter the circle*
It flowed gently through the land	*Teacher helps organize the children into a line, doing the flowing movements herself, inviting children to copy her*
The river flowed gently all day	*Teacher leaves the river, the children carry on*
And made gentle splashing sounds as it did	*Teacher invites children in the circle to make these sounds*
Tiddalick hopped up to the river	*New child takes on the role of Tiddalick*
And began to drink very noisily	*Teacher models noisy drinking sounds for the child to copy*
So noisily that it echoed across the land	*Teacher invites the children seated in the circle to copy these sounds*
Tiddalick hopped all the way along the river, drinking thirstily as he went	*Child does this, noisy sounds continue*
But as the frog drank more and more water, the river stopped flowing	*Teacher invites children in the river to stop still*
Then it got smaller and smaller	*Teacher invites children to make their bodies smaller*
Until it disappeared altogether	*Children crawl out from inside the circle quietly back to their seats*
Tiddalick looked surprised and said, 'Oh dear!'	*Child looks surprised and repeats 'Oh dear!'*
And his voice echoed across the land	*Teacher invites children in the circle to say 'Oh dear!', too*
'I've drunk the whole river'	*Child repeats, children echo*

'The water is gone'	*Child repeats, children echo*
'And I'm still thirsty'	*Child repeats, children echo*
'What shall I do?'	*Child repeats, children echo*
WHOOSH!	

Points to Consider

- There is no hard and fast rule on how to do the *Whoosh* successfully, but it must be playful and there should be a lot of laughter. This must not prevent the story from unfolding briskly or the children from listening. The story wand is a useful symbol here, in an activity in which the teacher is referee, storyteller and, indeed, magician! So use it authoritatively to 'conduct' the activities and bring about quiet when you need it.

- You will notice that I have added a lot of details that are not needed in the story but that are very helpful in the *Whoosh* as they involve all of the children very quickly. You will note, too, that they all signify action rather than description, as the narration must make it clear that children need to do something in response to what you say.

- Some children are happy to jump in and take the limelight; some are happy to join in but only with others; and some are shyer and more cautious. The example above illustrates how all three types of responses can be catered for.

- The scenes are short so that no one child or group of children is in the centre for long. This again helps share out responsibilities and stops children from becoming bored.

- With very young children don't attempt the *Whoosh* in this way. Instead, have them stand in a circle and take on different roles together as you go through the story with them. 'Once there was a frog called Tiddalick – let's all be that thirsty frog! He was so thirsty he began to drink up the river, just like this. Can we all be thirsty Tiddalick together?' And so on.

- The advantage of using the *Whoosh* with scenes from a story that children know is that they will understand what is happening more readily, even if they don't understand all of the verbal language you use.

- There is no need to do the whole story at once this way. As with every activity, it should not last any longer than children's concentration spans can manage.

- You will need to prepare your own retelling in advance and not just simply rely on the text in the storybook. In doing so, you can make sure you are recycling language and structures the children know, as well as introducing new or recently encountered vocabulary. Some of this vocabulary will come from the story itself, other new words can be revisited later. You will see above that I have used quite a lot of repetition. The language in a *Whoosh* is functional, not literary. We can revisit the literary language later by returning to the picturebook and reading it again.

Hot Seating a Character

Children can decide with you which character they would like to talk to from a story. You can then prepare some questions together that they might like to ask and that are not provided in the text itself. If the story is *Handa's Surprise*, they might wonder why Handa has to walk all of the way to her friend's house; why she carries the fruit basket on her head and if it is very difficult to do that; whether she was angry with the animals who stole her fruit; and what she might do in future to stop them stealing it again.[8] Such an exercise can tap into children's natural curiosity in a much more direct way than any dry discussion or straightforward questioning and answering. It can certainly help children understand the cultural and geographical background to the story; but it will be important for you to provide answers that are culturally sensitive and to avoid unintentional negative stereotyping in your answers. In other words, you will need to carry out some basic research if your own cultural background is very different from Handa's.

Points to Consider

- Preparing three questions in advance and deciding who will ask them means that, when you take on the role, you will not be met with silence.

- You need very clear signalling as to when you are in role and when out of role. Tell children that when you sit in the chair you will become that character and when you stand up again you will be their teacher once more. It will also help if you can have a visual sign that re-enforces this. As Goldilocks you might hold a doll; as Handa it might be a piece of tropical fruit or an empty straw basket. If you do this, however, be prepared for children to ask you about them.

- Any time you feel you need to, you can stand up and become teacher again. If the children have been getting overexcited or too noisy, you can ask them why they think you have had to stop being Handa and what you need them to do if you are going to carry on with this game.

- With very young children it might be easier for them to talk to a puppet. They won't mind at all if you are obviously providing the voice – you need not be a skilful puppeteer! They will often very happily look at the puppet rather than you when you are answering their questions.

- With children of all ages, make sure you ask them questions, too. So, as Handa, you might ask, 'How do you carry food if not on your head? What is your favourite fruit? What animals might you come across on the way to the shops?' and so on.

- Something most children of this age are very happy to join in with is when, once you come out of role, you immediately pretend that you have no idea about what this character has just told them. 'Did you meet Handa? Really?? What did she tell you?? That's interesting! Did she show you how to balance the basket on her head? No?? Oh, that's a shame …' and so on. In this way you are engaging children in a new discursive form, that of reporting back, using your own questioning to guide them in the process.

FIGURE 4 Questioning the teacher in role.

Teacher in Role

This is very similar to the above only more fluid and flexible. The key difference is that both you and the children will be in role and you will use your position in role to push children into reflecting on events, making choices and decisions. In the schemes in this book, I have tended to use this in a way that links very closely to hot seating as a means to focus on language and ease issues of classroom management.

Teacher in role is most commonly used to encourage children to practise different discursive forms of productive language usage that they otherwise might not have much practice of in the classroom. As an example, we might imagine the teacher taking on the role of Goldilocks's father, with the children in role as Goldilocks's classmates – something very close to their actual roles, but adding a fictional element. As her father you might tell the children that you are very worried about Goldilocks; sometimes she doesn't do what you ask her to. 'Did she tell you about what happened when she met the three bears? What did she tell you? … Is she naughty in school? Oh dear! What has she done? … How can I stop her being so naughty?' and so on. In this way, you can have children use their English to describe, explain and also give advice to an adult on how to manage a young child's behaviour – something they may have quite a few ideas about! Children can enjoy this kind of talk as it puts them in a more powerful position than usual and nicely inverts the normal roles of who is knowledgeable in the classroom.

Points to Consider

- With young children, it is often best to put them in some kind of collective role together for this kind of talk. Helpers and advisers of some kind, or friends, or observers who know more than the teacher in role does, as above.

- Your own questioning back to the children can help guide their inventiveness. So in the above, when the father asks about Goldilocks's behaviour in the classroom, if children are slow to respond, you might say, 'Well, she came home with some snack biscuits that weren't hers. Did she steal them?' If any child becomes too outlandish in their suggestions, you can modify them. 'Well she didn't break her leg because she walked home later. But she did have a big bruise and she was crying! What happened?? Did you see?' and so on

Children in Collective Role

Above I have suggested various collective roles that children can take on, and there are numerous stories that have such chorus figures in their cast,

characters, who share the same concerns, who are affected by a key protagonist in the same way, such as the other animals in the story of *Tiddalick*.
You might visit them in role as an animal from a nearby forest where all the
animals are miserable; you have heard that they are experts in making animals laugh, you tell them. Have they any suggestions for you to take back
and try out to cheer your friends up? Children might tell you jokes or try to
teach you some funny dance moves! You can keep up a miserable face for
some time and make children work hard to amuse you!

Ensemble Performance

You will see a few examples in the schemes that follow in which children act
out a story together in a more controlled, scripted way than the *Whoosh*.
With the youngest children, this will be short and you can control matters, as in the action songs outlined earlier, involving all of the children
physically and encouraging them to join in vocally when they can. Such a
performance will be informal, lasting no longer than a few minutes, but it
can also be rehearsed for a small audience of parents, perhaps when they
come to collect their children at the end of the day. With older children, the
scripted demands can become more challenging, but the principle remains
paramount that all children be involved and share responsibility for the success of the performance. In addition, you are advised:

- to avoid casting just a very few children in the major parts;
- to ensure that the demands are sufficient but not too challenging;
- to avoid lavish production values that take up too much time and
  are of dubious educational worth;
- above all, to make the whole experience one of enjoyment rather
  than endurance for all those involved.

Such performances are not a necessary part of each of the schemes that
follow, but they can be a useful way to make the learning visible and for
children to feel a great deal of satisfaction from being noticed and positively
appreciated.

Other Performative Strategies

Telling Stories

We saw earlier that one of Guy Cook's three metaphors for the kind
of authority the foreign language teacher should aspire to is that of the

storyteller. In the *Whoosh* we saw how that might work in action, but the more conventional ways of storytelling can be equally performative in their own, different ways.

Oral Storytelling

This form of sharing stories has been especially promoted, as we have seen, by Janice Bland and is particularly flexible as it allows the teacher to adapt the language to suit her audience and to introduce what Bland calls 'expressive prosodic features'. You may make use of hand gestures and facial expressions, give different voices to different characters and use your voice to reflect the atmosphere of the story – soft and quiet to build suspense; fast paced for a chase; a jolly tone for a comic tale and so on. Eye contact is crucial and one of the great advantages of oral storytelling, as there is nothing between the teller and the audience.

This kind of storytelling can be used in a variety of ways:

- to tell a whole story, provided it is not too long;

- to tell the opening part of a story, leading into other activities that will develop it through active participation, using some of the strategies we saw in the previous sections; and

- as a narrative link between scenes of a story that children are already performatively engaged in.

Props of various kinds can be used to illustrate meaning, provided they don't interrupt the flow of the story. A yellow ball to represent the golden ball in *The Frog Prince*, together with a frog puppet, perhaps; a rag doll to represent Tatia's doll in *Baba Yaga*; an old lamp or flagon for a story in which a genie is set free.

Picturebooks

As we have seen, picturebooks are widely promoted in TEYL, and I make much use of them in the following schemes. Apart from selecting a picturebook suitable for performative language teaching, how you present and read the story are equally important.

- You might spend some time before reading, asking children to look carefully at the cover for clues as to what the story might be about. This should be used to arouse children's curiosity, however, not as a vocabulary test.

- You may scan or use an online version of the book in order to make the pictures bigger if you have a large number of children in the class.

FIGURE 5 Captivated by the storytelling.

● Practise reading in advance so that you avoid stumbling, dropping the book and so on. Think of your role as that of a performer, a storyteller, rather than a teacher here and consider what you would expect if you were listening to a story being read to you.

● With very young children, simplify or adapt the language if necessary but only if necessary. Often the best picturebooks are beautifully written.

● I have heard some teachers of young children adopt the same jolly, rather patronizing tone for reading stories, no matter what the story is about; others I have heard read in a dull monotone. Both extremes are to be avoided, and you should think about the tone in which you will read as a means to underline meanings, create an appropriate atmosphere and hold children's attention.

● Make full use of the pictures for aesthetic enjoyment as well as language learning. You may return to individual pictures for particular scrutiny, asking simple, playful questions about them (How many mice can you spot? What colour is so-and-so's trousers?). In books such as *Handa's Surprise* much of what goes on is not told in the words but through the images, and there is rich language to be drawn out from revisiting different pictures. Do be careful, though; if you go through the whole book this way, your lesson is in danger of becoming predictable and boring.

● With very young children you may feel they cannot concentrate for very long as a group, in which case you can divide the reading up with a number of games and playful activities that relate to the events of the story in different ways. The scheme for *Max at Night* illustrates how this might work.

English Learning Area and Small World Play

I have grouped these two strategies together as they share two things in common: whereas other performative activities tend to be time bound, invisible apart from when they are being taught and enacted, these both remain constantly present during the length of a specific project; and they are both centres for improvisational, free play for children, far less subject to teacher direction than the others.

Many classrooms will have a home corner that may or may not be changed and adapted to suit specific projects. A role play area specifically devoted to English will have within it a range of resources that children have already experienced in their English lessons – puppets, materials, storybooks and picturebooks, toys, props, hats and other items of costume that have been part of the different stories they have experienced. Small groups of children can be timetabled to have free play time in such an area, to make use of the resources as they wish, with the proviso that this is an English speaking area, something that might be emphasized by them being asked to wear a particular badge when they go into it that states 'I speak English'. Adult intervention can be very helpful in such an area, but it should be supportive of the children's own ideas, not directive. In this area, children can have the opportunity to play with the different story worlds, perhaps creatively recombining elements of them in new ways. It can thus become a very good way of enabling the language of the different stories to have a creative, active afterlife in the children's collective imaginations.

Small world play, on the other hand, will have toys and models that reflect the world of a particular story that is currently being worked on. Toys, models, finger puppets, materials such as coloured cloth, shells or building blocks might all be present in a small play area situated in a corner, where two tables have been pushed together or, as I have sometimes seen, in a giant rubber tray. As with the role play area, children are invited to play creatively and freely with the items here which, unlike those in other interactive play areas, encourage them to play imaginatively within a specific fictional world. If the small world play represented the story of *Red Riding Hood*, for example, there could be a base of green sugar paper upon which were spread a number of plastic trees to represent the wood, with two model cottages one at each end. Finger puppets and/or toys or models of the different characters could be in place, with a few additional animals in the wood. There could be a small basket with different items of shopping. The cottages might be big enough for some furniture, like small doll's houses, with doors that can be opened and closed, so that different characters could knock on them and be allowed inside or denied entry! You might have drawn several interlocking paths through the wood. Once again, any adult intervention here should have a light touch, perhaps with the adult taking on a role with one of the finger puppets. As with the role play area, children will not necessarily act out the story at all but will play with possible variations and additional scenarios, exploring which is the longest path from each of the cottages, for example, even having the wolf attack and eat the hunter, or being chased by a bear that also lives in the wood! In which case, the adult helper could volunteer English words that help bring the event to life. 'Help! I'm being chased by a bear! Help me, Red Riding Hood!' and so on.

FIGURE 6 Small world finger puppet theatre for *The Frog Prince*.

Using Puppets

A range of good *glove puppets*, such as can be obtained online from companies such as Folkmanis puppets, can be a wonderful resource for teaching. A particularly friendly looking dragon might put in an appearance every so often when children are practising their spelling, for example. He struggles to get his spellings correct, but the children will willingly help him when he gets them wrong. Some animal puppets can represent characters from a story, as so many contain animal protagonists. You can introduce the puppet and have children ask them questions, in a hot seating exercise, which the puppet answers by nodding or shaking their head or whispering silently into your ear. When you 'repeat' what they have said to the children, you can act surprised, or concerned, or amused, depending on what line the children's questioning is taking.

Children will often love to play with these puppets and can do so later in the ELA. Here they can have the opportunity to go through such activities themselves, in which case your own performance with the puppet will be acting as a model for them to emulate. They will also like to play with *finger puppets*, which are popular these days and can often be bought cheaply. These puppets usually feature stock characters from fairy tales and a range of animals. Shy children may well find it easier to speak through such puppet play as a puppet can perform the same function as a mask, releasing them from language anxieties in the process. As a warm-up activity with older children, you might stand them in a circle and hand them a finger puppet, asking children to decide what it is called, how old it is and what it likes to eat. The children can then walk around, meeting and greeting and exchanging this information with other finger puppets. After a very few minutes they can be invited to sit back down and share with the whole class, or with their neighbour, what they have learned about someone else's finger puppet in the previous exercise.

For mini performance purposes, children can be invited to make *stick puppets* based upon the characters and environment of a story they have just been working on. These will be drawn on card, coloured in, cut out and taped to a lolly or other short stick. Such puppets can be used to bring a scripted version of a story, or part of a story, to life as children work in small groups with an adult helper, if necessary. You will see examples of this in the schemes that follow, but a brief return to the story of *Tiddalick* will demonstrate in detail how this can work with young children.

Let us suppose that there are three groups of five children working on three different scenes, telling the story of *Tiddalick* between the opening scenes, performed in the *Whoosh* and the climax, in which the Eel performs the dance that succeeds in making him laugh. Five children working on the first of these scenes have each made a stick puppet of one of the different animals that are illustrated on the opening pages of the book (there are eleven to choose from). The teacher has not drawn these, nor has she photocopied them; the children have copied and coloured them themselves, receiving advice and guidance. The script is prepared as follows:

The kangaroo said, 'There is no water left!'
The emu said, 'Tiddalick has drunk it all.'
The koala asked, 'What shall we do?'
The eel asked, 'Do you think it will rain?'
The snake replied, 'No! Look! The sky is very blue!'
The kangaroo cried, 'But I am so thirsty.'
All the animals cried, 'So are we!'
The emu said, 'If all the water stays inside Tiddalick ...'
'WE WILL DIE!'

As most of these children still have very limited reading skills, they only have very few lines to speak each and are expected to remember them rather than read them. The emu and kangaroo are the most confident of the children and have been given two lines each rather than one. The performance is rehearsed with the help of the adult assistant, who will, if necessary, speak the opening phrase of each line, looking in turn at individual children so that they know when to say their lines. If any child can't remember their line, she will mouth the words quietly as a prompt or, if necessary, say them

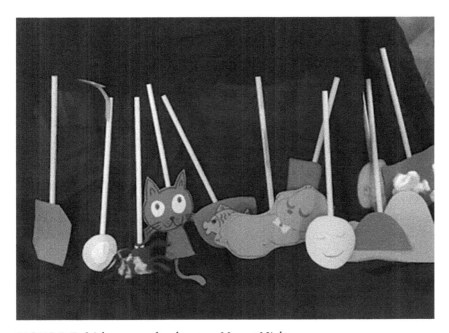

FIGURE 7 Stick puppets for the story *Max at Night*.

out loud while the child holds up their puppet. Children know they are all to say the last line loudly and clearly together.

You need not follow the above model exactly, of course – it depends on the competence of the children. For example, you might decide it is better for them to decide for themselves what their animals might say and write the script on a white board. Dividing the class into three groups with a short scene does, however, ensure that all are more or less equally involved and can enjoy other children's work as well as their own. It is important socially for you to emphasize this; that children need to be generous both as performers and as audience, in how they receive as well as give.

Music

We have seen examples of how action songs, games which involve singing and various playful activities that work on rhythm and rhyme can be integral to performative language teaching with young children. In fact, learning and singing songs together can be enjoyed in a number of ways. The lyrics of a song such as 'My Ship Sailed from China', which can be found on YouTube, tell of how the present of a fan is brought to the singer, which leads them to perform a different set of rhythmic actions each time the verse is sung. It can be adapted to sing of different presents other than a fan, presents that children can suggest before you sing the song, helping you work out what actions they will lead to. Popular songs can also be used and adapted or simplified. Tom Paxton's 'We're Going to the Zoo', for example, provides opportunities for groups of children to take a verse each and portray the different animals – the Bear huff-a-puffing, the Monkey scritch-scratching – as they sing. The chorus is very simple, and different percussion instruments can be chosen and added to accompany the different verses. The verses, too, might be adapted to fit different animals. To link with the story of Tiddalick, for example, the kangaroo could be 'hop-hop-a-hopping' and the eel could be 'roll-roll-a-rolling'. A longish song such as this will not be taught all at once, of course, and children can enjoy revisiting, then adding to it, over a series of lessons.

When introducing percussion and pitched percussion, as suggested above, it is important to do so thoughtfully and to encourage children to make use of those instruments that produce a musical effect that suggests the action. A drum might be very enticing for a young child because it makes a loud noise, but it does not convey any kind of effect that we might associate with a monkey scratching. But, once again, it is important that you modify what you can expect from children so they can meet your expectations; although we might expect an older child to be able to beat or shake out an appropriate rhythm to accompany the singing of 'scritch-scritch-scratching', this will be beyond most 3- or 4-year-olds.

The language and images in some picturebooks such as *A River* by Marc Martin are particularly evocative of sound; in this case the sounds that can be heard from the river as it flows from the city and its outskirts, through farms and fields, into the jungle, over a waterfall and out to sea.[9] The grinding of machines in the factories, the plumes of smoke that pour out from their chimneys, the murmuring of the water and the loud crash of waterfalls are all evocative of different types of sound. Older children can consider the meaning of such language and internalize it by experimenting with appropriate musical effects, with a selection of musical instruments previously selected by the teacher, if necessary, to accompany a reading. They can also add these as a layer over the words. So, for example, a group of children might repeat the word 'murmur, murmur, murmur' as they quietly tinkle triangles or run a beater softly across a xylophone. They should arrive at this performance not simply because you have instructed them, but through careful questioning that re-enforces key vocabulary. 'So for the murmuring water, do we want a loud sound or a soft sound? A harsh sound or a gentle sound? A jerky sound or a smooth sound?' and so on.

Music can also be used as an accompaniment to certain games, thus adding to the atmosphere and, consequently, to the enjoyment. In a scheme for *Where the Wild Things Are*, it could be used to control the children as they enact the rumpus of the wild things, for example. One child wears the crown in role as Max and, once he calls out 'Let the rumpus begin!' you might play a suitably fast and lively piece of music loudly over a speaker, with the instruction that the rumpus must end immediately once the music stops. Any wild thing that fails in this might be banished from the next rumpus! When the rumpus is to recommence, you can place the crown on a different child's head, so that a new Max can issue in the second rumpus. Using music in this way can help children enjoy the anarchic energy of being a wild thing in a way that is controlled, just as the wild things are controlled in the story by Max.

Movement and Dance

The exercise above with the rumpus is a simple way in which language, music and movement can come together within the performative context of a story. A more rehearsed use of movement with language can be exemplified once again through the story of *Tiddalick* to help children perform the Eel's dance that eventually makes the frog laugh. The story provides elegant vocabulary that we may wish to make use of. We are told that the eel began by moving slowly and gracefully; that she stood upright; that she began to weave and sway faster and faster before rolling over like a hoop, then twisting and spinning like a Willi Willi (a simile that you would be advised to omit in a British classroom!) and finally tying herself in a knot. You could make use of all or just some of this movement vocabulary to help children devise a series of moves and experiment with ways in which they can finally tie themselves in a knot, perhaps with a partner. As this is supposed to make Tiddalick laugh, you could ask them to add silly-looking faces to the knot they tie.

Drawing and Painting

Every early years teacher knows how important drawing, painting and colouring are for children and how much they can enjoy them. Such activities can find a place in performative language teaching for a number of purposes:

- as a natural way for children to respond to the story world – drawing characters or events from the story which can sometimes be displayed in the classroom, with or without writing;

- to record nominal vocabulary, such as the names of the animals in *Tiddalick* or of the fruit and the animals in *Handa's Surprise*; and

- to explore colour, light, shade and texture and learn the vocabulary that expresses them.

The distinction between these three purposes is important. In the first two, the quality of the artistic product is not a priority, rather its ability to help children record their responses to the story world and, in particular, help them record and recall aspects of the target language. The third purpose is different inasmuch as it is intended to teach children how to develop their mastery of the art form itself, through introducing and asking them to use language in ways that help them produce and talk about their own art work and that of others. We have seen this previously in the drama and music activities, which in their own ways have also been designed to serve the triple purpose of deepening children's experience of the story worlds; helping them learn the target language; and teaching them how to make use of the expressive potential of the different art forms. It is one of the principles of performative language teaching that language learning is at its most productive when the art forms work in partnership with, as well as in support of, the target language.

CHAPTER FOUR

Schemes of Learning: 3- to 5-Year-Olds

In the previous chapter I presented a range of strategies as the building blocks for performative language teaching in the early years, with examples of how they could be adapted to different story worlds and a few suggestions for organizing them into individual lessons. This and the following chapter will go further, exemplifying specific schemes of learning (SoLs), versions of which have been developed for teachers in MEIYI RKEC. I have, however, especially adapted them here for a more general readership.

Given the range of settings that teachers of EYL work in globally and the second language needs that different groups of children will require, it is, of course, impossible to present one individual SoL that will match all of their language and social needs. However, my intention is to provide schemes based on stories with huge general appeal to very young children; and activities aimed at matching the social needs and sensibilities of most. The language objectives will be clear and clearly sequenced and the activities arranged in an order to create a rhythm and pace of learning intended to harness young children's attention and keep them physically and mentally engaged with the learning. When following any of the schemes, you will, of course, need to consider how well they match the social and language levels that your own children are already at, for if the work is either too challenging or too simple they will quickly lose interest. If the children cannot play together in a co-operative manner, you will need to spend time developing their capacity and desire to do so; if their language knowledge is greater than the scheme allows for, you can look in the source stories for vocabulary and lexical chunks that will increase their language knowledge and adapt the activities accordingly, referring to the strategies in Chapter 3 to help you; if it is too complex for them, you can simplify the demands. Howsoever you make use of the schemes, adapting them and making them your own, while following their overall patterns and structures, will be a good way for you to learn how to create your own performative language resources in the future.

Some of the schemes are divided into a series of lessons, others provide a sequence of activities that you can divide into lessons yourself, dependent upon the amount of time you have with the children and their concentration levels. Remember, if you are organizing the activities into your own lessons, you will need additional activities to welcome children and refresh their memories at the start of the session; and calming, reflective activities to conclude.

Each scheme provides an introduction as to why the particular story has been chosen. This will concentrate on their aesthetic and human appeal for children of this age range as well as the opportunities they offer for language learning and language play. It will also list additional resources you will need to organize before teaching the scheme. For most of the schemes in this and the following chapter, I have also included a list of specific learning objectives under four headings:

- language for children to listen and respond to;

- new vocabulary for children to begin to speak;

- activities to consolidate previous language learning and develop fluency; and

- some specific linguistic competences that the schemes are intended to develop.

Those listed are rehearsed and practised throughout the schemes as they are presented. Your own may differ, in which case you will modify these specific objectives. These are important for assessment purposes and will be returned to in Chapter 6.

There will be a range of new games in the schemes, invented from possibilities suggested by the stories themselves. These will be explained clearly. If any games are derived directly from those described in Chapter 3, the descriptions will not be repeated, and you can refer back to the appropriate pages, if necessary, to remind yourself how to play them.

Max the Brave by Ed Vere

Max is a kitten who imagines himself as brave and fearless rather than as sweet and pretty and who dislikes the way people dress him in ribbons.[1] He knows he should chase mice but unfortunately doesn't know what one looks like. The book follows him as he asks a series of animals if they are Mouse or not. When he eventually does find Mouse and asks, 'Are you

FIGURE 8 The puppet responds to some simple questions

Mouse?' Mouse answers, 'Certainly not! I'm Monster!' and points towards a sleeping monster, telling Max that this is the animal he is seeking. Max tries to attack the monster, gets eaten and then sneezed out in the process, which leads him to flee and decide that chasing mice isn't as much fun as he had been led to believe. The book ends with him concluding that he doesn't have to be Max the Brave all of the time ... unless he is out chasing monsters! The final illustrations show him chasing the *real* mouse that had previously tricked him.

The story is illustrated simply and clearly in bold colours. Max as a character is appealing to very young children. He is vulnerable but adventurous and knows less about the world than they do. He goes on a quest, trying to make sense of his world, a journey similar to one they themselves are embarking on. Like the heroes of many more complex stories, he is tricked, faces danger, escapes and returns home, having learned an important lesson in life. There is a nice interplay between text and image in the story, the images often amplifying the meaning of the words in humorous ways. For example, when we are told that Max doesn't like being dressed in ribbons, we see him jumping angrily on a pink one. When we are told that he is fearless and brave, there is a large image of him standing straight and proud in a superman cape – evidently how he imagines himself to be, in contrast to the ribbons he is sometimes forced to wear. He thus shares characteristics with many 3-year-old boys but, rather than glorify infant machismo, the story is gently ironical. He is actually very polite in his questioning of the animals he meets and is not slow to run away when he realizes he is in danger. Any naughtiness is endearing, not malicious.

Much of the language of the story is structured in an additive way, as he moves from animal to animal, repeating the same question with minor differences each time. It lends itself very well, then, to learning and practising some basic questioning and answering structures and, as with many children's stories, learning the different names of animals. The sentences are short and simply structured, but there are also nonetheless some sophisticated alternatives to the word 'run' throughout, such as 'dash', 'scoot' and 'scurry'. These can be listened to and absorbed in numerous readings, even if the teacher chooses, as I have done, to just use the word 'run' in the activities.

There is a very good video available on YouTube, in which the author himself reads the story.

The session has been designed for children with very limited knowledge of and experience of English. Each session is between thirty and forty minutes in length. This may be too long for some classes and may need to be broken up into smaller units.

Resources

- A glove puppet (cat or kitten) for Max
- Cuddly toys, puppets or dolls for fly, mouse, elephant, bird, fish, rabbit, monster
- Different coloured ribbons (including pink) and a small 'superman' cape for Max; and one for the children
- A bag or box to hide the toys in
- Half a dozen hoops (for games) and a gym mat

Specific Language Objectives

Lexical chunks to listen and respond to:

Excuse me, please, who are you?
Who can show me ...?
Put on/take off (the ribbon)
Where is ...?
The Monster is coming!
Let's run together!
Get ready, get set, go!

Vocabulary and lexical chunks to speak:

Kitten/fly/mouse/elephant/bird/fish/rabbit/monster
Ribbon
Colours, including pink
Frightened; pretty; sweet; brave; big; small; loud; quiet
Yes I am/Yes you are/No you're not/No I'm not
That way!
Wake up!
I will eat you up!
Help me!

To revise and practise:

Greeting and saying names
Responding to various instructions and questions
Colours and those animal names the children already know
Happy/sad/angry
Performing the actions to 'Have You Seen the Monsters Sleeping?'

Competences:

Can respond to simple instructions appropriately
Can respond to more complex instructions with the help of visual clues
Can engage in simple, rehearsed speech exchange (saying name and greeting)

In final performance

Can repeat the lines clearly
Can perform the appropriate actions and gestures

Session 1

1. Sit children in a circle and begin with a simple greeting song, sung to the tune of 'Goodnight Ladies' (easily found on 'Walt Disney's Children's Favorites' on YouTube):

Hello, (child's name)
Hello to you.
Hello (child's name)
How do you do?

If the group is small enough, do this for all of the children, singing hello to each in turn. If not, sing it to one-third of the class and do the same for different children over the next three sessions.

2. Ask the children to stand and, still in a circle, play Show Me a Face using simple adjectives such as happy, sad and angry. Encourage individual children to show their face for the rest of the class to copy. Ask for more than one example for each face and ask which of these the children enjoy making the most.

3. Tell the children that the animal toys are now going to introduce themselves, holding each up in turn, saying, 'I'm bird!', 'I'm fish!' and so on in voices that suit them – a high pitch for the bird, a lower pitch and slower pace for the fish, for example. Then encourage the children to repeat each a few times in turn, copying the individual voices of the animals if they can. You will use these same voices for the animals when you read the story later.

   Repeat the exercise, asking children to help you complete the word 'I'm f... – that's right, I'm fish!' and then play the simplified version of Pass the Puppet round the Ring with three or four of the puppets, as described in Chapter 3.

4. Introduce the Max puppet as an English cat who speaks only English. Have the following conversation with different children, asking who would like to greet Max after you have modelled it first yourself:

TEACHER (as Max)	Excuse me, please, who are you?
CHILD	I'm (*they say their name*).
TEACHER (as Max)	Oh, hello X.
CHILD	Hello Max.

5. Play a version of Sharks and Fishes with the children, called The Monster's Coming!

6. Now tell the children that you are going to read them a story about Max and the other animals we have just met. Read *Max the Brave*, showing the pictures clearly as you do so and simplifying the language, if necessary. Pay particular attention to the animals and their names as you go through the book.

7. Bring children back into a circle and show them five or six coloured ribbons, fastened in a bow that can easily slip over the head and on to the neck of Max, the puppet. Have different children pull one out of a hat or bag to lay on the floor, saying its colour clearly each time. Children will already know some of these, so try to ensure that you are introducing some new colours to them, one of which should be pink.

   ● Ask 'Who can point to the blue ribbon/the red ribbon?' and so on.

   ● Say 'I'm going to take a ribbon and put it on Max – the red one. There! Isn't Max pretty?' performing the actions as you do so and sounding pleased. Take off the ribbon and repeat with a different colour. Then ask a child to choose and talk them through putting the ribbon on Max, using the same language pattern and saying, 'Max, you're sweet! Yes you are!' to the puppet.

- Still wearing the puppet, let this lead into the following dialogue:

CHILDREN	Max, you're sweet!
TEACHER (as Max)	No I'm not!
CHILDREN	Yes you are!
TEACHER (as Max)	But I don't want to be sweet! (Stamp your foot)

- Say 'Let's take off the ribbon. Who will put another ribbon on Max? Which colour shall we have this time? Let's see if Max is any happier!' Then repeat the above, perhaps saying 'pretty' instead of 'sweet' occasionally. Do this several times, encouraging individual children to talk to Max rather than it always being the group.

- If a child would like to take on the role of Max, encourage this, too, helping them with Max's words when necessary.

8. Show children Max's cape and have them help you put it on him. He is now Max the Brave! Ask if any of them would like to take Max for a flight around the circle. Each time a child volunteers, they will have to wait for you to say the words: 'Get ready, get set, go!' As they run, lead the children in clapping rhythmically and chanting 'Max the Brave! Max the Brave!' together.

9. Help the children find a space to stand in on their own. Ask them to copy you as you hold out your arm, like Superman, and call out, 'I'm Max the Brave!' Explain that you are all going to pretend to be Max and fly around the space when the music plays. Make it clear that there are two rules: they must show how skilful they are by not flying into any other Max; and they must freeze as Max as soon as the music stops, only setting off again when it resumes. Play this to suitable music, such as the theme tune of *Mission Impossible*. Praise individual children who manage to freeze on time.

10. Bring the children back together and look at the four opening pages of the book. Can they tell you in English what Max is thinking on each page, using the phrases they have learned in this lesson?

11. Children can be asked to draw two pictures of Max, one with the ribbon, the other with the cape.

FIGURE 9 Saying hello to Max the kitten.

Session 2

1. Begin this session with the first two exercises of Session 1, adding the adjective 'frightened' to Activity 2. Then play Pass the Puppet Round the Ring using the animal toys from the first session, making sure children remember their names before you play.

2. Display the animal toys and perform a simple mime for the actions of one of them, asking children if they can point to the one you are miming, saying its name if they can. Do this with a few of the animals, asking children to copy you together after each.

3. Read the story again. You may ask children to predict the animal which Max is going to meet next as you go through the book, seeing if they can recall from the first session.

4. Look again at the page where the rabbit points in the direction of the mouse and talk to the children about what is happening here. Then introduce a game called Help Max Find the Mouse! This will involve everyone running together from one wall to another. Begin in a group at one wall, giving the rabbit doll to a child and, wearing the Max puppet, ask, 'Where is Mouse?' The child with the rabbit doll is to point at one of the walls and say, 'That way!' You will then ask the whole class 'Where is Mouse?' to which they are all to reply loudly, 'That way!' The children then follow you at your command,

'Everyone, let's run (dash/scurry) to the wall! Get ready, get set, go!' Once there, look puzzled and say, 'But Mouse isn't here!' Then give the rabbit to another child and carry on the game, at least until you have run to all four walls.

5. Gather the children back in a circle, sitting them down and telling them they still need to help Max find Mouse. Look at the page with Fly and read it again. Then bring out the bag or box in which you have hidden the fly, making a buzzing sound with your voice and ask if a child would like to take it out. Wearing the Max puppet, lead the following dialogue, with the whole class in collective role as Fly, encouraging them to speak in the voice that they practised in the first session.

TEACHER (Max)	Hello, are you Mouse?
CHILDREN	No, I'm not Mouse.
TEACHER (Max)	No?? Then who are you?
CHILDREN	I'm Fly!
TEACHER (Max)	Oh, hello Fly.

Repeat this scripted role play exercise with the different animals, revisiting the relevant pages of the book each time, if necessary. Then place all of the animals in the bag/box and see if any of the children are brave enough to try this dialogue with Max on their own, speaking as whichever animal they pick out.

6. Ask the children to stand in space and copy and repeat after you: 'The Monster is BIG!' (making a big shape); 'The Mouse is small' (making a small shape); 'The Monster is LOUD!' (roar very loudly while you make the big shape); 'The Mouse is quiet!' (spoken quietly, with a little squeak). Then try putting these adjectives together: 'The Monster is big … and loud!' 'The mouse is small … and quiet' Play this a few times and start to pretend that you can't remember, asking the children to help you. 'The monster is big and … erm … quiet??? Is that right??' After a few rounds, children should have helped you recall all four adjectives more than once.

7. You can now play Mouse or Monster? A child enters the circle and becomes either a mouse or a monster, roaring or squeaking as they make a big or small shape. The other children have to say each time whether she is being Mouse or Monster and be encouraged to use the correct two adjectives to explain how they can tell. Model this first yourself.

8. Children can draw pictures of Max with Mouse and with Monster. They can be inspired by the illustrations in the book, by the puppets or by their imaginations.

Session 3

1. Look at the two pages where the monster is sleeping, read them aloud and ask what Max's mistake is (he thinks it is Mouse!). Then sing a new version of 'Have You Seen the Rabbits Sleeping?' as 'Have You Seen the Monsters Sleeping?' The words otherwise remain the same, apart from 'bounce' replacing 'hop', as this is a verb used in the book.

2. The following game is a fun way for the children to pretend to be eaten and then sneezed out by Monster. Two children sit in front of a gym mat and hold a hoop up between them. Explain to the class that they are in role as Monster and the hoop is its enormous mouth. One child is then chosen to be Max. The children repeat after you, 'Wake up, Mouse!' whereupon the two children as Monster repeat the words 'I will eat you up!' At this point Max jumps through the hoop uttering a suitable cry, such as 'Help me!' The monster is then to 'sneeze', saying 'Atchoo!' whereupon the child jumps back through the hoop and the class call out together in disgust 'Yuk!' This can be played a few times with different children taking the leading roles each time.

3. Play Rub Your Tummy If … focusing on whether the children like the animals that feature in the story in real life. 'Rub your tummy if you like Flies … Rub your tummy if you like Monsters' and so on.

4. Below is a simple song or chant. Its rhythm and tune are modelled on 'Flash' by the rock band Queen and can be clapped out rhythmically together. For each line, you sing or chant 'Max', the children respond with 'the Brave' and then echo the rest of the line after you, in which there are always four syllables, sung or chanted at equal length.

> Max … the Brave, wants to chase mice,
> Max … the Brave, went out searching,
> Max … the Brave, met a Monster,
> Max … the Brave, ran off back home,
> Max … the Brave, chases Mouse now,
> Max … the Brave, in his house now,
> Max … the Brave, THAT'S THE END NOW!

5. The following is a script for a short ensemble performance (see Chapter 3). It does not quote the book directly but simplifies the language and concentrates on making room for actions. It is very brief, but you may well need to work on it in short sections of no more than five or ten minutes. After every four lines, go back over what you have done.

The children are all to work in their own space and perform the actions with you, after you say the line. When it comes to the lines of dialogue, many children should know what these mean by now, so encourage them to repeat them after you. As you will work on this several times, it is important to keep it fun, to praise children when they do well and to encourage them to speak the lines, including the narration, only once they feel able to.

This is Max.	*Make a cat shape*
Max is a kitten.	*Hold the cat shape and mew*
Max wants to chase a mouse.	*Run on the spot*
But Max has never seen a mouse.	*Stop and look puzzled*
'Are you Mouse?'	*Ask a child nearby*
'No, I'm Fly. Go that way.'	*Move arms like a fly as they speak*
'Are you Mouse?'	*Ask a child nearby*
'No, I'm Fish. Go that way.'	*Make hand movements to show a fish swimming*
'Are you Mouse?'	*Ask a child nearby*
'No, I'm Bird. Go that way.'	*Flap arms like a bird as they speak*
Max sees a mouse.	*Hands as ears, in a squeaky voice*
'Are you Mouse?'	*Ask a child nearby*
Mouse tells a lie.	*Look displeased and wag finger*
'No, I'm Monster. Go that way.'	*Point and speak in squeaky voice*
Max sees a Monster. He thinks it's a mouse.	*Point to a child nearby*
The monster is asleep.	*Tilt head on to hands in gesture indicating sleep. Snore*
'Wake up, Mouse!' shouts Max.	*Point and shout*
The monster wakes up and roars.	*Make themselves big and roar*
Max runs away and hides.	*Run on the spot*
'Mouse is scary!' he says.	*Look and sound scared*
He won't chase Mouse after all.	*Wag finger and shake head*

The Little Red Hen

This is a simple, popular tale, in which a hard-working little hen plants some grain that grows into wheat, cuts the wheat and takes it to the miller to be ground into flour and then carries the flour to the baker to be baked into bread. Finally she takes the bread back to the farmyard to eat. At each stage she asks a pig, a cat and a rat if they would like to help her, but each time they refuse until the very end. By this time, of course, it is too late, for having done all of the work herself, the hen decides to eat all of the bread herself.

Teachers of very young children will like this tale for the example it provides of how we use the processes of nature together with human technology to produce our food. They will, in particular, appreciate its simple moral message – that working together and helping each other, unlike laziness, will bring benefits to everyone, values that fit very well within any classroom ethos! Of course, I have previously warned against the use of openly moralistic tales, but this little fable has much in it that appeals to very young children. Structurally, it establishes a formulaic, repetitive pattern that alters accordingly as the story progresses. This serves to sustain interest as it leads to a predictable and satisfying denouement, a twist in the tale that children appreciate for its abrupt 'serves them all right!' effect.

For the purposes of language learning, it is an excellent example of the kind of traditional tale that we saw Janice Bland promote in Chapter 1, as its formulaic story pattern and use of additive language will help young children predict and join in vocally with the telling. I have also included this scheme here as it makes very evident use of a range of activities outlined in Chapter 3, in particular the use of rhythmic chanting.

The specific learning objectives are self-evident. The children are meant to understand the key vocabulary, particularly the nouns, at the heart of the story and should be able to join in vocally with the choric chanting in the various exercises that lead to the shared, ensemble performance at the conclusion of the scheme.

A simple, well-illustrated version of the story can be found in the Well-Loved Tales series, published by Ladybird.[2]

Resources

- Copies of the Ladybird version in Well-Loved Tales
- Stick puppets for the hen, the cat, the rat and the pig. They need to be robust enough for the children to handle
- A small bag of wheat grains; a small sheaf of wheat; a small bag labelled 'Flour'; a small loaf of bread (*Note*: these should be made of plastic or take the form of clearly illustrated stick puppets.)
- A shoebox for the introduction to the storytelling and a tambourine

1. Bring the children into a circle and stand there together to play a round of Rub Your Tummy If You Like Eating ... Provide four or five examples, the last one being Rub Your Tummy If You Like Eating Bread. Then play Shake Your Hands If You Like to … (e.g. run, go to school, play with friends, watch TV, help). The last one is the one you must conclude with, as it is what the animals refuse to do in the story. Talk a little about what children like to help with before telling them that this story has some animals in it that don't like to help at all!

2. Now sit children down in front of you and show them the stick puppet of the little red hen, telling them that it is her story which is, in fact, called *The Little Red Hen*. Have the other animal puppets on hand in the shoebox and ask different children to pull them out one at a time. Hold them up each time and make sure children know what each is called. Tell them that they all lived in a farmyard together and show them the first page of the book.

    Now *read the story* making sure that everyone can see the pictures on each page.

    Once you have finished the story, ask what the children think of each animal by holding up stick puppets of the rat, cat and pig, asking: 'Who thinks they are good friends to the Little Red Hen? Why not? Hands up if you think they are lazy/greedy/mean?' Then put these puppets down and hold up the hen puppet and ask: 'Who thinks the little red hen is lazy?/greedy?/mean? If you were her, would you eat the bread yourself or share it? Why?'

3. Back in a circle, play Pass the Puppet Round the Ring with the four animal puppets. As these are very young children, you may need to pause for them to pass the puppet at the end of each line. This will include four passes in all, so if there are sixteen children, each of them will have held a puppet once. Do about four rounds of the game, organizing it so that as many different children as possible will hold up a puppet at the end of each round.

4. Have children stand to play a version of Pass the Clap around the Ring. Introduce this with a rhythmic question, also clapped out: '**Little** Red **Hen**, **Little** Red **Hen**, **who** will **help** the **little** red **hen**?'

    Going from left to right each child in turn will act as one of the animals, saying 'Not I' or 'Not me!' as they clap. When it arrives back at you, tell the children that we will now go back round the circle in the opposite direction, answering this time as the helpful children we are, saying each time, with a happy, friendly face 'I will!'

    Once you have done this, repeat the game again, saying that you will time it to see how long it takes to go round one way then back again. You can then play the game in future lessons to see if you can do it a little faster each time.

5. Have the children stand in space. Explain that you will now play a game in which they will move about and that, when you tap the tambourine, they are to crouch in a ball on the ground, trying to make themselves as small as a grain of wheat. Play this two or three times, making sure that they move carefully through the space, listening out for you and staying still and quiet in their own space when they shrink into a grain of wheat. This may take some time if the children are not used to such play as yet.

6. Have the children stand in a circle again and tell them that, in this game, we will all do what the animals failed to do, which is help the little red hen to do all of her jobs. Everyone is to clap out and chant together: 'Little Red **Hen**, Little Red **Hen**, **we** will **help** the **little** red **hen!**'

Then give the children the following instructions, miming them first yourself and having children copy you. Do this activity on the spot so that children don't travel from their places in the circle.

> *First we will plant the grain. Everyone, let's plant the grain.*
> *Next we will cut the wheat. Everyone let's cut the wheat.*
> *Then we will help the Little Red Hen carry the flour …*
> *Now we can help her eat the bread!*

All of these actions can be clearly mimed. And of course we all look very happy when we eat the bread, as it is so delicious!

7. This activity can now be repeated, first clapping out the words for each job in turn, to the same rhythm as before:

Little Red **Hen**, Little Red **Hen**, **we** will **help** you **plant** the **grain!**
Little Red **Hen**, Little Red **Hen**, **we** will **help** you **cut** the **wheat!**
Little Red **Hen**, Little Red **Hen**, **we** will **help** you **carry** the **flour!**
Little Red **Hen**, Little Red **Hen**, **we** will **help** you **eat** the **bread!**

At the end of each line, there is a pause as you lead the children through the correct mime together.

8. This activity can be repeated now or later as a version of Simon Says called The Little Red Hen Says but only when you judge that most of the children will remember what each of the actions is and how to mime them. You can call them out in any order and more than once. Children only perform the mime if you first say, 'The Little Red Hen says …' of course!

9. Ask the children to stand in their own space. Repeat Activity 5, before telling children that they will now grow into the wheat, as in the story, to be tall and strong! When ready, they are to listen to

you as you shake the tambourine, gradually growing into the wheat. Mime how to do this with them the first time, showing them how to stand tall and strong (and still!). Then you can go round as the little red hen and cut each one in turn, at which each child is to fall to the ground.

Play the complete game a couple of times more, now and later in the scheme, as children will enjoy this very much!

10. Ask the children to sit in a circle and teach the following rhyme, again clapping out the rhythm as you do so. It summarizes the story. You may feel that you will need to look at the pictures again, of the mill and the miller, the bakery and the baker; but for such young children, the sequence of grain→wheat→flour→bread is what matters, not how each is made.

> The **Little** Red **Hen** plan-**ted** the **grain**
> The **grain** grew **in**-to **wheat**
> The **wheat** was **cut**
> The **flour** was **made**
> And **baked** into **bread** to eat!

Teach this one line at a time, asking children to repeat it each time after you.

11. Children can now be invited to draw pictures showing how they have helped the little red hen. You can also talk with them about the things they do to help at home – tidying away their toys, washing their hands before a meal, carrying the shopping out of the car or off the bus, perhaps. This conversation may well happen in their mother tongue, in which case you will need to offer them the English for a selection of their answers (no more than five!). You can use the sequence of miming games, as illustrated above, for children to move from showing that they understand and can respond to what you say, to being able to copy what you say and speak as they do the actions. They can draw one or two pictures that show them helping at home this way. You and any adult assistants can scribe a sentence for each of these illustrations, working alongside small groups of children, who should each help you decide what should be written. These illustrations, mounted and labelled neatly, could make a nice classroom display.

12. Clapping rhythms to help children remember phrases is something we can do a lot of in this scheme; and we can, as we shall see below, build these into a short ensemble performance. Children will be able to appreciate that the cat, rat and pig are lazy, greedy, mean and

unhelpful; and that the little red hen works hard, walks far and is happy. A series of short descriptive sentences can be clapped out for children to echo, as exemplified below. The rhythm, as usual, is four claps a line. The first vowel sounds in the words 'lazy', 'greedy' and 'nasty' have been extended in order to fit the rhythm.

> The **cat** is **mean** and **laaa-zy**
> The pig is mean and greee-dy
> The rat is mean and naa-sty
>
> The **lit-tle cat** is **not** help-**ful**
> The lit-tle rat is not helpful
> The lit-tle pig is not helpful
>
> The **little** red **hen** works **ve-ry hard**
> The little red hen walks ve-ry far
> The **little** red **hen** is **so** ha-**ppy!**

You need not do all of these at once, or exactly as above, and you must ensure that the children do understand what they are chanting with you and that they chant it properly! You can repeat the sentences, going back and forth with these phrases. I have separated the chant into three groups of three lines, each group sharing identical syllabic rhythms.

13. This story is ideal for *small world play*. You can set this up with the help of the children. Have items such as a small plastic farmyard, including other animals apart from those in the story if you like, as well as the mill, the field of wheat, the baker's shop. There can be trees alongside paths that the red hen has to travel from one job to the other. Small groups of children can be given time to play out their own stories as well as this one, with a light touch from yourself or an adult assistant, who can play alongside them in the English language.

14. *Ensemble performance.* The example given below includes the voice of you, the teacher, providing most of the narration, with the children joining in those parts they have worked on during the scheme. As with all of the performance scripts offered in this book, it can be readily adapted to fit with your children's abilities. I propose that it will be best to perform it in the round, with you and any adult assistants standing in a circle with the children to add support or model any physical responses. Any audience should sit in their own circle around the outside.

Script for *The Little Red Hen* Ensemble Performance

This is the little red hen (*child holds up the stick puppet*).

She lives in a farmyard with a cat, a rat and a pig (*different children hold up each in turn as they are mentioned*).

One day she found some grains of wheat (*child holds up the grains*).

She asked the animals, 'Who will help me plant the grain?'

Little Red **Hen, Little** Red **Hen, who** will **help** the **little** red **hen**? (*all children*).

'Not me!' 'Not me!' 'Not me!' (*all children, as the puppets are held up in turn*).

So the little red hen planted the grain herself (*children mime planting the grain, apart from the child who holds up the stick puppet*).

The puppets are now passed around the circle to the game Pass the Puppet Round the Ring, which should be sung by the children as they do so. This will ensure that different children are holding them in the next section.

The grains were very small (*children, apart from those holding puppets, make themselves very small*).

But they grew and grew and grew tall and strong into wheat (*children grow to the guidance of the tambourine, as in Activity 9, above. Teacher holds up wheat or a picture of wheat*).

One day the wheat was ready to be cut.

The little red hen asked, 'Who will help me cut the wheat?'

Little Red **Hen, Little** Red **Hen, who** will **help** the **little** red **hen**? (*all children*).

'Not me!' 'Not me!' 'Not me!' (*all children, as the puppets are held up in turn*).

So the little red hen cut the wheat herself (*child with the stick puppet goes around the circle pretending to peck each child who falls to the ground when she does so*).

The puppets are passed around the ring again, to the song.

The wheat (*teacher holds up wheat*) now needed to be made into flour (*teacher holds up a bag of flour*).

The little red hen asked, 'Who will help me carry the wheat to the mill to be made into flour?'

Little Red **Hen, Little** Red **Hen, who** will **help** the **little** red **hen**? (*all children*).

'Not me!' 'Not me!' 'Not me!' (*all children, as the puppets are held up in turn*).

So the little red hen carried the wheat to the mill herself (*children mime carrying wheat*).

All children chant rhythmically as the puppets are passed around the circle one at a time:

The cat is mean and lazy (*cat puppet is passed around*).

The pig is mean and greedy (*pig is passed around*).

The rat is mean and nasty (*rat is passed around*).

When the miller had ground the wheat into flour (*teacher holds up the bag of flour and gives it to the child who is holding the hen puppet*), the little red hen asked, 'Who will help me carry the flour to the baker to be made into bread?'

Little Red **Hen, Little** Red **Hen, who** will **help** the **little** red **hen?** (*all children*).

'Not me!' 'Not me!' 'Not me!' (*all children, as the puppets are held up in turn*).

So the little red hen carried the flour to the baker herself.

All the children chant rhythmically as the child with the hen puppet and the flour walks once around the inside of the circle.

The little red hen works ve-ry hard.

The little red hen walks ve-ry far.

The little red hen is so ha-ppy.

And soon the flour was baked into delicious bread (*teacher holds up the loaf, smells it and goes 'hmmmmm' with pleasure; the children echo this*).

And the little red hen asked, 'Who will help me eat the bread?'

Little Red **Hen, Little** Red **Hen, who** will **help** the **little** red **hen?** (*all children*).

This time the animals all shouted:

'I will!' 'I will!' 'I will!' (*all the children should call this out several times, jumping up and down in excitement, stopping immediately when the teacher bangs a tambourine*).

'No you will not,' said the little red hen, 'I will eat it myself!'

And she did! (*all the children repeat this, ending with a groan – 'Ahhhhh!' They then conclude with the chant below. For this they should turn and face the audience. As it is chanted, the grain, wheat, flour and bread can be held up by different children exactly when their words are spoken*).

The **Little** Red **Hen** plan-ted the **grain**
The **grain** grew **in-to** wheat
The **wheat** was **cut**
The **flour** was **made**
And **baked** into **bread** to **eat!**

Children bow together!

Max at Night by Ed Vere

This is the second of three picturebooks about Max the kitten.[3] As in the first, Max's naivety leads him to embark on a quest, this time in search of

Moon, not Mouse, as he wants to say goodnight to her before he goes to sleep. Once again, he asks variants of the same question along his journey: 'Have you seen Moon?' but, as he is asking inanimate things, such as a tree and rooftops (also a dog, who, perhaps fortunately, is sleeping), he never receives a reply. His journey leads him to climb higher and higher, and finally, when he is on top of 'the highest of the high hills' the wind blows the clouds away, revealing Moon, who thanks Max for his goodnight wishes but whispers that there is no need for him to come looking for her again as she can always hear him from home. So Max, by now very sleepy, makes the return journey and is soon curled up, snoring, fast asleep.

As in *Max the Brave*, this story symbolizes very young children's own journeys as they learn to understand the world about them, being in the genre of those bedtime stories that affirm the necessity to explore outside the home, with the underpinning reassurance of a safe return home to bed. For TEYL, it offers the same pattern of question and answering we found in the first Max story, with further possibilities for extending vocabulary and also the chance to practise comparative adjectives, such as *high, higher, highest*. I have further used this scheme to exemplify how a range of simple songs can be adapted to different stories; and how a retelling of the story can be broken up into very short episodes, each supported by performative activities that enable language practice.

Resources

- The Max puppet

- A small box

- Dolls or puppets for fish, spider and dog

- A crescent moon, perhaps cut from polystyrene and simply coloured, light and about nine inches tall

- Cotton wool balls, at least one per child, for the clouds

- Lolly sticks or similar, sticky tape, card and coloured pencils for making stick puppets

Specific Language Objectives

Lexical chunks to listen and respond to:

Climbing over, climbing up; falling
Feeling sleepy; drinking milk
To bark

Vocabulary and lexical chunks to speak:

Bedtime; Moon; fish; box; spider; building; hill; rooftop; wind; clouds
Tall; taller; tallest
High; higher; highest
Blow the clouds away; blow a kiss
Smiling; sleepy
Climb; creep

To revise and practise:

Brush (my/your/his) teeth; clean ears/face/hands/nose/neck
Where are you?
Here I am
Goodnight

Competences:

Can give and respond to simple instructions
Can join in with singing some simple songs in English
Can speak a line in a simple ensemble performance

1. Read the story to the children, simplifying or reducing some of the text if necessary. Concentrate on encouraging them to understand the meaning and the pattern of the text. You may refer to the pictures using a similar language structure each time – 'Look, Max is climbing over the dog … Look, Max is climbing up a tree'. When you have finished, check that children have more or less understood what the story is about and tell them they are going to act it out together, one section at a time.

2. Look at pages 1–4, which show Max feeling sleepy and preparing for his bedtime by drinking his milk, brushing his teeth and cleaning behind his ears. Discuss what the children can see, matching the English to the pictures. Then have them stand in a circle and play Show Me … Max Feeling Sleepy; Max Drinking His Milk; Max Brushing His Teeth; Max Cleaning His Ears.

    Play more games with this vocabulary, such as Simon Says and Do What I Say, Not What I Do. Later, for revision, you might adapt Knights, Dogs and Trees to incorporate these images.

3. We can, of course, add to this vocabulary of cleaning. Max is one of those anthropomorphic animals who is as much human as cat, so we can include *face, hands* and *feet* (rather than *paws*), *nose, neck* and so on to the parts of the body he must clean. Children can stand in a circle and respond to your instructions, as above.

Then tell them that sometimes Max is late going to bed and so has to clean himself very quickly. Repeat the game but quicken the pace of the instructions.

If the children enjoy this and are ready to use the vocabulary themselves, you can try putting them in pairs, with one of them giving instructions to the other to make sure they clean themselves thoroughly. Then repeat this with children reversing roles. If the children can manage the language but are not yet socially ready for such pair work, you can ask for volunteers to take on your role and help them give instructions to the rest of the class.

4. Look at pages 5 and 6 together, where Max says goodnight to *Fish*, *Box* and *Spider*. Introduce the objects and put them on display where all the children can see them. Have children repeat the names for each and play some games to help them practise saying the words. In Kim's Game, for example, children are asked to close their eyes while you remove one item. Once they open their eyes, they have to tell you which is missing.

    Wearing the Max puppet, ask children if they can help Max say goodnight to each in turn. If the objects could reply, what would they say to Max?'

5. Look at pages 7 and 8 together, in which Max asks the Moon where she is. Ask the children to take the part of Max's echo, echoing what you say and how you say it. Call out 'Moon, Moon, where are you, Moon?' a few times, each time at a different volume, commenting on how good they are at being his echo. Then choose a child to be blindfolded in the middle of the circle, holding the Max puppet. Play some nocturnal music, such as Debussy's 'Clair de Lune', while the children pass the polystyrene moon behind their backs. When the music stops, remove the blindfold and the whole class is to call out together 'Moon, Moon, where are you moon?' As in Pass the Tambourine, Max has three chances to guess who is hiding the Moon.

6. Teach the song 'Little Moon, Where Are You?' to the tune of 'Tommy Thumb':

    Little Moon, little Moon,
    Where are you? (*point upwards, to the sky*)
    Here I am, here I am (*make a crescent moon shape with your hands*)
    Goodnight to you (*put finger to lips on 'to', point to the children on 'you'*)

    You can repeat this with *fish* and *spider*, inventing different hand movements for each when singing 'Here I am'.

7. Read from page 9 to page 12, in which Max meets and climbs over the sleeping dog. Explain that if the dog was not asleep, he would bark. Let the children hear what a bark sounds like before asking to hear what convincing dogs they can be on your instructions. 'Let me hear you bark together once; three times' and so on. Use the tambourine to help them be good dogs and stop when you command!

   Now sing the action song 'Have You Seen the Dogs Sleeping?' adapted from 'Have You Seen the Rabbits Sleeping?' Encourage the children to sleep in the shape of the dog in the book and, at the end of the verse, instead of just singing 'and stop!' you will sing 'and stop … and BARK!'

8. Look again at pages 13–18, where Max climbs up a tree, then a tall building, then the highest of high hills. Tell children that you are going to show them a *tree*, a *tall building* and a *high hill*, just using your body. They are to see if they can tell which is which. Once they can, instead of copying the shape on their own, tell them that they have to make it with a partner – two people, one shape! Actively help with this, having some pairs watch and copy others, if necessary. Play Show me … a few times, then play the game described below, calling it Hills and Trees. For this, children will need to be able to move about the space and work with their partner.

   - Put the children in groups of four. Two of them are to make a tree shape, two a hill shape. The tree stands in front of the hill.

   - If you call out 'Trees', the trees are to run off together, holding hands, and find a new hill; if you call out 'hills', then the hills must find a new tree.

   - No one is ever 'out' in this game, but you can challenge the class by timing how long it takes each time for them to complete the round. Emphasize that you will only stop counting when they are properly in new positions, standing still and silent.

9. Sit children in a circle and ask for two pairs to come into the circle and show the class their tall buildings. Congratulate them on being *tall* and show the class how one building is *taller* than the other. Do the same with another two pairs, then, on the third pair, ask, 'Which is the taller?' to see if children are able to understand. Then, if they are ready, introduce a third pair and demonstrate 'tall, taller, tallest' in the same way.

10. Revisit pages 19–24, where Max finds the Moon when the wind blows the clouds away and teach children the following short song, adapted from the chorus of the sea shanty 'Blow the Man Down', though sung far more slowly and gently. Have them take a breath and blow where indicated.

Blow them away, blow them away,
Blow, blow, the clouds away
Take a breath and blow
Blow them away, blow them away,
Blow, blow, the clouds away
Take a breath and blow

We can now have a lot of fun by combining this song with a game to see which child can blow their own cloud furthest away.

- Line up four children and give them each a cotton wool ball that you have fluffed up to be light and to look like a cloud.

- They are to kneel on the floor with their 'clouds' in front of them while they and the rest of the class sing the first two lines of the song, whereupon they take one breath and see how far they can blow their cloud across the floor.

- They then move up to wherever it has stopped and the final two lines are sung, whereupon they blow it again.

- You can mark the distance the furthest cloud gets to with a small piece of tape and write the child's name on it.

- Repeat this so that all of the children have a turn. This way we can see who the windiest child in the class is!

11. Repeat Activity 9, this time with the hills and using the adjectives *high*, *higher* and *highest*.

12. The verbs *creep* and *climb* are used to describe Max's return journey. You might set up a little obstacle course with mats (as rooftops) and soft blocks (as tall buildings) for children to enact a version of this journey, explaining what they have to do: 'creep across a rooftop … climb over a tall building …' then let them complete it to the tune of *Mission Impossible* again. Alternatively, you could use much quieter music and ask children to make the journey stealthily. This would allow you to speak over the music, reminding them to creep, to climb and so on, thus re-enforcing the vocabulary.

13. Ask children to sit in a circle and call upon volunteers to re-create the environment of trees, high hills and tall buildings using their bodies.

Hand the Max puppet to another volunteer who is to follow your instructions. 'Max can you climb up a tree? Can you climb down a tree? Can you climb up another tree? Can you jump to a tall building? Can you creep over the roof? Can you climb down the tall building?' and so on.

Repeat this with a different child as Max and start to encourage the children in the circle to help you by suggesting the next instruction.

14. Teach children the following action song, sung to the tune 'My Ship Sailed from China'.

I climbed up a rooftop and what did I see?	*Make a rooftop with hands*
I saw the moon, smiling at me	*Use both hands to make a crescent moon and smile as you sing*
I thought I'd climb higher to blow it a kiss.	*Blow a kiss from your hand*
So I began climbing like this	*Mime climbing*

You can repeat this verse using 'tall tree' and 'high hill' instead of 'rooftop'. A final verse could be:

When I reached the moon, what did I see?	*Point upwards*
The funniest face, smiling at me.	*Show an exaggerated smile*
I couldn't go higher, I blew it a kiss,	*Shake head, blow kiss*
Then I began falling like this … aggggh!	*Slowly fall to the floor*

Ensemble Performance

You could make a simple, ensemble performance of this story using stick puppets, dividing the class into groups and organizing the work as described in Chapter 3. The puppets will include the tree, tall buildings and the high hill as well as the dog, the box, the spider and, of course, the Moon and a cloud. There can be individual puppets showing Max doing different things – drinking his milk, brushing his teeth and so on.

If you were to invite parents into the classroom to see it, you could incorporate some of the singing into the performance at the appropriate points of the story.

The performance text will need to be much shorter and simpler than the text in the book; and, in your own version, you can amplify the repetition, thus making it simpler for children to speak and understand. For example, the first three lines might be:

This is Max. Max is a kitten. It's his bedtime and he is sleepy.
Max drinks his milk. He brushes his teeth; he cleans his ears.
Max says 'Goodnight Fish! Goodnight Box! Goodnight Spider.
Goodnight Moon.'

FIGURE 10 Performing *Max at Night* with stick puppets.

As he makes his journey, his words to the dog, tree, tall building and hill can be practically identical, as he wishes them goodnight and asks if they have seen Moon. In each case, the dog/tree and so on 'says nothing'. You can repeat the words 'climb' and 'higher' at each stage of his journey as he moves from 'tall building' to 'tallest building' and from 'high hill' to 'highest hill', thus revisiting the vocabulary children practised throughout the scheme, giving them added purpose in this little performance. The performance can end as Max climbs the stairs and into bed.

'Goodnight Max!' says Moon. But Max says nothing. He is asleep.

We're Going on a Bear Hunt by Michael Rosen and Helen Oxenbury

This is one of the most famous and well loved of picturebooks and will be used across the globe in a range of early years settings where English is taught.[4] Written in the first-person plural (the 'We' of the family who go on the hunt), the journey takes us through a series of obstacles, each of which must be crossed: long grass, a cold river, thick mud, a dark forest and a snowstorm. The final obstacle is a cave in which the family, to their surprise and terror, discovers an actual bear. Quickly they all race back home, through the same obstacles in reverse order, pursued closely by the bear whom they manage to shut the door on just in time. They all jump into bed, hide under the covers and resolve never to go on a bear hunt again.

There are many reasons for the book's popularity. As a story, it follows the pattern of quest→discovery→danger→safe return to bed, which, as we have seen, characterizes so many popular stories for young children. This time, however, the journey is that of a family, not a lone individual, and the danger is not really a danger as the bear is evidently harmless. It is clear from the wonderful illustrations that the bear really only wants to be friendly, and there is poignancy in the final illustration in which it is depicted walking back to its cave, by the sea, alone. The details in the illustrations do, indeed, add subtle nuances of meaning to the simple narrative. If you pay particular attention to the baby in a reading of the story, for example, you will notice a journey of shifting emotional responses throughout and a clear indication that, in its innocence, the baby alone appreciates the true nature of the bear. In this case, experience is exciting, but what the family learns from it is somewhat ambiguous.

Language Objectives

The language of the text, its musicality, rhythmic energy, choric repetition, additive pattern and implied variety of pace make it ideal for children to join in physically as well as verbally, enacting the journey as well as speaking it. Importantly, such work can introduce very young children to the ways in which poetry and verse accentuate what is, in fact, the natural spoken rhythm of English, in ways that will most probably be quite different from their own first language. This will be significant for those who eventually proceed to study English at advanced levels. On my travels I have come across many mature students and teachers who speak and understand English very well but who admit to having little or no sense of how to read or appreciate poetry written in English.

The straightforward aim of this scheme is for children to understand, know and be able to speak as much of the text as possible by the time it is concluded. In doing so, they will absorb lexical chunks and grammatical templates such as prepositional use (over, under, through) and a use of the imperative (quick, run! etc.) that can be recycled in future language activities.

Resources

- Five or six differently coloured teddy bears or beany bears
- Six hoops, two of which should be brown
- Differently coloured PE bands, enough for each child (see Activity 8 below)
- Two lengths of light, coloured cloth, one blue and one white
- Narrow strips of thin, green plastic or stiff, green card to represent the long grass
- Different animal puppets/toys
- Gym mats
- A doll's house, with small dolls or figurines

1. Have the teddy bears hidden around the classroom before class starts. Send the children on a bear hunt with the instruction that, when they find one, they are to come and sit down. If possible, hide enough bears for every child in the class. You can always have the children hunt with a partner, to halve the number you need.

FIGURE 11 'Are you scared of these bears?'

Talk in English about the bear they have found. Is it a big bear or a small bear? A brown bear or a blue bear? A good bear or a bad bear? A friendly bear or a scary bear?

Play Pass the Teddy Round the Ring, singing 'Who's got the brown bear?' 'Who's got the blue bear?' and so on after each round of the chorus.

2. Now read the book to the children, making sure that they can see the pictures as you read. After you have finished, ask about the bear in this story – its colour, its size and whether they think it is a friendly bear or a scary bear.

3. Tell children that you are going to play a game in which they will pretend to be the family that is frightened of the bear. Play a version of Sharks and Fishes with the hoops spread on either side of the floor. For the first round the family is walking; next they are skipping; then they are hopping. Instead of calling out 'The Shark is coming!' call out 'Oh no it's a bear!!' as the signal for the children to run into a hoop to escape.

4. Stand the children in a circle and play Scared/Not Scared by showing them a physical shape and face to copy for each before playing games such as Show Me What I Say, Not What I Do to bolster comprehension.

5. *Learning the chorus*. Tell the children that we are going to pretend to go on a bear hunt, like the family in the story. Stand them in a circle and teach them to chant the four lines of the chorus, from 'We're going on a bear hunt' to 'We're not scared'. Emphasize the rhythm – 'We're **go**-ing on a **bear** hunt' – by stamping one foot, then the other, on the stressed beats, to exaggerate the rhythm of a walk. Keep to this stressed rhythm throughout the first three lines, with a slight pause before 'We're not scared'.

    Incorporate an appropriate gesture for each line – for example, peering from one side to the other with your hand over your eyes for the first two lines; spreading out your arms to indicate what a beautiful day it is for the third line; standing upright, using the 'not scared' image from the previous activity for the fourth line. Alternatively, you might have children clap out the strong rhythm on different parts of their body – legs, chest, arms – as they chant together.

    Repeat this a few times until children are familiar and reasonably competent with it, changing volume from very quiet (not to attract a bear) to quite loud (to show how 'not scared' they are!).

6. *Learning the language of the journey*. It is fun to do this physically, making use of the onomatopoeic words that describe each stage. Although many are invented, they nonetheless present good

possibilities for children to play with the phonology of English in expressive ways. Have the children stand in a circle and lead them through the following:

- For the *grass*, stand up tall, with your arms straight in the air and sway, whispering 'swishy, swashy' as you do so.

- For the *river*, spread your arms out and gesture a flowing motion, saying 'splish, splosh' as you do so.

- For the *mud*, act as though your feet are getting stuck.

- For the *forest*, stand in a tree shape, and use your arms (as branches) to mime snagging and tripping 'invisible' passers-by.

- For the *snowstorm*, make a dance in the air with your fingers and hands as snowflakes, blowing as you utter 'hoo whoo'.

- For the *cave*, have the children all link arms together and bend over to form the shape of a large cave.

Then play Show Me and other associated vocabulary games to re-enforce understanding and further encourage children to speak the words associated with each stage of the journey. If you play

FIGURE 12 Long wavy grass.

Simon Says, rename it Bear Says, holding a teddy bear and pretend it is the bear giving the instructions.

7. *Over, under, through.* When faced with each obstacle of the journey, the family realizes that they can't go over or under it but always have to go through it. The following activity will help children practise the three prepositions physically.

Sit the children in a circle. Come to the centre and hold a hoop. Ask different children by name to come out and go over, under or through the hoop according to your instruction, saying each time: 'You have to go ___ it.'

After a few turns, you can ask children seated in the circle to prompt you as to which instruction you should give. Later, you might leave the hoop in the ELA for children to play this on their own, or you might build it into a further activity, having children sit in smaller circles of five or six, taking it in turns to give and receive/act out instructions.

8. *Getting through each obstacle in turn.* The coloured PE bands are intended to represent the different parts of the journey. For example, light green for the grass; blue for the river; brown for the mud; dark green for the forest; white for the snowstorm; black for the dark cave.

Help children to learn which is which through the following short activities:

● Repeating after you 'Blue is for river' and so on as you hold up each band in turn.

● Choosing the right coloured band as you say 'River' or 'Mud' and so on.

● Completing your sentence as you pick up and show them the bands in turn. 'Blue is for ...'; Brown is for ...'.

Then play the game below:

(a) First play a round of *huggy* to get children into five groups of more or less equal size.

(b) Distribute a different set of coloured bands to each group for them to wear over their shoulders, making use of all of the colours above, apart from the black. The five groups will then represent the different parts of the journey. The group wearing the light green bands will be the long grass; the white bands, the snow storm and so on.

(c) In order to start the game, the children wearing the light green bands are to spread out in a line across the room and are told that they will try to tag their classmates as they run from one wall to the other, attempting to get there without being touched. They are not to catch and hold on to any child, simply to try and touch as many as they can.

(d) Once all of the children have made it to the opposite wall, you can ask for any child who managed to avoid being tagged to put up their hand. The class can help you count the total number aloud.

(e) You can then repeat this activity by having children try to return through the grass again before moving on to the next round.

(f) The game continues with the group in the blue bands, representing the river, next taking the centre, then on to the brown bands and so on.

(g) Before each round, have children echo you, or chant with you, the relevant text for each obstacle, from 'Uh-uh! …' through to '… We have to go through it!'

9. *The journey to the cave.* For older children who are used to working in groups, the following exercise will be enjoyable.

Have separate zones set up in the teaching space to represent the different stages of the journey. For example, long strips of thin, green plastic or stiff card for the grass; a large, blue cloth for the river; a large, white cloth for the snowstorm; brown hoops for the mud.

Put the groups of children into their correct zone, according to the colour of their bands. Then instruct each group to perform a simple action that will represent their zone – picking up and waving the strips of card for the grass, picking up the white cloth and billowing it up together for the snowstorm and so on. Assist as much as you need to and encourage them to accompany their actions with the appropriate phrases – 'swishy swashy' for the grass and so on.

Go through the journey again, proceeding in order around the circle. All of the children can join in with the words for each stage, from 'Uh-uh!' up to and including 'We've got to go through it!' whereupon you help the relevant group perform their actions, leading them in making the appropriate sound effects – 'hoo whoo' and so on.

10. '*Tiptoe, tiptoe – what's that?*' Hide the different animal puppets around the teaching space before the children enter it. Tell them in hushed tones that there is a bear hiding somewhere, as well as some other friendly animals. 'We need to see if we can find where the bear is hiding.' Group them together and lead them through the space very quietly, 'Ssshhhh! Tiptoe, tiptoe, tiptoe.' Show them how tiptoe works, moving from one foot to the other on the tip of your toes as you say the word over and over again. Every so often you will stop them and say 'Ssshhh', pointing and asking 'What's

FIGURE 13 Being chased back home.

that?' Ask a child to go and have a look. There will be a cat, a frog, a bird, a monkey, perhaps – they can pick it up, show and tell you what it is and put it back. If they find the bear, the class is to call out together 'Oh no, it's a bear!' before running back to the safety of an area previously designated as home – some mats in the centre of the room, for example. Here they can all crouch down and hide until you tell them it is safe. If the children want to play it again, tell them before doing so to keep their eyes closed while the bear finds a different cave to hide in.

11. *Going through the cave.* This can be represented physically by having children stand opposite a partner, joining hands with them and then stretching their arms upwards to make a small, narrow passage between them both. If you line two or three pairs of children opposite each other, this becomes the cave for other children to tiptoe through in turn.

12. *Practising the sequence of the journey there and back.* Have the zones set up again and practise going through each space together, uttering the appropriate phrases but this time more quickly. The words are: 'We're going through the grass – swishy, swashy; we're going through the river' and so on. Once they have all gone through the cave (formed as above) say, 'We're going back now. Ready?? Quick! Back through the cave. Tiptoe tiptoe' and so on thus practising the language of the return journey, as presented in the book.

For a more advanced try at this, change the tone and the pace of the journey, speaking slowly and quietly as they approach the cave, then loudly and more quickly on the return journey.

13. *Back home*. Sit the children around the doll's house. Use some small toy figurines, one for each child, if possible. Practise the language 'Open the door/shut the door/up the stairs/down the stairs/into the bedroom/out of the bedroom/into bed/out of bed.' You can do this with different figurines, demonstrating first, then asking the class to repeat the phrases after you. Then see if any child will volunteer to follow your instructions: 'Aminah, what is your doll called? Good. Can he open the door? And shut the door behind him? Very good!' before moving on to another child. The children can then take the lead, giving instructions to you or to another child.

    These actions can also be mimed – opening the door, running upstairs, hiding under the bedclothes and so on. You can take the lead in this, miming with them while calling out the instructions in an excited voice.

14. It may be possible now to *perform the whole story together*, using the zones to represent the places, with the cave later being formed in the centre of the room. First of all read the whole story again, encouraging children to join in with you. As far as possible, when you perform the journey, children should speak the words with you.

    If you decide to present this to parents, have different groups take on responsibility for enacting the grass, the river, the mud and so on for the others to travel through. A child can represent the bear by holding out a large teddy and chasing the children back home, but do rehearse this before any formal presentation. Every so often there could be a pause to allow the bear to roar very loudly. You can make the ending quite sad by having the bear return slowly to his cave and say, 'I only wanted to be their friend!'

    Instead of a physical ensemble performance you might use stick puppets, as in the previous scheme *Max at Night*.

15. *Further possibilities*. Given the ambiguous nature of the ending of the picturebook, the following activities allow for some further exploration of its implications. The children will only need fairly basic English to engage in them.

    - Make a physical image of the bear, sitting back in his cave and looking sad. Come out of the image and ask the children how the bear is feeling. Tell them that this sad, lonely bear can speak English and ask them what questions they would like to ask it. Then take up the image again and let the children question you. For further guidance, see the section 'Hot Seating a Character' in Chapter 3.

FIGURE 14 Performing the story with stick puppets.

- After the exercise, if the children are able to read and write a little, you could explain that the bear can speak but cannot write in English. Can the children compose a short letter to the family on its behalf, explaining that it only wants to be friendly and would like them to visit the cave again? You, of course, will scribe this for them.

- In a later session, take on the role of the family's worried father or mother. Explain that your daughter opened and read a letter supposedly written by the bear. Read it aloud to the children, and say your daughter wants the family to visit the cave again but that you are not sure whether this is a good idea. What advice do the children have for you? Don't make this too easy for them and conclude by saying that you will have to think about it before you make a decision.

- Help the children create different final images for this new story, according to the different ideas they have. If the family went back to the cave, what would happen? If they didn't, what might the bear do? See the section 'Imaging a Scene' in Chapter 3 for further guidance.

Goldilocks and the Three Bears

This is such a well-known story that no summary is necessary, though a decent, short version of it can be found on the internet at dltk-teach.com.[5] I have already used the tale quite extensively in Chapter 3 to provide examples of how a number of performative strategies can work in practice. As the tale provides more opportunities for repetitive, additive yet enjoyable uses of language, I am giving it some further attention below by sketching what a scheme for this story might look like. I am including less detail than in the previous schemes in the hope that you will by now be able to flesh out the ideas yourself to best suit your children's needs and interests.

Specific Language Objectives

Through the activities presented below, the children should learn how to speak most of what the three bears say in the story; to use phrases like 'too hot, too cold, too hard' and 'just right' appropriately; and a variety of new nouns for things that belong to the three bears in their cave. These can vary but might include cigar, cup of tea, brush and comb, various toys for baby bear and so on. The children can also be introduced to the two rhymes about Goldilocks presented in Chapter 3, the one as part of a circle game, the other as a clapping game. These will introduce a range of vocabulary and lexical chunks to do with clothing and parental reprimands. You can present the specific learning objectives you choose to concentrate on in your planning in the form previously suggested in the two Max schemes.

Resources

- Three teddy bears of different sizes and dressed as mummy bear, daddy bear and baby bear; or three stick puppets that are readily identifiable

- A doll with yellow hair to represent Goldilocks (NOT a Barbie doll – she will always be Barbie to the children!)

- Pictures/flash cards of a bowl of porridge, a chair and a bed

1. Prepare a version of the story that suits the language level of your children but keep the strong patterns of three throughout. Tell your version orally to the children, using the teddy bears or stick puppets as visual aids as you do so. Give the characters very distinctive voices. Mime being Goldilocks tasting the porridge, sitting in the chairs and so on so that the meaning of phrases like 'too hot/too hard/just right' are very clear.

2. Chant the action rhyme 'Teddy Bear, Teddy Bear' together but use one of the three bears for this and change the lyrics accordingly – 'baby bear, baby bear turn around' and so on. Repeat this in future lessons with a different bear each time.

3. Play Show Me and other various vocabulary games to illustrate and practise the phrases: 'this porridge is too hot/too cold/just right'.

4. Play The Bears Are Coming, with the children as Goldilocks and the hoops as cupboards to hide in.

5. Play Pass the Puppets Round the Ring with the three bears and Goldilocks.

6. Use the different bears for children to help you, speaking their phrases in the wrong voice. Children will enjoy correcting you if you hold up the daddy bear and speak in baby bear's voice, for example.

7. Tell parts of the story again, with children helping you to get the words and also the voices right for the three different bears. If you make use of the teddy bears and also pictures (of porridge, of a chair, of a bed), you can then hold up a bear in one hand, a picture in another and children can tell you what the bear is saying here and you can encourage them to speak in the appropriate voice.

8. Have three hoops and place the three different bears in each. Then have nine or twelve objects that evidently belong to different bears, for example, a child's book, a toy, a doll and packet of sweets for baby bear. Try not to be too sexist for mummy and daddy bear, but do make them as gender specific as you can – a man's razor and a man's hat for daddy bear, for example. You can include items like a cigar and a cup of tea and let children help you decide whom they belong to.

   You can now do quite a few activities with these items.

   ● Play a version of Kim's Game, in which children close their eyes while one child as Goldilocks 'steals' an item and hides it behind her back. Children are to try to spot the one she has taken. Once they have it right, they all clap and chant rhythmically together: '**Gold**ilocks, **Gold**ilocks, re-**turn** that **hat!**' (handbag, razor, toy etc.).

   ● Play a similar game, but this time in the voice of the three bears. Children have to decide which voice to use as they say, 'Who has stolen my cigar? (book, doll, hat etc.)

   ● As a variation of this, you can have children practise the three verbs eating/drinking/smoking by just leaving the cigar, the tea and the sweets in different hoops. This time children are to say, in the appropriate voice, 'Who has been smoking MY cigar!'

and so on. You can then mix the items up, for example, putting the cigar in baby bear's hoop so that they have to say, 'Who has been smoking MY cigar' in the voice of baby bear, which should greatly amuse them.

- You can play the same game only this time using the verb 'playing with', as with 'Who has been playing with MY toys!' 'Who has been playing with MY razor!'

9. You could have children *sculpt images* of Goldilocks and compose a *character rap* for her, as described in Chapter 3.

10. You might teach children the rhyme *Goldilocks wore pink socks*, as described in Chapter 3, and play the game to go with it.

11. You could do the *teacher in role* activity as one of Goldilocks's parents, as described in Chapter 3.

12. *Studying threes*! Children can think about how many sets of three there are in this story. Some are to do with characters and objects: three bears; three pots of porridge; three chairs; three beds. Others are to do with sequences: Goldilocks tries three lots of porridge, three chairs and three beds, which is itself a sequence of three. Three lots of questions are asked in another overall sequence of three (Who has been eating/sitting/sleeping …?). All of these can be used to make a large display. Mathematically minded children (of which there are a few!) may well be very taken with this!

CHAPTER FIVE

Schemes of Learning: 5- to 7-Year-Olds

Introduction

The following schemes are generally longer and more complex than those in the previous chapter. The stories are sometimes lengthier and the language more varied, as are the range of teaching approaches. I also suggest a number of activities that involve some simple reading and writing for those children who are becoming literate in English at this young age. There is much that remains similar to the earlier schemes nonetheless. The key resources are picturebooks and traditional tales; and two of the stories involve principal characters having adventures that lead them into dangers and difficulties, which they manage to overcome before returning home. The aesthetic appeal of the stories for very young children and their capacity to inspire enjoyable, performative teaching and learning remain of central concern.

The language objectives are presented in the same format as in the previous chapter but are selective and also variable in these more complex stories. It may well be that the class will already know some of the lexical chunks I present as new language; it may be that some of the more expressive vocabulary needs more re-enforcement than the scheme offers; it may be that suggestions I put in the list for 'speak and understand' may be modified to 'listen and respond to' or vice versa. Sometimes rather than present specific vocabulary I point to more generic lists, as in the case of listing opposites in the first of the schemes. Importantly, these schemes attempt to make more space for children to develop discourse skills, making productive use of their English language resources, notably in their dialogues with the teacher in role. One final point is a very important one: the stories should be returned to later and read again and again. Just as children enjoy favourite bedtime stories, they can enjoy listening to favourite classroom stories. Hearing language repeated in expressive ways through stories they enjoy and understand will serve to increase their vocabulary over time.

As in Chapter 4, the schemes are either divided into individual lessons or presented as a list of ordered activities. Either way, you will need to look at them carefully, regarding them as guidance rather than as scripts to follow slavishly. They will need your own commitment and vitality if they are to come alive in the classroom.

The Opposite by Tom MacRae and Elena Odriozola

This delightful picturebook, described by Stephen Fry on the cover as having 'all the hallmarks of a classic', tells the surreal story of Nate, a young boy who wakes to find an Opposite on his ceiling one morning.[1] This mischievous little creature – rather like a bogle from traditional English folk tales – reappears at intervals during his day, causing havoc by making the opposite happen to what Nate is intending to do. At breakfast, instead of his milk pouring over his cereal, it splashes over the table and ceiling. At school, when he is painting, the paint sprays over the floor, ceiling, walls and even the teacher. Adults can't help Nate because they are unaware of the Opposite's presence. Nate finally solves the problem by stating the opposite of what he wants to happen. As a result, everything goes into reverse; the paint is on his picture, not the floor, and he is able to make the Opposite disappear by saying how much he would like it to stay forever. Life carries on as though the Opposite was never there, but there is a twist in the tale. The next morning the same thing happens; the Opposite reappears, and Nate has to say that he hopes the story will go on forever and ever in order for it to end abruptly.

The illustrations in the book are simple, almost cartoon like, and the Opposite itself is easy for a child to sketch – hooded, with a long, straight tunic and tiny legs and feet. It is a manifestation of the forces that very young children often face as their struggles to control the material world often end up with the kind of mess and confusion that insensitive adults are likely to scold them for. This is another tale in which adults do not understand the child's problem, and the child needs to exercise wit and cunning to get rid of the bullying menace of the mischievous Opposite. The story could just as readily be about a little girl called Natalie; there is nothing gender specific about this little boy's behaviour, nor in the resources he draws upon to sort out his world.

The activities below integrate drama, music and art. All should be taught if children are to gain fully from the language work. In addition, there are some playful suggestions that you should make use of in your general teaching with the class for the duration of this scheme.

Specific Language Objectives

Lexical chunks to listen, understand and respond to:

A range of vocabulary relating to opposites expressed in the superlative form, such as: messiest/tidiest; naughtiest/best behaved; dirtiest/cleanest; clumsiest/most careful; laziest/hardest working

Other adjectival opposites, from the simple 'loud/quiet' *to the more expressive* 'stormy/peaceful' *and* 'upside down/right way up'

Vocabulary and lexical chunks to speak and understand:

A full list of opposites chosen by the teacher to re-enforce and develop children's understanding of the concept and the range of their vocabulary

Here, there, anywhere

Correct use of prepositions of place such as: *on* the ceiling; *in* the corner; *at* the door
Expressive verb forms relating to the appearance of the Opposite, including: staring; grinning; hissing; blinking; baring teeth; shrieking; disappearing in a puff of smoke

I mean to say
  The opposite happened
  You're not usually so lazy/clumsy/messy

To revise and practise:

A range of adjectives and verbs expressing opposites, such as: big (biggest); small (smallest); stand (jump) up/sit (lie) down

Competences:

  Can discuss the quality of sounds made by different musical instruments
  Can describe clearly the Opposite and his appearance
  Can help perform a version of the story with musical accompaniment

Resources

- Three stick puppets modelled on different appearances of the Opposite. These should be quite large, about 60 centimetres tall. We should have one each for *staring*; *grinning*; and *hissing*
- A4 paper and coloured pencils
- Coloured paints and plastic bottle tops

Session 1

1. Play Go/Stop/Show Me with the words *big*; *small*; *happy*; *sad*; *fat*; *thin*. Model for the children, if necessary, or have them copy particularly good examples shown by different children.

2. Ask a child to demonstrate what *big* looks like, then ask the class what its opposite is. When they answer, ask for another volunteer to demonstrate what *small* looks like. Using these visual examples, say 'the opposite of big is small ... and the opposite of small is ...?' Children should be able to tell you. Do the same activity with the other pairs of opposites to show clearly what the concept of an *opposite* is.

3. Sit the children down and show them the cover of the book, where we see Nate standing upright, staring intensely at the Opposite, which is hanging upside down from the ceiling, smirking at him. Tell them the title of the book and explain that it tells the story of a little boy called Nate and a creature called the Opposite. Ask them which of the figures on the cover is Nate and which the Opposite. How can they tell? Just from its picture, do they think the Opposite is naughty or well behaved? Why?

   Now read the story. Make your reading expressive of the surprise and annoyance caused by the Opposite and also of Nate's innocent sounding pleasure as he learns how to get rid of it.

4. Teach children the following song about the story. The tune is the same as 'Wind the Bobbin Up'. As with that song, there are actions/responses to accompany each line. Children are initially to be taught the actions rather than the words – they will pick the words up soon enough, and you can invite them to join in as and when they are ready to.

   You will need to sing the song and model the actions first. These should be clear and simple. Shrug and look puzzled, arms out to the side, palms upwards for the first line; look slowly around with your finger poised to point for the third line; for the other lines, you just need to point to appropriate places in the classroom.

   > *Where's the Opposite? Where's the Opposite?*
   > *Here, there, anywhere?*
   > *Spot the Opposite, Spot the Opposite,*
   > *Here, there, anywhere.*
   > *Is it on the ceiling, is it on the floor,*
   > *In the corner or at the door?*
   > *Under the table, on my chair?*
   > *Staring at me over there!*

5. Read the story again and have children tell you where the Opposite is in the pictures when it appears. The song above re-enforces the correct use of prepositions of place, so ask children to draw upon these when answering your questions. You can ask the children to figure out from the illustrations what it has done before you read the actual text. The story is not long and should be read a few times while you are working on this scheme.

Session 2

1. Have the three Opposite stick puppets prepared. When the children enter your class, ask them if there is any evidence that the Opposite might be hiding in the classroom somewhere today. Make sure that there are two or three clues; perhaps a picture on display is now upside down; perhaps your name is spelt backwards on the whiteboard; perhaps the date is written in reverse and so on. Ask a child if they can find where the Opposite is hiding. Have the *staring* Opposite hidden somewhere that is not too difficult to find (don't introduce the other two puppets yet). Then lead the children in the song together, as in the last lesson, asking the child who is holding the Opposite to stand somewhere in the classroom, with the puppet behind her back. When children start singing the last line, she is to hold it up so that everyone can see and point to it.

   Children will like this and most will want a turn with the Opposite. You can perform the song twice more now, introducing the 'grinning' and 'hissing' Opposite puppets. Ask the children each time if they know from its face what it is doing. The last line of the song must change each time; rather than 'Staring at me', the children will sing 'Grinning at me' or 'Hissing at me'.

   Be playful in the way that you choose the child who will hold up the stick puppet; for example, say 'I mean to say, shall I choose the messiest child?' Children are to reply together, 'No, the opposite!' At which you respond, 'So what is the opposite of messiest? Yes, tidiest, that's right!'

   Perform this song once a day for the remaining duration of the project. Always play this same verbal game to select the child, but make sure you choose a different child each time, using a different pair of opposites to do so (dirtiest/cleanest; noisiest/quietist; nastiest/ nicest etc.). Let the child you select choose which Opposite puppet they want to hold up, and make sure the class knows what they should sing for it.

2. Tell the children that they are going to spend the rest of this session learning how to look and act like the Opposite. You can have them *stare* like the Opposite and *grin* like the Opposite, and *hiss*, modelling this very clearly with them. They should quite quickly be able to use this language themselves now. Then introduce *blinking*, *baring your teeth* and *shrieking* in a similar way and play some of the usual games to get them used to these new words.

3. Sit children down and explain that they are going to use music to help the Opposite disappear. Have an assortment of musical instruments in front of you and introduce the exact words of the sentence from the book that describes how the Opposite disappeared in a puff of smoke. Talk with children about the kind of sounds that might accompany each of the verbs – blink, shriek, hiss – and the phrase 'puff of smoke'. Do the actions, vocally making sounds that signal clearly what each means before asking them to choose an appropriate instrument that can make a similarly apt sound. Make sure their choice is thoughtful and makes sense, even though it might not have been the one you would have made yourself. So you might say:

> *Now that we know what blink means, do we want a long sound or a short sound? A quick sound or a slow sound? A loud sound or a quiet sound? Do we make a loud noise when we blink? Right, so we need a quiet, quick, light sound. Which instrument shall I choose to make that? How shall I strike it? Mateo, you have a go. Can you try again, only this time can you do it more quietly?*

You may choose also to do the *musical notation* activity here, as referenced at the end of this scheme. Once you have all four sound effects ready, you should have four different children perform each in turn as you speak the sentence. Direct this clearly, so that each occurs in a pause just after you speak the word. Perform this sentence at least three or four times so that different children can have a turn. Ask the class to join in with you speaking the words as soon as they can.

4. Now, or in a later session, this can be extended to incorporate movement. Look at the appropriate page and talk about the shapes the Opposite makes for 'shriek' and 'hiss'. Ask, 'Can any child copy them? Can we all do it? How about for "blink" and "disappear in a puff of smoke"?' Again, try to ensure the gestures chosen are clear, clean and can be done as an ensemble. You can now try this a few times, with some children playing the music and the others doing the actions. Vocal sound effects can also be used, but make sure they don't interfere with or drown out the musical instruments – the two should complement one another.

Session 3

1. Play Go, Stop, Show Me ... with the words: *go/stop*; *stand (jump) up/sit (lie) down*; *look happy/look sad*. Hopefully, when you ask, children should notice that these have been paired as opposites. After a few rounds, tell children that they are going to play it again only this time, when you wave your magic wand, they are all to become the Opposite. 'So what will you do when I say "Go"? That's right, you will stop!' and so on. Insist that they will need to think very carefully each time – it is hard to be an Opposite! Congratulate them when they play it well. Wave your wand again to turn them back into the good children you are used to in this class, the ones who do what you ask and not the opposite!

2. Teach the children a new song, or chant, about the Opposite. The example below is modelled on the verses of the Beatle's song 'Hello Goodbye', but there are a number of Opposite songs, especially composed for children, readily available on YouTube. You can make your version short and sing it in different lessons with different pairings of opposites each time.

   Initially, the vocabulary should mainly consist of words the children already know, and they should be able to help you complete each line, you telling them the first word, the children telling you the second, before you sing or chant it together. It will be very good if, in later versions of the song, you incorporate newly learned vocabulary that re-enforces what children are currently learning. The Beatles begin by pairing yes with no and stop with go, very appropriate vocabulary for this young age range. It will be even better if you can provide gestures for each word that re-enforces the meaning – a slow nod of the head for 'yes', a slow shake of the head for 'no', arm outstretched, palm forward for 'stop' and so on.

   Below are some easy opposites you might incorporate into your version. I have begun with 'I say ...' rather than 'You say ...' to allow you to pause, giving space for children to call out the relevant opposite in a call/response version, best attempted once children have already learned it through the previous exercises.

   I say laugh, you say cry;
   I say low, you say high
   I say up, you say down
   I say smile, you say frown
   I say big, you say small
   I say climb, you say fall
   I say short, you say tall
   I say none, you say all

3. Look at some of the different illustrations of the Opposite throughout the book. Tell the children that they are going to draw and colour their own Opposite, then discuss with them what they see and how they can tell it is an Opposite from its appearance. You should help them note its long, thin arms and short, thin legs; the shape of its face at the top of a single tunic; the shape and position of its eyes; the shape and position of its nose; the thin line for its mouth. You could also look at the inside cover of the book and talk about the different shapes and positions it has on these pages.

Children should now be given a piece of A4 paper and told that their own Opposite should fill the length of this, as they are all going to become part of a big display. Talk with them carefully about the shape they want it to be, the colour of its tunic and also the kind of expression they want – grinning, baring its teeth and so on. Avoid drawing the shape for them, but it will help if an adult can sit with small groups of children and talk with them so that they are guided to think about what they want to draw and how to draw it.

Session 4

Complete the artwork for the display outlined below once children have their Opposites finished.

1. Study the design on the inside cover of the book, which shows red, circular flowers atop of long, thin stems, which curve in from all four edges of the page. Among them float seven different manifestations of the Opposite. Show this to the children, and trace your finger along the 'lo-ong, curvy line' of a stem, and then along others, repeating this phrase each time. Tell children they are all going to draw their own flower on a big sheet of display paper attached to a wall or to a board that is at their height; and that they are going to practise making it big enough before they do.

2. Have them stand up in space and mirror you as you stretch out your arm and sketch a line through the air, repeating the phrase 'lo-ong curvy line' with you as they do. Try this several times, from different angles and with different curves, before asking children to show you their own long, curvy line, sketched in the air. Then put a felt-tip pen in your hand and show how you are now going to draw this on the large sheet of paper, before inviting one or two children out to do it themselves. The rest of the children should be asked to draw their own carefully, one at a time, with the teacher guiding them to where might be a good position, away from others, each time.

3. Meanwhile children can be asked to cut out their own Opposites and attach them to different parts of this display, again looking

for where there is space and also to complement and contrast with others – upside down, horizontal and so on.

4. Children will also, during this period, be experimenting with how to print the round flowers, using suitably sized plastic bottle tops and different coloured paints on a piece of A4 paper before choosing one of the colours to use for the flower on their own stalk. They can also put two or three different fingerprints of paint along the length of their stalk to represent leaves.

5. Once the picture is completed and displayed, congratulate children on their lovely work and encourage them to look at it carefully by asking questions such as: 'Which is the biggest Opposite? Who can spot the smallest? How many Opposites are there altogether? How many are smiling? How many are baring their teeth?'

Preparing for and Performing the Story in Class

You can now begin to work on a simple ensemble performance of the story, using the text below and some musical instruments. As in examples provided in other schemes, the teacher will narrate and the children will each pretend to be Nate or the Opposite and perform an appropriate action or gesture for each line. This can be created and rehearsed one or two sections at a time. The children should contribute their ideas as to how it should be performed physically, as well as musically, and should be invited to join in the narration with the teacher. Be appropriately expressive in your facial expressions, gestures and in the way you speak the words of each of the characters.

Prepare for the musical effects by talking to the children and helping them choose appropriate instruments for each sound. It would be best if this were done in small groups, each taking responsibility for a different scene. You can guide the children with questions as in the example below:

Now, we need a sound for lying in bed. Should that be a loud sound or a quiet sound? A stormy sound or a peaceful sound? So which of these instruments might give us a quiet, peaceful sound? OK, so Maria, you give me a quiet peaceful sound on the triangle when I give the signal. Very good! Now, what about a very different sound for the Opposite happening? Something loud, like an explosion. Maybe we can use two or three instruments for this, all being played together. Let's see if we can make loud, crazy sounds but you must stop immediately when I give the signal. Ready??

In this way you help the children to think and choose appropriate sound effects but also exercise enough control so that the performance can proceed enjoyably, acting rather like the conductor of an orchestra. Below I have noted where these effects should happen in the first scene only. This pattern should be repeated with new sounds in the second and third scenes. I have provided possible actions for the first scene purely as an example.

Nate was lying down in bed.	*Musical effect, as above. Children lie down on the floor*
Nate's dad said, 'Nate, get up!'	*Children sit up and look at teacher*
But then the Opposite happened!	*Children say this with you. A loud musical effect*
Nate stayed lying down.	*First musical effect repeated and children lie down again*
Nate's dad said, 'Nate, you're not usually so lazy!'	*New musical effect for lazy*

Nate was at the table, pouring the milk.
Nate's mum said, 'Nate, be careful!'
But then the Opposite happened!
Nate spilt the milk on to the table.
Nate's mum said, 'Nate, you're not usually so clumsy!'

Nate was in school, painting a picture.
Nate's teacher said, 'Nate, paint on this clean piece of paper.'
But then the Opposite happened!

Nate splashed the paint on the table	*Music,*
on the walls	*Music*
and on his teacher!	*Music*

Nate's teacher said, 'Nate, you aren't usually so messy!'

Nate had an idea and said, 'I mean to say, the Opposite isn't standing here!'

But then the Opposite happened.	*Music*
The Opposite bared its teeth.	*Music*

Nate said, 'I mean to say that I do hope the Opposite will stay here forever.'

But then the Opposite happened.	*Music*
With a blink	*Music,*
a shriek	*Music*
and a hiss	*Music,*

the Opposite disappeared in a puff of smoke.

The last line, of course, has already been prepared in Session 2.

Further Activities

1. Use more music and art activities to explore opposites. In music, as above, we can consider loud/quiet; long/short; light/heavy; high-pitched/low-pitched; stormy/calm and so on.

2. In art, you can look at bright/dark colours; thin strokes/thick strokes and so on. These can be considered as part of a task for children, like Nate, to paint a picture of their favourite animal.

3. You should consider making a display of all these opposite pairings on the classroom display board. For a visual display of the music, children can be asked to provide their own notation for their particular sound effects. Again, the teacher should work with small groups here and guide them.[2]

4. Think of opportunities for you as teacher to make playful use of the vocabulary and phrases repeated throughout the story in your usual class time. Below are a few possible examples:

   > *'Yoko / Hao yue, you're not usually so messy/lazy/clumsy/well behaved/noisy/quiet' and so on*
   > *I mean to say …*
   > *I have SO enjoyed teaching you math today and I DO hope I will teach you math forever and ever and EVER!*

5. Another very nice idea for art work is to look again at the page where the Opposite disappeared 'in a puff of green and yellow smoke'. Discuss with children how this is represented visually and tell them that sometimes the Opposite might disappear in different coloured smoke and that they are going to paint pictures to show how! Let them choose from: yellow and red; yellow and blue; red and blue. Always start painting with the paler colour.

   You will need to experiment with this yourself first, as the approach will depend upon the coloured paints you have and the paper you use. You will need to use paint mixed with water and may find that the paper will have to be wet first.

6. Nate, we are told, was very good at pouring his own milk. Children can be seated in a circle and asked for suggestions about what they are very good at doing at home, things that they or their parents are pleased with. Note a few suggestions, then go into the centre and mime Nate pouring his own milk. Ask how they could tell what you were doing here. Then ask if any child can mime either what they are good at doing at home, or anything that anyone else suggested in the previous discussion. If necessary, work with volunteers, having them whisper to you what they have chosen and then miming the activity alongside them.

The Tale of Peter Rabbit by Beatrix Potter

Beatrix Potter is one of the most well established and best loved of children's authors.[3] It is not just the charm of her stories and the exquisite quality of her illustrations that distinguish her but also the quality and economy of her language. It is for this reason that I am including *The Tale of Peter Rabbit*, undoubtedly one of the most famous of all children's stories, so established as a classic that it features in the opening chapter of *English Literature: A Very Short Introduction*, written by the celebrated English academic Jonathan Bate.

When setting off to pick blackberries with his three sisters, Peter is warned by his mother not to go into Mr McGregor's garden and reminded how his father had 'an accident' there and ended up being put in a pie by Mrs McGregor. Although his three sisters obey their mother, Peter immediately runs off to the garden, squeezes under the gate and begins to feast on a variety of vegetables. However, inevitably, he is spotted and given chase by Mr McGregor, very nearly caught, has to hide in a can of cold water and eventually finds his way back home after a series of narrow scrapes. When tangled in a gooseberry net, he loses his new jacket and shoes, which Mr McGregor later uses to dress a scarecrow. On returning home, Peter is not very well and is sent to bed with a spoonful of camomile tea. His sisters, by contrast, have milk and blackberries for supper.

Bate expresses admiration for Beatrix Potter's style, the detached, matter-of-fact voice with which she narrates her tales that influenced later writers of adult fiction such as Evelyn Waugh and Graham Greene. He also sees in Peter Rabbit a fully rounded character, neither good nor bad, but 'at once naughty, adventurous and innocent'.[4] These adjectives could equally apply to Max the kitten, of course, and are at the heart of their appeal as fictional characters to children. Bate contrasts Peter, who has a human name (as does Max), to his well-behaved sisters Flopsy, Mopsy and Cotton-tail, their conventional rabbit names indicating, from the outset, that they are not the central figures in this story. In fact, they quickly turn out to be what many children would see as 'good-goody', appreciated by adults, perhaps, but completely uninteresting as fictional characters as they know their place and are content to stay in it. They will never get into the kind of scrapes and adventures that characters such as Peter will. This focus of interest is sometimes unappreciated by those serious-minded educators who see themselves as curators of children's moral imaginations. Potter's deftly ironic lightness of touch even seems to elude Ellen Handler Spitz in her generally excellent study *Inside Picture Books*.[5] For all her perceptiveness and sensitivity, Spitz is not very good on irony and provides a rather pious and somewhat heavy-handed analysis of this tale. Irony, I would argue, is part of Potter's charm and key to what children find amusing in her tales.

The illustrations that Potter painted herself are also integral to this charm. Not only are they brilliantly observed and executed in their detail, they are a potent visual introduction to the English pastoral ideal that characterizes much of English poetry and literature. Like many illustrations in the best children's picturebooks, they serve the dual function of re-enforcing and also complementing the narrative. In the second picture of the story, for example, we see Peter's mother with the three sisters grouped around her, evidently listening to her advice (which, we suspect, has been proffered many times before) in contrast to Peter, who stands apart, looking outwards at the reader, clearly not listening to his mother. There are also motifs that occur in the illustrations, delightful little details that convey a pattern of meanings, like the various birds that follow Peter on his adventure. We see a blackbird cheekily pecking at the blackberries that the sisters have just picked and dropped into a basket and, later, a curious robin standing protectively over each of Peter's lost shoes. It is the urging of 'friendly sparrows' that rouses Peter to escape just in time from the gooseberry net. Best of all, the lost jacket and shoes with which the farmer dresses the scarecrow, rather than repelling the birds, serve instead to attract all of them to his field, where they happily peck away at his seeds and gaze up in fascination. They contrast with the white cat, whom Peter feels it safer to avoid, and the little mouse that can't help him open the garden door. The cat is a domestic animal, the mouse a house dweller; the birds are the freest of animals and consequently most at home with Peter's urge for freedom to explore the world. The illustrations depict them as his sympathetic, spiritual allies.

As with other tales for young children, the central character ends up safely tucked in bed; but once again Potter's irony is notable. The final chronological image of the story is, in fact, part of the book's front matter, where Peter is shown to be hiding under the bedclothes, evidently trying to avoid having to take the camomile tea, which his mother has at the ready for him. This contrasts with the book's final image, on page 69, which shows his three sister rabbits enjoying their feast together. Whether children have ever tasted camomile tea is beside the point; it is clearly less appetizing than what his siblings are enjoying, domestic rewards denied to this returning young hero.

In the scheme that follows, I am proposing that the children do quite a lot of work to become acquainted with the story and aspects of its language before they actually listen to it. As it is quite lengthy, I have divided its presentation into three episodes. Many of the activities are devised to help children look closely at the illustrations, as they are so integral to a full and enjoyable understanding of the tale. I strongly suggest that you relax and spend some time reading this story and study the illustrations for your own enjoyment before turning to the scheme below. You may wish to edit some of the pages, particularly the lengthy narrative later in the story. There is also an officially published board book that presents a faithful but shorter version for very young children.[6]

The specific language objectives below are ambitious and also flexible. I have included a deal of expressive vocabulary, verbs and adjectives and some specific nouns, for the food and drink, which may be unknown to the children even in their own first languages. It is a good idea to have samples of the real thing here, and children might appreciate them more if they can be coaxed to share a small taste of a 'Peter Rabbit Salad' and a spoonful of camomile tea! Children can enjoy and absorb some of this vocabulary and be encouraged to use it if they can. In fact, it is quite selective and a range of other vocabulary will be used in the games and the story itself. So it will be easy for you to expand the language objectives if you wish. The games and activities based around specific phrases can be modified and simplified if necessary, but Peter's adventures, amplified by the activities, should contextualize it to make much of it generally comprehensible to the children.

YouTube will provide you with the chance to show pictures from the book projected large on to a whiteboard, but copies of the original book are essential for children to be able to hold and look at for themselves and for some of the small group work. There is also on YouTube a good animated version that incorporates this story with its sequel, *The Tale of Benjamin Bunny*.[7] This can be enjoyed as a final activity, once children have thoroughly explored the story through active engagement.

I provide a number of page references throughout the scheme. These apply to the original and authorized edition, published by Frederick Warne. You will need to have your own copy of the story handy to make proper sense of the lessons plans.

Specific Language Objectives

Lexical chunks to listen, understand and respond to:

Feeling sick; wriggling out of a net; peeping over the plants
A dose of; a spoonful of; a cup of; a plate of
Twitch; flick

Vocabulary and lexical chunks to speak and understand:

Pie; blackberries; lettuces; radishes; beans; camomile tea
Shed; rake; watering can; bush
Put in a pie
Beware; take care; doesn't care
Stop thief!
Digging; squeezed/squeezing; wriggle/wriggling; waved/waving; push; rush; sneeze
Panting, out of breath; shivering with cold; trembling with fright
Scritch-scratch
Quite: for example, quite new; quite tasty
What are you doing?

Adjectives/phrases to describe Peter's embarrassment at the end of the tale

To revisit and practise:

Previously learned vocabulary such as: jacket; buttons; shoes; new; to spot; to hide
Numbers; likes/dislikes (food)

Competences:

Can infer and discuss meaning from illustrations
Can recount the events of a story they know to interested parties
Can predict what will happen next in a story

Resources

- Real or plastic vegetables – radish, lettuce and so on or, if necessary, flash cards

- A rabbit glove puppet

- A Peter Rabbit jacket to fit the puppet; also a larger jacket, with a pair of shoes, for the scarecrow game later

- An old-fashioned hat for Mr McGregor

- Various percussion, pitched percussion and simple musical instruments

- An apron for teacher in role as Mrs Rabbit

- A small door, kitchen cupboard sized (see Session 4)

- A dressing-gown belt for the cat game in the same session

- An ordinary jacket that is rather too small for you

Session 1

1. Begin by asking children about rabbits, and tell them that you will be working on a story together about a rabbit called Peter, who had a mother and three sisters. Then show them the picture on page 9, where Peter has turned his back on his mother's advice. Can they spot which one is Peter? Is he a good little rabbit or a very naughty rabbit? How can they tell?

   See if you can make a *still image* of that picture together, with you or the teaching assistant as Mrs Rabbit and four children taking the part of the three sisters and Peter. Tell them what Mrs Rabbit says to the children here (the writing on page 9). Speak it as though you were Mrs Rabbit. What do they think the three sisters might be saying in reply? What about Peter? Ask if they can think why she might not want them to go to Mr McGregor's garden, before telling them it is all to do with what happened to Mr Rabbit, their father. Then show them the picture on page 10 (of Mrs McGregor serving up rabbit pie), and see if they can tell what her warning might have been before you speak her words on page 11. Turn back to the earlier illustration. Do the children think the sisters will obey their mother? Then show the picture on page 17 and talk about what they are doing (picking blackberries), making sure that the children understand that the sisters are doing as they have been told. (And note the naughty blackbird!)

2. But will Peter obey her? Show them the picture on page 18, where he is evidently hurrying somewhere. Where do they think he is going? And what happened to his father there?? Should he be going there?? At this point, you can teach them the following short chant, to a regular four-beat time. The beat can be clapped out on the syllables marked in bold.

> *Put in a pie by **Miss**-us Mc-**Greg**-or*
> *Naugh-ty Peter **Rab**-bit should be-**ware**!*
> *Put in a pie by **Miss**-us Mc-**Greg**-or*
> *But **naugh**-ty Peter **Rab**-bit does-n't care!*

3. Next we look at page 21 and talk about what Peter is doing (*squeezing* under the gate); what will he find to eat in the garden do they think? What do rabbits like? Gather some suggestions and then say, 'Well, let's find out!'

   Get children on their feet by squeezing under a pretend gate (like Peter) and then play Rub Your Tummy if ... Include four or five items of food that you know children will like but also introduce *lettuce*, *radishes* and *beans*, then produce the rabbit puppet and ask, 'Do we think that Peter Rabbit will like these? Well, what will he like??' Have the lettuce, radishes and beans handy (or flash cards) and have the puppet nod or shake its head when you ask: 'Peter, do you like radishes?' 'Peter do you like chocolate?' and so on. Children can join in and ask the puppet questions about likes and dislikes of food. Then ask, 'Peter, have you eaten any of the radishes in Mr McGregor's garden?' The puppet will nod. Then ask, 'How many? Can you clap how many??' As the puppet claps, you and the children count out loud. Become more and more incredulous as the number grows up to and past five. Do the same with the lettuce and beans, then ask, 'Peter, how do you feel after eating all those radishes, lettuces and beans?' At this you can make the puppet look ill by having his paws grasp his tummy, and the children will tell you readily enough that he feels sick. Ask, 'Peter, is there anything you can eat that will make you feel better?' At this, the puppet can whisper in your ear and point to a flash card showing parsley. 'Parsley!' you say. 'Are you going to look for some parsley in the garden now?' As the puppet nods say, 'Well, Peter, do be careful!'

4. Briefly go over what the children have learned from this activity, and then tell them that, while looking for parsley, Peter found something – or rather someone – else. Can they guess whom? Show them the picture on page 26. Make sure they understand that this is Mr McGregor, the owner of the garden. What do they think will happen next? Then show them the next picture, where he is chasing Peter with a rake. What will happen to Peter if he is caught, do they think??

   Now organize children into a chase game. Have a farmer's hat to place on a child. Whoever wears the hat is Mr McGregor, and the other children must escape being tagged by him. When you take the hat and put it on someone else, we will start a new round with a new Mr McGregor. Begin each round with everyone calling out together 'Stop thief! I'll put you in a pie!' When children are tagged, they are to stay still until set free. Each time a child sets someone free, they are to say 'Peter, run!' as they do so. While playing this game, play the old song 'Run, Rabbit, Run' by Flanagan and Allen, which might well have been written about Peter Rabbit!

5. End the session by sitting children down and asking what they think will happen to Peter. Explain that, in the next session, we will find out whether he ended up in a pie or not!

Session 2

1. Recap the story and teach the children to sing the chorus of 'Run, Rabbit, Run', perhaps changing the words to 'Run, Peter, Run'.

2. Have the children stand in a circle and tell them they are going to see what happened to Peter in the story as he ran away from the farmer. Have children mime along with you as you actively narrate the following.

   Well Peter ran as fast as he could but first he lost a shoe in the cabbage patch. ... Then he lost his other shoe amongst the potatoes ... and then he got caught in a net. He wriggled and wriggled and had to pull off his jacket and leave it behind to escape from Mr

McGregor. Then he rushed into a shed and jumped into a watering can to hide. But the can was full of water and Peter began to shiver ... Mr McGregor came into the shed. Would he find Peter?? Peter was very frightened. He wasn't safe yet ...

3. Sit children in a circle. Ask them what has happened in the chase so far. At this point they don't need to understand all of the vocabulary. This will be returned to and re-enforced in the activities that follow. For now, it is enough for children to understand the key points of action (running; losing shoes and jacket; being trapped and escaping; hiding in a watering can). If necessary, talk them through these actions again, then tell them that there was a very small window in the shed. If Peter could jump out of the can and escape through it, he would be safe. Then play the chase game The Farmer and the Rabbit. As the signal to start each round of the chase, say, 'Presently Peter sneezed', whereupon the whole class will shout 'Kertyschoo!' (as on page 43), and you will respond with: 'Mr McGregor was after him in no time ... Go!' The aim is for Peter to return to his place before being tagged. He also needs to jump through a hoop (the window) held by the teacher in front of his place before sitting down again. If the farmer tags him before then, he will be cooked in a pie. Play this game three or four times and see how many pies the farmer might have had at the end of it. You can play it again, of course, in subsequent lessons and keep a tally of the pie count!

4. Now children can be read the story so far, up to and including Peter's escape from the tool-shed (pages 44 and 45).

5. After this, play a round of Show Me as a means of recapping the story so far. This will also revise a lot of good vocabulary and can include the following: '*Show me Peter squeezing under the gate ... Good. Show me Peter eating radishes.*' We can also include the following: *feeling sick; running from Mr McGregor; wriggling out of the net; hiding in the watering can; jumping out of the window.* Follow the usual sequence for introducing such new vocabulary and make use of a selection of the games to re-enforce it.

   You can also play Show Me for Mr McGregor's actions – digging his garden, chasing Peter, waving a rake, looking under the pots. This, too, can be played again in later sessions, as What Are You Doing, Mr McGregor? In this game, you go into the centre of the circle and mime one of these activities. When you stop, the children are all to ask together, 'What are you doing, Mr McGregor?' You give one or two wrong answers first and the children shake their heads and say, 'No you're not!' When you finally give the right answer, they say, 'Yes! You're waving a rake!' and so on. When any child is ready to play Mr McGregor, they can wear the hat and take on the role.

6. It will also be a good time now to do a number of re-enforcement activities of vocabulary, particularly of the fruits and vegetables we have met so far, through drawing, colouring and labelling. If children are fairly good readers by now, they can do some cloze procedure exercises, too, for example, matching different verbs with the correct sentence, as below:

> Peter … out of the net.
> Peter … into the tool-shed.
> Mr McGregor … a rake.
> Peter … out of a window.
> (rushed; jumped; waved; wriggled)

Session 3

1. Teach the children the following chant, which has the same rhythm as the one taught earlier in Session 1.

> **Chased** through the **gar**-den by **Mis**-ter Mc-**Greg**-or,
> **Quick**, Peter **Rab**-bit, **run** and **hide**!
> **Chased** to a **shed** by **Mis**-ter Mc-**Greg**-or,
> **Quick**, Peter **Rab**-bit, **hide** in-**side**!

2. It will be a very nice activity at this point to create an ensemble performance of the story of Peter's chase through the garden, through words narrated by the teacher and sound effects created from pitched percussion instruments played by the children, with the teacher acting as musical director as well as storyteller. So, for example, children help you choose the instrument to make the sound of each shoe dropping; of Peter struggling in the gooseberry net; of the splash of water as Peter jumps into the can; of the footsteps of Mr McGregor coming into the shed and searching under the pots. They can tell you when there needs to be vocal sound effects (e.g. the sneeze). All the children should have something specific to rehearse and perform, sometimes in small groups. You could make a sound recording of the final performance for the children to listen to and feel proud of later.

Session 4

1. Begin by playing the round of Show Me from Session 2 as a means of recapping the story so far.

2. Remind children that, all this time, Mrs Rabbit was back home and knew nothing of what Peter was up to. You can now go into role as Mrs Rabbit, back from the shops, cooking in her kitchen. For this you can just put on an apron and mime some simple cooking. Be talking to yourself, saying that your good little daughters have now come home but no one knows where Peter is. Then notice the children and explain that you are preparing some bread and milk for supper, to go with the blackberries that the good little rabbits have brought home. This is Peter's favourite. But where is he? Try to engage children in a dialogue, encouraging them to tell you in detail what has happened in the garden. Be incredulous at first, but then make it clear that you are cross with him for being so disobedient but also very worried, reminding the children what happened to his father. As the children explain that he successfully hid in Mr McGregor's tool-shed and escaped through the window, you are slightly relieved. So he should get home safely, shouldn't he? Do the children agree?

3. When the dialogue has run its course, come out of role and tell children that, at that very moment, Peter was hiding in the garden, *panting and out of breath; shivering with cold; and trembling with fright*. Give each of the three phrases clear and distinctive gestures as you say them – use 'Brrr!' to emphasize cold and rattle your fingernails against your teeth to emphasize fright. Then get children to perform these with you and play some of the games such as Simon Says and Do as I Say Not as I Do to ensure that children can understand and differentiate between them.

4. Tell children that Peter faced three more challenges if he was to escape safely from the garden. First of all he found a door in the wall that a mouse could squeeze under but he couldn't. It was locked but could he push it open, perhaps? Holding a small door, such as one from a kitchen cupboard or a bathroom cabinet, invite a child, pretending to be Peter Rabbit, to try to push it open. The children are to call out rhythmically, 'Push, Peter Rabbit, push, push, push!' as the child tries and you are to make sure he fails, of course, by holding it firm! Three different children can try and, after the third effort, tell children Peter had to give up and started to cry. Have them all sob like Peter.

5. Then tell the children that Peter began to walk across the garden and saw a white cat looking down at some fish in a pond. The cat wasn't looking at Peter, but it had a tail that 'twitched as if it were alive'. Use the dressing-gown belt (a white one, if possible) as the cat's tail to show the children what 'twitch' looks like, followed by 'flick', saying each word as you perform the actions and then invite the children to join in with you. Say that you are going to play the

'tail as if it were alive'. Make it flick across a specified space, such as a gym mat, and invite one child at a time to volunteer to be Peter and try to get past the cat without the tail actually touching them. Each time, say 'twitch and FLICK!' The child can only begin to cross the mat on the word 'twitch' and the rest of the children can call out 'Flick!' with you. You can add a commentary such as: 'Peter didn't want to be chased and scratched by the cat so he tried carefully to get past without being noticed or touched by its tail as it went twitch and FLICK!'

6. Tell the children that Peter had to take another route across the garden, to avoid the cat, and so crept underneath some bushes. Suddenly he heard the sound 'scritch-scratch'. He peeped over a bush and saw Mr McGregor busy working. His back was turned towards Peter and beyond him was the gate! There are a few ways in which you can play a chase game to represent Peter trying to escape from Mr McGregor for the second time. The simplest is to play The Farmer and the Rabbit again, only instead of Peter having to jump through a hoop as window, he has to crawl under the hoop as a gate. This time, the children introduce each round by repeating with you. 'Scritch, scratch, scritch, scratch – Mr McGregor spotted Peter!' Then you say 'GO!' and the chase is on.

7. After a few rounds of the above game, ask children whether they think Peter will actually escape this time, under the gate. Ask them to show hands three times: if they think he will; if they would like him to; if they think he deserves to get away. You can ask any child who seems to have an opinion to explain their thinking for this last question. Now you can say that they will find out what happened – and read from pages 42–3 (a small recap of him hiding in the shed) to pages 58–9 (where Peter finally slips under the gate and escapes).

8. Remind the children that this is not yet the end of the story. What will happen when he gets home? We shall find out next time!

Session 5

1. Recall with the children where you left off last time, then play a round of Show Me as a means of recapping the second part of the story. This will also revise a lot of good vocabulary and can include the following:

   Show me Peter panting out of breath; shivering with cold; trembling with fear. Show me Peter pushing at the door; peeping over a bush at Mr McGregor; squeezing under the garden gate; running off home.

Do these in the correct order as above, then mix the order up and do them as a sequence of activities where you first get children to tell you which one you are doing, before individual children volunteer to mime one for the rest of the class to work out. You can also, of course, choose three of the actions for a version of the game Knights, Dogs and Trees.

2. Ask children what they think will happen to Peter once he gets home. Encourage more than one idea then ask for them to help you make a possible picture of this together. You can help organize volunteers into an image of Mrs Rabbit and Peter, encouraging them to think carefully to show what each will feel like and helping with/ noting the vocabulary. 'Ah, see, Mrs Rabbit looks very surprised (cross, shocked, upset) and Peter looks tired (happy, hungry, exhausted).' Again, encourage different possibilities. It will also be fun if you can have them imagine and show you different ways in which the three sisters might react (feeling sorry for Peter, perhaps, but also maybe giggling a little ...).

3. You can now read the rest of the story, from pages 58–9 through to the end.

4. Discuss what the children think of the ending, in particular, the fact that the sisters get what Mrs Rabbit told us earlier is Peter's favourite supper, while he is given only camomile tea. Do they think he will like this? Show them the picture at the front of the book, where we see him hiding under the bedclothes while his mother gets ready to give him the tea. This shows clearly that he doesn't like it at all. Ask children to help you make a list of the kind of food that we know will get Peter to lift his head out from under the blanket and look happy, as well as perhaps one or two more examples of medicine that they can imagine might make him pull a face and hide. When you have a few examples in each list (including camomile tea, of course), play a game in which children either hold up both hands with a miserable face, as though they are Peter hiding under the blanket, or pull their hands down, smiling, as though they are peeping out from under it, ready for a treat. Speak as Mrs Rabbit, saying, 'Peter, here is your dose of camomile tea' or 'Peter, here is your cup of milk' or 'Here is a plate of blackberries' and so on, with children responding appropriately each time. There will be correct and incorrect ways of responding here, of course, so do check and rectify any misunderstandings. You may wish to play this again with different children taking on the voice of Mrs Rabbit.

5. Discuss with the children whether they feel sorry for Peter, or whether they think he has what he deserves. Make sure that you don't pass judgement or say what you think – let the children respond for themselves.

Session 6

1. Here is the final chant of the scheme, which again has the same clapping rhythm as the previous two:

   Safe back **home,** your **goody**-goody **sis**-ters
   Drink their **milk** and **eat** their **bread.**
   Cam-omile **tea** for **naugh**-ty **bun**-nies,
   Pe-ter **Rab**-bit, **go** to **bed!**
   Go to **bed** and **hide** your **head,**
   Pe-ter **Rab**-bit, **go** to **bed!**

2. Introduce the rabbit glove puppet as Peter's cousin, Benjamin Bunny. As Benjamin, tell the children that you just went round to play with Peter, but his mother has told you that he is in bed. Say that, on the way there, you noticed what looked like his blue jacket and new shoes on a scarecrow in Mr McGregor's field! Do they know anything about that? In this way, encourage them to retell the story once again through the questions you ask. (Unlike Mrs Rabbit, Benjamin is quite amused by what the children tell him.) When they have finished, ask, as Benjamin, if they think it will be possible to get the clothes back. Would they like to try??? After all, Mr McGregor has gone out with his wife, you saw them leave, and it's only a scarecrow …

3. Play a version of a game called the Keeper of the Keys, in which the scarecrow is 'guarding' the jacket and the shoes, which can be placed on a small table or chair in front of the scarecrow. Whoever plays the scarecrow (the teacher or teaching assistant initially) can hold two pieces of rolled-up sugar paper to act as the scarecrow's arms, wear an old hat and a blindfold (one through which you can actually see a little; a more effective one for any child who plays the scarecrow in the future). Either arm might swing out to hit the child trying to retrieve an item of clothing at any time. Make it difficult for the children without ever hitting them when they are this young. Allow one child to retrieve just one piece of clothing each time, which means that three different children will have a turn.

4. Children can then bring the jacket and shoes to the teacher-in-role as Mrs Rabbit, wearing the apron again. She asks them how they got them and is rather shocked. How did they know they would be safe? Whose suggestion was it? Ah, Benjamin Bunny's – he is almost as naughty as Peter! Inspect the jacket and be shocked as it is dirty and some of the buttons are missing. How did that happen, do they know?? And, oh! it is damp and has shrunk. How might that have happened? Well, you are not rich enough to be able to buy a

new one for Peter. He will just have to wear the jacket as it is, even though it is too small for him now!

5. If possible, have a jacket that is too small for you and put it on, commenting that, like Peter's, it has shrunk in the rain. Say this is how Peter will feel and look miserable and embarrassed. Get the vocabulary out of the children and have them imagine the kind of things his three sisters might say to him, and how they will look when he has to wear it. What kind of look will he give them if they giggle or make fun of him? Create these images with the children and maybe add some speech to them.

6. Show the children the animated version of Peter Rabbit and Benjamin Bunny, discussing afterwards their understanding of the second part of the story.

Follow-Up Activities

Children should have at least one more reading of the whole story now. Some further activities will enhance their language work as well as their understanding and appreciation of the story.

1. The whole class can create a large display as a map of Mr McGregor's garden, with pictures and words, using the book as a guide as to where they should place things. The animals and events can be included in it. It will be best done by children making their own observational drawings of the different vegetables, organized and clustered by the teacher into a cabbage patch, carrot bed and so on.

2. Make a small world play garden, where children can use plasticine or play dough to represent different vegetables and place them in different parts of the garden. They can work in groups of two or three to play out the story with small plastic figurines. This can be guided by an adult first of all and later repeated as an independent activity.

3. Make cards out of the different illustrations, without the text. Place the cards face down. Have different children take out a picture each, and each time talk together about what part of the story it is illustrating. With each subsequent card, discuss, too, where it should be positioned to help them sequence the story through the cards. You can do this with children in small groups, according to ability, with anything from three to six cards each time.

4. 'It was a blue jacket with brass buttons, quite new.' This is a lovely little sentence with its detached, ironic tone. Introduce four or five adjectival phrases such as 'quite friendly' for the robin and

'quite wet' for Peter hiding in the watering can. Other possibilities include: quite tasty, quite cross, quite twitchy, quite frightening, depending on what your children can manage.

Have cards made to illustrate sentences, such as those below that can be completed by such phrases. Invite children to complete them with the appropriate phrase above. Some of the cards can come from illustrations in the story. For the others, some simple sketches will suffice. This can just be an oral exercise, with children completing what you say.

> 'It was a blue jacket with brass buttons, quite new.'
> 'It was a large radish …'
> 'It was Mrs Rabbit and she was …'
> 'It was a large, white tail …'
> 'Farmer McGregor had an angry face and looked …'
> 'Peter sat there shivering …'
> 'It was a tiny robin …'

Have a worksheet prepared to allow children to do this exercise through reading and writing, if they are able to.

The Shopping Basket by John Burningham

John Burningham has produced a number of classic picturebooks, many of which feature adults who consistently fail to appreciate the powerful imaginations of young children and the bizarre trials and adventures that life has in store for his child protagonists.[8] In this story, Steven is an ordinary young boy who is sent to a corner shop by his mother to buy six eggs, five bananas, four apples, three oranges, two doughnuts and a packet of crisps. On his way he passes a number of different landmarks such as railings with a gap in them, a dog kennel and a door to a house where he has been asked to drop in a note from his mother. On his return home, however, he finds different animals blocking his way, and they each demand that he give them different items of food from his basket. Near the dog kennel, a monkey wants all five of his bananas; by the railings, a pig wants his doughnuts and so on. Steven manages to trick each of them in turn but, in the process, loses one item of food every time. For example, he suggests that the monkey is too noisy to catch a banana without waking the dog up; and that the pig is too fat to squeeze through the railings if Steven threw a doughnut through them. In each case, the pictures illustrate what happens: the monkey is trapped by the dog on the roof of the kennel; the pig gets stuck in the railings; and Steven is able to carry on home. Similarly, Steven is able to trick all the other animals that confront him. On arriving back home, however, he is scolded by his mother for taking so long. We are left wondering what she will say when she discovers that there are fewer items in the basket than she asked for; and if she will ever believe Steven's explanation.

The story is a comic take on the classic hero quest, a journey in which the protagonist is sent on a mission and is confronted by a series of unexpected dangers that must be overcome in order for him to return home safely. From the illustrations we see that Steven is no archetypal hero. He is plain looking, wears glasses, is dressed in cheap clothes and has the kind of physique that will never win any playground fights. Like that great mythic hero Odysseus, his key virtues are quick thinking and cunning and the ability to remain calm in the face of a crisis. Unlike Odysseus and other famous heroes, however, he never threatens or makes use of violence and there is no evidence of hubris, of overbearing pride or arrogance. These are, in fact, vices displayed by his opponents; the monkey threatens to pull his hair, the pig to squash him against the railings and Steven makes use of their arrogance to defeat them. In each case, the bullies are ignorant of their limitations and this leads to their downfall, albeit always in a comic fashion.

There are many features that make this an ideal text for language learning. As well as opportunities for revising and extending vocabulary, the language is repetitive in ways that reflect the pattern of the story itself. For example, the exchanges of dialogue between Steven and each of the animals are always similar in their ordering and in their sentence and grammatical structures, with each animal voicing a different threat, then being told they have a different fault and being offered a different challenge by Steven. This comic pattern of 'same but different' can help maintain children's interest by harnessing their understanding and encouraging anticipation. It also lends itself very readily to the range of performative strategies at the heart of this book.

The book was written in 1980. Steven is white, working class and male. His mother is a busy housewife with a young baby and the corner shop is owned by Mr Diwali and his family, who are evidently British South Asian. Although these are only peripheral figures in the story, some educators may decry them as gender or cultural stereotypes that need to be challenged. Perhaps this might be a relevant, sensitive issue in some EYL classrooms, but there is a balancing act to be had here. I agree wholeheartedly with the need to challenge unhelpful stereotypes, but this can be done through selecting a range of picturebooks and topics, not by censoring classic stories such as this, which contain so much of value for young children. For this purpose, I have referenced a number of websites in Chapter 3 that list a range of picturebooks promoting diversity, some of which can be used for performative language work and others simply read and enjoyed. I would also wish to re-emphasize another point I made in Chapter 3 – that, as soon as you begin to enact these stories, visible, physical attributes such as ethnicity and gender become blurred with the original. After all, there is no reason why Steven could not be Black or female; the story's power remains the same.

Specific Language Objectives

To listen, understand and respond to:

Acting out sections of narrative that describe what happens in the pictures
Understanding the content of a letter

Vocabulary and lexical chunks to speak and understand:

Door number 25; the gap in the railings; the full litter basket; two men dig-
ging up the pavement; the nasty dog; Mr Diwali's shop
Verbs: hug (the breath out of you); pull (your hair); thump; butt; squash; whack
Future tense: I'll … (hug you, squash you etc.)
Adjectives: brave, clever, cunning, calm
Discourse skills: explaining to Steven's mother what has happened
Discourse, pragmatics, literacy: helping write a letter in response to the
teacher who lives in number 25.
Matching adjectives and nouns semantically and phonetically: sneaky snake,
crawling crocodile and so on.

To revisit and practise:

Items in grocery store, specifically: eggs, bananas, apples, oranges, doughnuts, a packet of crisps; numbers 1–30
Animals, specifically: bear, monkey, kangaroo, goat, pig, elephant. *Also*: tiger,
crocodile, snake, lion, scorpion, gorilla, horse
Singular/plurals
Adjectives: slow, noisy, clumsy, stupid, fat, short. *Also*: hungry, greedy,
scary, terrifying, lazy, sneaky, crawling

Competences:

Can give instructions that follow a given sequence
Can use appropriate language to describe a character's attributes
Can help compose a written letter to argue a specific case

Resources

- A wicker shopping basket

- A variety of flash cards and plastic items of food. You will need
  more than one for each to reflect the fact that Steven has to buy six
  eggs, five bananas and so on

- Flash cards depicting the places Steven has to pass on his journey.
  These are illustrated on the second and third pages of the
  picturebook and can be copied, cut out and enlarged

- A pillow or large cushion
- Small, cuddly toys to represent some of the different animals in the story
- Worksheets for the additional activities

Sequence of Activities

1. Below are listed a variety of circle games to begin each of the lessons you devote to this story. You can choose the most appropriate for the language level of the children you are working with. They are presented in order of difficulty. I suggest that you do no more than two in the initial session before moving on to the second activity. In later sessions, you can use these as warm-up exercises and for revision.

   - Sit the children in a circle and play the game I Went to the Market, altering the word 'market' to 'shops'. Each child is to complete the sentence with a different item (an apple; some sweets etc.). This will generally include vocabulary the children already know. At the end, see if the children can go round the whole group and say together everything that they bought.

   - Play In Mr Diwali's Shop There Are … You need real or plastic items or flash cards in a basket for this game. Children pass the basket around to music. When the music stops, a child takes out an item and places it in the centre of the circle (and later in the ELA, set up as a shop corner, I suggest). Include *apples*; *bananas*; *oranges*; *eggs*; *doughnuts*; *a packet of crisps*, as these are in the story.

   - Have two bags prepared, one containing number cards from 1 to 10, the other pictures of the different items listed above. One child pulls out a number and tells you what it is; another pulls out an item and tells you what that is. Ask 'What have I bought?' Answer: you've bought six eggs/five packets of crisps and so on.

   - Have plastic items in the centre of the circle and a shopping basket similar to the one Steven has in the book. Ask different children for a different amount of items each time, for example, '*Can I have four eggs please?*' They are to place them in the basket and the game continues until there are different numbers of each item in the basket. At the end of the lesson, the basket can be reintroduced and children can be asked to recall how many of each item you bought before counting them out.

2. Tell children that in the story you will be acting out together there are different animals. Play Go/Stop/Show Me … a bear; a monkey;

a kangaroo; a goat; a pig; an elephant. You may well need to model some of these for them to copy. Later, as in previous schemes, you can play Steven Says (instead of Simon Says) and Show Me What I Say, Not What I Do.

3. Read the story, giving the animals specific voices that suit the adjectives Steven uses to describe them (e.g. the bear has a slow voice; the monkey a loud, noisy voice; the goat has a stupid voice).

   As usual, you can read the story more than once during this scheme, and again in later weeks, once it is completed. Children will enjoy returning to it and, once they know a lot of the language, they can join in with you as you read, predicting what comes next.

4. Have flash cards prepared for the places Steven has to pass, namely: door number 25; the gap in the railings; the full litter basket; two men digging up the pavement; the nasty dog; Mr Diwali's shop. Place them in the shopping basket.

   - Pull the cards out one at a time and have children repeat what they are as you place them in the circle.

   - Ask them to help you sequence the cards in the correct order, then hand one each to different children so that a child can be asked to take the basket round the circle as a way of performing the narrative adapted from pages 2 and 3. Speak it slowly and ask children to help you. '*Steven set off for the shop and passed door number 25 … then walked past the gap in the railings etc.*' Do this two or three times, with different children taking the part of Steven each time.

   - Mix the images up so that Steven's journey will take him haphazardly across the circle rather than around it. Can a child tell him where he should go next so that the order stays the same as in the story? '*Steven, go to door number 25; now go to the gap in the railings*' and so on.

   - Play this again but the class are to say, 'Hurry! Hurry!' after each instruction. The child telling him where to go next has to try to make Steven complete the journey as quickly as possible. You can time the children to see who is the quickest at this.

   - You can start to ask the class to predict where Steven should go next, repeating what is suggested (and if necessary correcting it).

   - Children can later be encouraged to play this in small groups in the ELA.

5. *Whoosh* the part of the story where Steven returns from the shop and meets the animals. Concentrate on what the animals say and what happens each time, simplifying the dialogue, for example:

The bear said: 'Give me an egg or I'll hug the breath out of you.'
Steven said: 'You're too slow to catch an egg if I throw it!'

You can also add descriptive emotional words to each animal.

The bear was angry and said, 'Me, slow??'

You will need to provide the missing narration, which should follow a recognizable pattern throughout. I suggest you use three sentences followed by a vocal sound effect each time. For example:

So Steven threw the egg. But the bear was so slow it couldn't catch it. The egg landed on his nose. Smassssssshhhhh!
So Steven threw the banana. The monkey jumped after it but was very noisy. It woke the dog. GRRRRROOOWWLLLL.

Note: It may well be best to whoosh this journey in two separate sessions, with Steven meeting the first three animals in one session, the next three in the following session.

6. Sit the children in a circle. Put a pillow or a large cushion in the centre and explain to children they are going to do to that pillow what the animals threaten to do to Stephen. Refresh their memories then ask children the question. '*If you were the bear and this was Steven, what would you say to him?*' Answer: '*I'll hug the breath out of you.*' Ask for a volunteer to come into the circle and make the threat and then carry it out with the pillow, which you are holding, if necessary. Do the same with volunteers for the other animals. Have a time limit of five or ten seconds each round, with the class counting in together, '1, 2, 3, HUG!' or '1, 2, 3, SQUASH!' and so on. They can then clap out the time and chant the verb rhythmically together as the child performs the action with the cushion.

   You can continue the game, or repeat it later, by having individual children instruct volunteers which animal they are to be, in any order. The volunteer must each time make the appropriate threat and, unlike in the story, carry it out! (For the goat and pig, you might just concentrate on the verbs 'butt' and 'squash' rather than the whole phrase.)

7. The adjectives Steven uses to describe the different animals are: *slow*; *noisy*; *clumsy*; *stupid*; *fat*. Also the trunk of the elephant is described as *too short*.

   Model each of these for the children taking the part of each of the animals in turn. When you say '*Me, fat??*' they respond '*Yes, you are fat!*' and so on. Each time you say '*Me, slow??*' '*Me noisy??*' clearly demonstrate physically that this is exactly what you are! Don't try to look like a goat or an elephant here, concentrate on demonstrating the qualities emphasized by each adjective. For example,

> the bear speaks slowly and takes one slow pace forward
>
> the monkey speaks loudly and does a couple of loud monkey calls
>
> the kangaroo stumbles as he jumps
>
> the goat just looks and sounds stupid

Now repeat this representation of the animals, this time with the children copying what you do and what you say, followed by a selection of the usual games for learning new vocabulary in this active way.

8. Play a tag game in which different animals chase Steven. Have little toys or puppets for the chaser to hold and tag children with. There is no need in this game to act or move like the animals, but the class can call out together what the animal shouts at Steven before each round of the chase: '*I'm the goat and I'll butt you!*' '*I'm the monkey and I'll thump you!*' and so on.

9. Put children in groups of three. Ask each group to show a different still image, using only their bodies, of one of the places that Steven passes on the way back home and the animal that he finds there. One group can be told to '*show me the kangaroo and two men digging*'; another group told to '*show me the pig and the gap in the railings*' and so on. Ask each group to recall what their particular animal says to Steven and to show, in a second image, what happens to them in the picture in the book. Circulate and help children as they work on these.

   Now sit the children in a circle and ask one group to come into the centre and show you their first image. Rather than asking the group to show you their second image now, you might first of all act out with them the part of the story that ends in that image. If so, take on the role of Steven and provide the narration that you went through earlier, encouraging children in the circle to join in as you narrate. The words underlined below indicate where you might pause to encourage children to suggest what you should say next. The children in the centre should act out what you say, as in the *whoosh*. So, for example, with the group enacting the pig and the railings, a 'script' would include everything that the pig and Steven say on the page beginning 'Give me those doughnuts', followed by the following, which describes what happens next:

   > *So Steven put the ... <u>doughnuts</u> through the ... <u>gap</u>. The pig tried to squeeze through but was too ... <u>fat</u> and he got ... <u>stuck</u>! Uuuuughhhhhh!*

10. Tell the children that you are going to pretend to be the man or woman who lives in number 25. Just play the role as yourself here, in your own voice. Steven's mother has sent you a note. Read it out loud. If children can read, have it enlarged on the whiteboard for them to see it as you read. You may care to use or adapt the following:

> *Dear (your name)*
> *I am very cross with my son, Steven.*
> *I sent him to the shops and he took a very long time – he is so lazy and slow!*
> *He also brought me too few eggs, too few oranges, too few apples, too few bananas and too few doughnuts!*
> *He is so naughty and he told me a ridiculous story about what happened on the way home.*
> *He said different animals tried to bully him but he was too clever for them.*
> *He is such a liar!*
> *What shall I do with him to make him behave?*
> *Yours sincerely*
> *Steven's mum*

Discuss this with the class. We all know the story, what really happened. Is she right about Steven? No, of course not. What do *we* think he is like? Hopefully you will get vocabulary from them, words such as nice, cool and so on, but you should encourage them to think of some precise words to describe the virtues he displays in this story – in particular, *brave, clever, cunning* and *calm*. Scribe for the children as they help you write a reply on the white board. Create this together but encourage them to be precise and clear in their language. The letter you write MIGHT read something like the example below, but DO NOT use this as a template to copy.

> *Dear Steven's mum*
> *I think you are being unfair to Steven.*
> *I saw what happened.*
> *Steven is not lying.*
> *Some animals did try to bully him.*
> *He was very brave because he did not run away.*
> *He was not naughty but clever and cunning.*
> *He was not lazy but very calm.*
> *Because he was brave, clever and calm he came home safely with a lot of food.*
> *I think you should be proud of your little boy!*
> *I am sending round the children from his class with this letter.*
> *Yours sincerely,*
> *(Your name) from house number 25.*

11. In a subsequent lesson, have this reply written on a large piece of paper and remind children why you wrote it. Tell them they are going to give the note to Steven's mother and we shall see what she has to say. Then take on her role, with the basket in your hand and looking a little harassed. Tell the children that you are very cross with Steven as he took so long to get home with these things. You have sent him off to take the baby for a walk. '*Have you seen what he brought home?*' Take items out of the basket in the order of the story and get cross that each time there is one item missing. '*I asked for six eggs and there are only five, look! One, two, three, four, five!* (Ask them to count aloud with you) *What happened to the other one? Do any of you know???*' Be astonished at their story and encourage them to retell it with the right amount of detail. In the end admit that this is exactly what Steven told you and that, if the teacher who lives in number 25 also saw it, then it must be true. Ask children what you should say to Steven, now that you know that you were wrong to disbelieve and get cross with him.

12. If the class is capable, and if their reading and writing skills are sufficient for you to note vocabulary on a whiteboard for them to read, you might now consider varying the story a little. What other items might be bought and how many each time? You could look together at the illustration of Mr Diwali's shop and see what else he sells, making a list and choosing from them.

13. You might also do an exercise of matching an adjective with an animal. Have two lists, as below.

Snake	hungry
Lion	greedy
Crocodile	scary
Tiger	lazy
Scorpion	sneaky
Gorilla	terrifying
Horse	crawling

    Children match these up phonetically (i.e. sneaky snake; lazy lion etc.). What might they threaten to do to Steven if he doesn't give them something? You could do a cloze procedure exercise before having children read out their threats to the teacher in role as Steven.

14. The song below allows you to practise different types of shopping – for sweets, for vegetables, for fruit, for toys and so on. It is an adaptation of *Charlie over the Ocean* (see Chapter 3) and is played the same way, only with altered lyrics.

First of all ask the children to make a list of nice food and treats that they would like to buy from the shops. You can use this to teach some new vocabulary for treats they don't know the English for yet. Alternatively, have some flash cards that you hold up and use to prompt them for each round of the song.

Then teach them the new lyrics for the song, as below. As it is a song in which each line is sung by a leader and then repeated by the class, this should be easy to do.

> *Steven went out shopping*
> *Shopping for his mummy.*
> *Steven bought some chocolate (toffees/ice cream/lollies etc.)*
> *You can't catch me!*

Another variation is to have a puppet, for example, a large snake of the kind that can be bought from folkmanis puppets online, called *Sneaky Snake* (see the exercise above). This can have a different game-like element to it. Spread some items on the floor in the middle of a circle. Go through what each item is with the snake puppet evidently showing that he wants to eat them all. Each time you finish a verse, name a different child whose task is to grab the item you mention and return to the circle before the snake can bite it or the child as she is running back! The singing proceeds as above, but instead of repeating the final line after you, children sing it with you and wait for you to name the child who is to run into the circle:

> *Sneaky Snake went shopping*
> *Shopping with no money*
> *Sneaky Snake likes chocolate*
> *But so do we ... Mahmud!!!*

Whereupon Mahmud runs into the circle and the race is on! It is a good idea to always let the child win but only just!

The Emperor's New Clothes by Hans Christian Andersen

This famous story needs neither introduction nor summary, and I propose that you use the original version to work with rather than any of the anaemic alternatives that have occasionally been rewritten for young children.[9] I suggest that part of its appeal for them lies in the naughtiness that pervades the entire tale, from the roguish weavers to the naked Emperor at the end; and, once again, in its irony, the fact that the children know more about what is going on than the main character does. This time, however, he is not

FIGURE 15 The Emperor and his servant.

a kitten, like Max, but the most powerful authority in the land, which adds to the drama.

The tale provides an opportunity for children to consider the vanity and foolishness of this particular tyrant and the fear that motivates those who serve him to pretend to believe in one big lie. But these are young children so any such exploration must be playful and enjoyable, as must be the obvious opportunities the story provides for a range of language activities associated with clothes and dressing up. A dressing-up box is an essential learning aid in this scheme, with items such as a crown, a cloak, a sword included along with the usual hats, slippers, scarves and so on. But much can be made of miming and pretend, of playing with clothes that aren't actually there, as this is precisely what the two swindlers in the original story do so well.

Specific Language Objectives

To listen, understand and respond to:

Put the (crown, slipper, cloak etc.) on my (head, foot, shoulders etc.)
You can't see them
Magic
Minister
Storytelling by the Emperor (teacher in role) and in the whoosh

Vocabulary and lexical chunks to speak and understand:

Use of 'so' as an adjective of degree, as in: so great, so handsome etc.
Items of clothing, such as: crown, scarf, slippers, sunglasses, cloak
Use of past perfect tense: he has put on a scarf, jacket etc.
The (shoes/shirts/socks/coats etc.) are made of (silk, leather, gold, silver, diamonds).
Long live the emperor!
The rhyme: 'The Emperor loves to have new clothes'
The weaver's got ...
Pretend/pretending
Fine, wonderful
Look! The Emperor has no (shoes, socks, clothes etc.)

To revisit and practise:

Descriptive adjectives for the Emperor, spoken and written
Items of clothing; colours; parts of the body

Competences:

Can take the lead in a number of language games that have been modelled by the teacher
Can correct descriptive errors deliberately made by the teacher in role
Can draw a picture accurately following verbal instructions
Can predict what might happen next in the story
Can read lines in the correct sequence in a short performance

Resources

- A crown
- A dressing-up box
- Small samples of rich-looking cloth and fake jewellery
- A4 paper and coloured pencils

The activities are sequenced for this scheme under four headings in which the children meet the Emperor, explore his wardrobe, encounter the trickery of the rogue weaver and help perform a finale to the story.

Meeting the Emperor

1. Go, Stop, Show Me ... Play this game with the words *clever*, *brave*, *strong*, *rich*. Point to and describe any particularly clear examples, copying one of them yourself and having all the class do the

same, or helping with your own suggestions, thus clearing up any misunderstandings. For rich, for example, you might pretend to be counting money, with a big smile on your face; for clever, you might show a thoughtful face, pretending to be reading a book in one hand and holding a pen in the other. Children then sit down and help you recall the descriptive adjectives used in this game, which you can list on the whiteboard. Read them aloud in turn, asking children after each word to raise their hand if they would like to be described as such. Then ask if there are any other describing words they would like to be called, adding them to the list before requesting advice to help you show what these look like. For handsome or beautiful, for example, you might pretend to hold a mirror and look pleased with your reflection. Children are quite likely to think that such a person is not likeable. They may not know the word 'vain', but they are likely to feel it and the following exercises will help develop their appreciation of its meaning.

2. *Emperor, you're so great!* Show a crown to the children and tell them it belongs to a very powerful emperor who likes to be flattered and praised with any of these words. Rehearse with them how to say, 'Emperor, you're so handsome/brave/strong etc.' emphasizing that they must sound as though they mean it! Then put on the crown and have individual children volunteer in turn to praise you. If they say 'Emperor, you're so strong!' adopt the 'strong' stance

FIGURE 16 The Emperor is so vain!

used in the previous game and say, 'Yes, I know. I am so strong!' Do this for four or five examples before inviting children to volunteer to wear the crown and be the Emperor themselves as the game continues.

3. *Dressing the Emperor.* Take on the role of Emperor and sit in a chair, telling the children that this is your throne. The dressing-up box should be close by. Command different children to bring you something from it. 'You! Bring me my crown! Put it on my head! Now bow! Now sit!' and so on. Other items can include a scarf, slippers, a sword, gloves, sunglasses. When you come out of role, ask the children to recall and repeat together examples of what the Emperor said and how he spoke. A child can then volunteer to be the Emperor and, with your prompting as and when necessary, the game can be repeated.

   If necessary, sing a version of the action song 'Head, Shoulders, Knees and Toes' before this to refresh the vocabulary for parts of the body.

4. *The Emperor on the wall!* This version of the drama strategy *role on the wall* consists of an outline of the Emperor drawn on a large roll of white paper that you have attached to the classroom wall. Children can begin to suggest a list of words and phrases to describe the Emperor from what they have learned about him so far. You should help them extend their vocabulary and also their accuracy. So, for example, if children suggest 'handsome' or 'brave', you need to push them to appreciate that this is what he likes to hear and may not be true. 'He thinks he is handsome' or 'he likes people to say he is handsome' would be more accurate. 'He is proud' or 'he is big-headed' might be added, of course – and even 'he is vain'. As the scheme progresses, you can add more and more words and phrases to this list as and when appropriate.

5. *The deaf servant.* A fun extension to Activity 3, when revisited later, is for you to take on the role of a servant (or courtier, or minister) who is hard of hearing, who gets the items wrong and/or puts them in the wrong place. If the emperor says, 'Servant! Put the crown on my head!' you can speak to the children watching in the circle: 'Put the crown on his leg?? Well, he is the Emperor, I must do as he says.' This can initially be played with an adult helper in role as the Emperor, who holds a rolled-up sheet of sugar paper as a stick with which she can beat the courtier over his back each time he gets it wrong. Children will very much enjoy helping the courtier to hear correctly, as well as seeing him continuously get things wrong, and will love to play this game later in small, supervised groups or in the ELA. It is also a good activity for character exploration

FIGURE 17 Enjoying being in role as the Emperor.

and vocabulary extension, children being asked to add to the list of words that describe the Emperor, most of which will now be far from flattering!

The Emperor's Wardrobe

1. *The Emperor gets dressed.* Stand in the centre of the circle with the crown on your head, pretending to take something out of an imaginary wardrobe and put it on in front of an imaginary mirror, admiring yourself as you do so. The children have to suggest what the Emperor has just put on and then repeat it together. 'He has put on a coat/a scarf/gloves' and so on. After a few examples, invite different children to take on the role of the Emperor and do the same.

2. *The Emperor has a hundred …* Sit in a circle and then list together different items of clothing that the Emperor will have in his wardrobe. A child is invited to choose one item from the list, and you then lead the following chant, clapping on the stressed syllable: 'The **Emp**'ror has a **hun**-dred shoes (socks, hats etc)! **Long** live the **Emp**'ror!' The children repeat, each time chanting and clapping as one.

You can now introduce small examples of rich-looking cloth or materials that are passed around the circle and named one at a time. These include gold, silver, silk, leather, diamonds. After playing some of the usual vocabulary games, the chant is repeated and changed thus: 'The **Emp**'ror has a **hun**-dred shirts! The **shirts** are made of **silk**!' 'The **Emp**'ror has a **hun**-dred gloves! The **gloves** are made of **sil**-ver!' and so on.

3. *Creating and exploring a 'word-robe'.* Children are given a piece of A4 paper and a range of coloured pencils and asked to draw and label a specific item to be found in the Emperor's wardrobe. These are then spread over a clear space. Working now in pairs, one child is to keep their eyes closed and be led around the imagined wardrobe by their partner, who, by reading what is on the floor at a particular point, will help them imagine the colour and texture of different items of clothing. You can give them a simple language structure for this. *Here is a shirt – it is blue and made of silk; here are some shoes – they are white and made of silver* and so on. After a while the activity is paused to allow children time to talk together about what they recall from the journey. When they carry on visiting the rest of the wardrobe, their roles are reversed.

The Rogue Weaver

1. Now you can begin to tell the story, in the voice of the Emperor. You can do this by putting on the crown and sitting on your throne, telling children before you begin that the Emperor is very excited today – just listen to what he has to tell them.

   In my version of the story, there is just one weaver, not two, as it makes some subsequent activities simpler. Although I am following the story and saying that the weaver is male, that need not be the case. If you yourself are female, you can alter the gender of the weaver and, if you wish, that of the ministers and servants who are duped by him.

   Your narrative could progress like this:

   Something very interesting happened to me today. A weaver came to see me. Do you know what a weaver does? He makes clothes – shirts, jackets, trousers, socks, dresses – all kinds of clothes. Well, he has come from a city far away where he learned how to make magic clothes, magic in a special way. He can make clothes that not everyone can see. If you are stupid, you can't see them; if you are foolish, you can't see them; if you are not clever enough to work for me, you won't be able to see any of the clothes he makes. But, if you are clever enough to work for me, you will be able to see them! Isn't that fantastic? Now I can find out who is clever and who is stupid in this palace. Now, let me see. Hands up if anyone here thinks they will be clever enough to see these clothes, hands up high …

There are a few things you can do to continue. If everyone puts their hands up, you can proceed immediately to the next activity; if some don't, you can ask why not. If they haven't understood the English, you can do some translanguaging with the help of the children who have understood. If they say they think they are not clever enough, you can be nice to them and say you are sure they are cleverer than they think. If they say they don't believe the weaver's story, you can act surprised and probe them as to why not. You can do all of this still in role as the Emperor, or – more easily, perhaps – by coming out of role and reflecting upon the Emperor's story with the children. However, make sure that you do it playfully, as though you don't know what will happen next. 'Really? Do you think the weaver might be lying? Oh dear, why??'

2. You can teach the children the following chant, which has the same rhythm as 'My Mother Said I Never Should' (see Chapter 3).

> The **Emperor loves** to **have** new **clothes**
> That's **something that** the **weaver knows.**
> He's **making clothes** that **you** can't **see**
> Unless you're **clever** – **oh** dear **me!**
> **Are** you **clever? Are** you **not?**
> **Can** you **see** what the **weaver's got?**

You can go through this a few times, clapping to the stressed beat. It may also help to have children stand as they do it and stamp a foot as well as clap. If it is too hard for some to learn it all, concentrate on getting them to know the last two lines as this feeds directly into the game below.

3. Ask the children to stand in space, with one child next to you and the dressing-up box at the front of the class. Have about eight items in the box and show children what they are, if necessary repeating each after you as you put them in the box. The children now chant the last two lines of the above rhyme together, clapping to the beat, after which you call for them to close their eyes. The child then selects something from the box and hides it behind their back, whereupon the rest of the class open their eyes and have three chances to guess what it is. Each time they are to use the same

sentence structure: 'the weaver's got the sunglasses' or 'the weaver's got the hat'. You can change the child playing the weaver after one or two rounds.

4. You can now *whoosh* the next section of the story, taking the example in Chapter 3 as a model for how to make it work. The following is offered as a possible guide.

> *Now the weaver, as you have probably guessed, was only pretending to make clothes in his room. In fact what do you think he was doing instead? (You can draw upon children's ideas here) Yes, he was smoking, drinking tea, eating biscuits and playing cards. If a minister was sent to see his work, he would knock on the door. As soon as the weaver heard the knock, he would hide his cigarette and his tea cup and shout 'Come in!' When the minister entered, the weaver would pretend to be working very hard and very fast, moving his foot up and down, his leg up and down, his arms up and down, his fingers up and down and breathing very hard.*
>
> *WHOOSH*
>
> *The weaver stopped pretending to work and pointed to the invisible clothes he was pretending to make. 'Isn't it fine? Isn't it wonderful?' he asked. Well the minister looked very hard. He walked right up and tried to touch. 'Don't touch!' shouted the weaver, smacking his hand away. 'You might tear it!' The minister turned his back on the weaver. 'Oh dear,' he said. 'I can't see anything! I must be stupid! Ssshhhhh!! No one must know!' He turned back to the weaver, 'Of course! It is a fine, wonderful shirt.' The weaver smiled. 'It's not a shirt,' he said, 'It's a pair of trousers.' 'Of course,' said the minister, nodding his head, 'a fine, wonderful pair of blue trousers.' The weaver frowned. 'But they aren't blue,' he said, 'they are green!' The minister only nodded his head very fast, 'Of course, of course!' he said, 'A fine, wonderful pair of green trousers! I'll go and tell the Emperor.' He walked to the door but, as he opened it, the weaver called out, 'Tell the Emperor I need a lot more gold. To buy more fine, wonderful cloth.'*
>
> *WHOOSH*

5. Check that the children have understood what has just happened in this *Whoosh*, then ask them whether they think the minister will tell the Emperor the truth, that he couldn't see anything at all! Why/why not? Then tell them that he sent more ministers to see the weaver, so let's see if any of them can catch the weaver not working!

The children now spread out in space. Ask them if they can remember some of the things that the weaver was doing when he wasn't pretending to work. Then play Go, Stop, Show Me, calling: 'Show me the weaver smoking/drinking tea etc.' Once they can do this, introduce the call, 'The minister is coming!' Whenever you call that out, they are immediately to stop whatever they are doing and pretend to be working very hard making clothes. Ask them if they can remember some of the movements the weaver did when he was at his loom. Have them rehearse these before playing the game. When you call out 'The minister is coming!' do it loudly and urgently, then take on the role of the minister briefly, inspecting the weavers and commenting, 'Well, you are very busy, I see …'

You can also agree with children in advance what they will say to the minister if he asks what they are weaving. If they say a shirt, say 'Yes! Tell him you are making a fine, wonderful shirt!' Whereupon they will practise the answer: 'It's a fine, wonderful shirt!' When playing the game, you can ask the whole class to answer in chorus, or individual children you think are capable of answering on their own. Always speak in the role of the minister here, 'What are you making? A fine, wonderful shirt?? Ah, of course it is!' and so on.

Play about four or five rounds of this before continuing.

The Emperor's New Clothes!

1. For the following exercise, children will need easy access to blank A4 paper and coloured pencils so this might be best done at their desks, outside of drama time.

   Tell them that all of the ministers who visited the weaver were too frightened to tell the Emperor the truth, that they could actually see nothing at all. Instead, they always told him they had seen different, wonderful items of clothing. In his excitement, the Emperor asked them to draw a picture of what they hadn't in fact been able to see; so they had to remember what the weaver had told them and draw that.

   Now say that you are going to pretend to be the weaver and that you are going to describe three different pieces of clothing and the children have to draw what you tell them. *But* their drawing must be beautiful in order to please the Emperor! To make this a fair exercise for them, tell them that, unlike the weaver, you have three pictures in front of you that you will describe, so the children can compare their own drawings with the original once they have finished each.

   You can make this as difficult or as easy as you like, depending upon what vocabulary your children understand. You can also change the demands for different ability levels and do the exercise in small groups. For example, a simple task will involve three instructions, such as: "This is a shirt. The sleeves are short. Its colour is green.' You could even use hand gestures to help the children here. More difficult would be: 'It's a shirt with short sleeves and six white buttons. It has stripes that are light green and dark green in colour. The collar is white.'

You can also have a series of cards made of different clothes and ask children to play this in pairs as an exercise in later lessons or as a game in the ELA.

2. Play a game in which you show the children one of the cards, or an item of clothing, and get the details wrong. Be falsely confident each time. 'Ah, look at this! It's a hat, isn't it! No??? Erm, well what is it then? A pair of socks?? Right, a yellow pair of socks! No?? A blue pair … Ah, so it is!' This could be more fun if you pretend to be the short-sighted servant whom we met in the earlier game. He has been asked to tidy some of the old clothes in the Emperor's wardrobe to make way for the new clothes when they are ready. 'So what do I tell the Emperor this is again???'

3. Sit children in a circle and tell them that finally it came to the day the Emperor had been waiting for – the day of the royal procession, when he would walk through the city and everyone would line the streets to cheer him as he passed by. Relate the next section as

FIGURE 18 'Could you draw the clothes described by the weaver?'

a *whoosh*, perhaps, or just in your own voice, with appropriate movement and expression.

> *Very excited, the Emperor called for his new clothes to be brought to him. The weaver entered, pulling behind him a big suitcase. He put the suitcase down, opened the lid and proudly lifted up a pair of … Nothing!! The Emperor stared and then looked about him. All of the ministers were smiling and clapping, pretending they could see something fine and wonderful. Could he really be the only stupid person in the palace? Surely not! But he certainly had to pretend or everyone would think that he, the Emperor, was not as clever as them. And that was impossible, of course. No one could be allowed to think that he, the Emperor, was stupid! 'Here,' said the weaver, 'take off your trousers and put on this fine, wonderful pair!' The Emperor want pale. What should he do?*

4. Ask the children what they think the Emperor *should* do and then what they think he *will* do. Tell them that he took off all of his

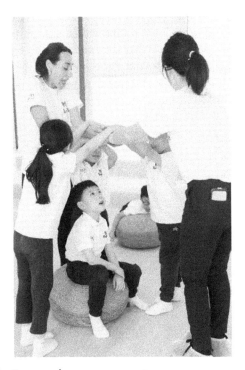

FIGURE 19 The Emperor has a new crown!

clothes and put on these invisible clothes that he thought everyone could see apart from himself. Then he stepped out with his ministers and guards on to the streets, where all of the people were lined up to cheer him. Ask, if they were in the crowd, what would they do? What would they call out to him? What do they think the Emperor might do then?

5. Make a list with the children of all the clothes the Emperor should be wearing, from his feet up to his neck. This list can then be used to complete a series of sentences, each beginning: 'Look! The Emperor has no ...', as in: 'Look! The Emperor has no shoes!' 'Look! The Emperor has no socks!' culminating in 'LOOK! THE EMPEROR HAS NO CLOTHES!' You can tell the children how all of the grown-ups pretended they could see his new clothes, but that all the children were honest and called out what they could really see. Gather the class in a semicircle in front of the outline of the *Emperor on the wall* (see the earlier exercise), then lead them in this activity. Point, looking by turn shocked/amused/alarmed, varying the volume and asking children to copy exactly what you do and say and the way that you say it with each sentence. Do this more than once if the children are enjoying it.

6. If children can read English by now, you can have these lines prepared and written down on individual slips of paper which you can then distribute so that the exercise can be repeated with individual children pointing and leading the call rather than you.

7. As a concluding exercise, children can draw and add speech bubbles to this final image of the story.

CHAPTER SIX

Performative Language Teaching and Assessment for Learning

So much has been written in recent years about the assessment of young English language learners that this chapter could take up as much space as the preceding chapters put together.[1] Many of these publications reflect the attention that the recent global growth of TEYL has received from researchers and specialists in the field. In order not to be swamped by this growing area of scholarship and research, I intend to focus squarely on issues of assessment that relate directly to the schemes of work within this volume. This will nonetheless require some initial consideration of a range of general issues relating to assessment, its forms and purposes and how it relates to learning, as well as more specifically how the assessment of these schemes might be aligned with objectives that attempt to map out content and progression in EYL. Above all, the chapter is meant to be of help to practising teachers and will therefore intentionally avoid advocating modes of practice that are over-elaborate, time-consuming and not directly related to the evaluation and improvement of learning.

Assessment: Forms and Purposes

Assessment is generally regarded as having a crucial role in the young-learner classroom.[2] It has a range of interrelated purposes, namely: to identify what young learners are capable of and what their next steps of learning ought to be; to help teachers evaluate their own teaching and improve the effectiveness of their lessons; and to help them record accurate data that is informative for themselves, professional colleagues, parents and other stake-holders, including the individual learners themselves. Such record-keeping is now an integral part of a teacher's professional accountability but should never detract from the core aim of assessment, namely, to help further children's learning. In the case of young learners, we can go so far as to say that any assessment that does not contribute to this is probably a waste of both the teacher's and the learner's time.

Assessment can be either informal or formal and can have formative or summative intentions. Informal assessment will happen while teaching and learning are taking place, as the teacher observes, responds to and offers support for and feedback to groups or individual children. Such observations will naturally influence future planning and interventions. Summative assessment is often more formal, taking the shape of a test of some kind, with the aim of gauging what individual learners have learned from a particular unit of study.[3] Of course, formal testing of very young learners is problematic and written tests for 3-year-olds are out of the question. However, the kind of performances suggested at the end of some of the units in Chapters 4 and 5 can be seen as enjoyable forms of summative assessment that integrate learning in English with social skills and the performing arts.

'Evaluation' is another term that relates to the process of assessment but has nuances that are importantly different. If assessment tends to focus on recognizable, identified criteria of attainment, evaluation considers broader issues of 'value-added'. Considering the educational value of a programme of learning for a child or group of children will necessarily overlap with assessing what they have attained from a set of identifiable targets or objectives but will also take into account important observations that underpin or complement such objectives. If a child or a group of children evidently enjoy an activity, respond positively to a lesson, engage deeply with a story or demonstrate commitment to a task, these are all likely to contribute to their confidence as learners, overall well-being and positive attitudes to being in school. Such results cannot easily, or usefully, be broken down into a learning ladder but will be seen as fundamentally significant by most teachers. They are often particularly emphasized by teachers who value the role of play and the arts in the education of young children. Such teachers will often look for evidence of them when they evaluate their own lessons. For this reason I tend to use the term 'evaluation' when referring to the effectiveness of a lesson or scheme of learning and 'assessment' when considering what learning there has been.[4]

'Progression' is integral to assessment for learning. In the previous paragraph I have used the term 'learning ladder' to indicate how assessment criteria are often broken down into units that support an idea of linear progression through a specific scale of attainment.[5] These often take the form of 'descriptors' of the knowledge, skills or abilities that plot learning in some kind of sequential order of rising competence. Such 'criterion referencing' is used, for example, in models of progression offered by the influential Common European Framework of Reference for Languages, or CEFR.[6] Necessary as such frameworks for progression are, however, they are insufficient in themselves to help teachers ensure that children make progress in their learning.

Contexts for Assessing EYL

I have previously proposed that the schemes in this book should be considered as complementary to a structured course in language learning rather than as constituting an entire course in themselves. In MEIYI RKEC, Chinese children are being taught English in an immersive context for 50 per cent of their school day. This is supported by a published course in English, the popular Pearson's *Backpack Gold*. Assessment of English takes place within the structured learning afforded by this course but also within the curriculum content taught in the immersive curriculum, of which drama is one aspect. In non-immersive programmes, where children are being taught English for just one or two hours a week, assessment will relate directly to a structured course of some kind, perhaps a published course such as Pearson's or an in-house model. Should schemes such as those proposed in this book be adopted or adapted to complement such core English courses, their assessment, too, might at times align itself with learning in these course programmes.

Examples of how this can work in a simple way can be found by referring to the section entitled 'Scope and Sequence' in the Teacher's Book for *Backpack Gold Level 2*. Here the learning objectives for each scheme are clearly mapped out. Unit 7 entitled 'Favourite Foods', for example, and unit 8, 'Fun at the Zoo', could be readily complemented by the story *Handa's Surprise* and the related drama activities outlined in Chapter 3; or by aspects of the schemes in *Peter Rabbit* and *The Shopping Basket*, as they all deal with the units' stated objectives of likes and dislikes for different foods; and learning the names, traits, capabilities and features of different animals.[7]

For those minority language learners in mainstream education in English speaking countries, assessment will relate to the core English curriculum and be supported by targeted objectives, such as are provided in the UK by the *EAL Assessment Framework for Schools*.[8] Here descriptors for recording the progress in English for children with EAL are provided under the four strands of language knowledge, namely listening, speaking, reading and viewing, and writing. At primary level, each of these contains fifty descriptors of specific competences arranged on ten levels, many of which are constantly revisited in the schemes throughout this book. So, for example, under the heading 'Listening', statements include 'Can understand single words or short phrases in familiar contexts' and 'Is beginning correctly to interpret intonation, stress and other culturally-specific, non-verbal communication'. It would be relatively straightforward to feed assessment information gathered from the schemes in this book directly on to such records. With regard to these two descriptors, for example, children are constantly being asked to respond appropriately to different words and phrases, whether to instructions, in games, or through different miming activities. They are also given regular opportunities to practise and interpret facial and gestural communication and to observe and respond to different plays of intonation and stress in English, as the teacher in role conveys emotions such as surprise, bewilderment and annoyance.

The examples above illustrate how progression in language learning is often presented as a *map*, with talk of 'mapping children's progress' being quite common. If performative approaches to TEYL are to contribute to such mapping, however, they will do so in ways very different from standardized courses. For example, the two descriptors from the EAL framework cited above are drawn from opposite ends of the level descriptors for listening, the former from the early development stage, the latter from the top end of the scale, described as 'getting ready for the next band'.[9] They illustrate how performative approaches will often cut across linear maps of progression. They differ, too, from graded course work which will often emphasize the instrumental, transactional aspects of EYL, whereas performative approaches will include a strong emphasis on expressive language objectives, which may be presented as much higher on the 'learning ladder' in such models. For example, songs and rhymes connect 'stress intonation and rhythm', identified in the CEFR as prosodic features rated at the higher end of the intermediate 'independent user' competence level rather than at the level of the beginner or 'basic user'.[10] Furthermore, stories in these schemes have been chosen for their human interest rather than as vehicles for graded language practice; verbs cover a range of expressive subtlety, including emotive vocabulary such as *grab*, *snatch*, *dash*, *wriggle* that bring stories to life and that can shape children's playful movement work; and the social skills that underpin successful communication and co-operation are given particular prominence.

Documenting and Acting Upon Assessment

Any attempt to assess thoroughly all elements of learning runs the risk of becoming cumbersome and impractical. Carmen Becker provides a compelling example of this in her account of the implementation of the European Language Portfolio, or ELP.[11] This was launched in 2007 to provide a form of assessment that would help with the dissemination of the CEFR. The ELP was intended to act as a record of the individual learner's achievement in language learning, to celebrate their experiences as learners, to provide a valuable source of information and to aid with transfer to the next class. The portfolio consisted of three parts: a language passport, to record their language-learning experiences at home and in school, including their mother tongue; a language biography, to record specific proficiency levels in listening, speaking, reading and writing; and a dossier, to include examples of work completed and so document their learning processes. In all three parts, learners were to be involved centrally in the compilation of the portfolio, selecting the examples of work for the dossier, for example, and completing a work diary for the biography.

The ELP was designed to promote a new learning and assessment culture and offered a range of laudable democratic learning opportunities: promoting learner autonomy and self-responsibility, for example, and recognizing the importance of affective and social processes to complement cognition. However, in her evaluation of a large-scale pilot project in which the ELP was implemented in Germany, Becker found that both its uptake and its effect on actual practice were very limited. There was no evidence of a paradigm shift towards competency-based teaching; existing coursebooks remained dominant; and primary teachers reported having very little confidence in their learners' self-assessment skills. Ninety per cent of teachers reported that their teaching practice remained unchanged, stating that the ELP had not been integrated into their daily teaching and regarding it as a time-consuming add-on.

Becker remains committed to the values and principles of the ELP and outlines the kind of support and training that teachers would need in order to change their practice so it could be successfully implemented. Her chapter remains sobering reading, however, for anyone promoting a new kind of pedagogy and recommending ways that assessment can be integrated within it. For the remainder of this chapter, I will nonetheless attempt to do this by using two of the schemes, one each from Chapters 4 and 5 , and considering how assessment can be incorporated into everyday teaching in simple ways that can help record attainment but, above all, act as an aid to learning. In doing so I will focus squarely on the assessment of English language, as this is the key point of interest for anyone making use of this book.[12]

Assessment for Learning Example 1:
Max the Brave

The language learning objectives for each scheme have been included at the beginning of each in ways that focus principally on vocabulary extension but that also include a selective group of competences. Other vocabulary and language competences may well come into play during the teaching, but it is necessary for both learning *and* assessment to prioritize where any new learning is to be focused. That is why I have emphasized that such a sheet will have to be adapted, particularly under the third subheading, *to revise and practise*, as this will depend on what your class has already covered.

The following page illustrates how such a sheet can be readily adapted to act as a working document intended to aid assessment for learning throughout your teaching of the scheme. Rather than prepare one for each child, I propose that you prepare just three sheets, with three different headings, namely *secured*, *developing* or *emerging*, and ensure that there is enough space at the bottom of the sheet for you to be able to write the names of children in your class in relation to the level of learning assessed. This list of names on the three levels can then be altered where appropriate as you work through the scheme, as illustrated below.

After the first session, you can highlight on each sheet the language objectives that have been covered, then decide which of the children's names should be written on which sheet according to how you have seen them perform. As an example, let us consider the performance of three different young learners: Li, Hao yue and Lian. Li is confident and linguistically gifted, quickly understands new vocabulary and enjoys speaking English. She will most likely have *secured* the new learning very quickly. If she and other children like her fail to do so, then it is more than likely that the scheme in its current form is not well matched to this particular class. Hao yue was engaged throughout the class but has been less quick to understand and has struggled to remember new words and phrases; she will thus be added to the *developing* sheet. Lian has found it difficult to repeat any of the words and phrases and joins in activities mainly by observing and copying her peers. Her name will be added to the *emerging* sheet.

The reason for having just three sheets is purely practical. If you have twenty different sheets, one for each child, individually named, they will be far less useful to you as working documents. As well as being more time consuming and probably no more accurate in terms of an ongoing record for each child, the fact that children are grouped in graded categories can signal to you quickly which of them need re-enforcement or additional support. Realistically, you will know that certain children are likely to remain in the emerging group while others will tend to establish themselves very quickly in the secured group; but you will have observed others who might move up a grade if given some specific attention. You can select such small groups of children for focused additional support and language practice before teaching the next session of the scheme, concentrating on the specific objectives you have observed them needing practice in. In the case of *Max the Brave*, they may need to practise the greeting song; or be reintroduced to the various animal puppets, repeating one or two of the vocabulary games again; or they may need to revise their colour vocabulary. This could be a ten- or fifteen-minute task for you or the teaching assistant while other children are doing simple drawing or colouring activities or, in the case of the higher achieving group, a worksheet with some straightforward extension activities. In this way, you can cross out individual children's names from one sheet and add them to another as and when your observations judge them to have moved up a level. Ideally, when the scheme is completed, there will be more names on the secure sheet than on the other two, with some names on the developing sheet that were assessed as emerging at an earlier stage in the scheme.

This is not a scientific exercise but one that depends upon you observing, intervening and providing additional support as and when necessary. Using such a process thoughtfully can sharpen your professional know-how and make teaching and learning more effective in your classroom. It is an example of how a simple assessment map can shape the journey of learning.

The final list of names you have on each sheet at the end of this particular unit can act as a form of summative assessment for the scheme. The competences, too, can be seen as secured, developing or emerging, and the final performance can contribute to this summative assessment as a kind of test that in no way should diminish children's enjoyment of the activity.

Scheme: *Max the Brave*

Specific Language Objectives

(*Secured* or *Developing* or *Emerging* written here)

Lexical chunks to listen and respond to:

Excuse me, please, who are you?
Who can show me ...?
Put on/take off (the ribbon)
Where is ...?
The Monster is coming!
Let's run together!
Get ready, get set, go!

Vocabulary and lexical chunks to speak:

Kitten/fly/mouse/elephant/bird/fish/rabbit/monster
Ribbon. Colours, including pink
Frightened; pretty; sweet; brave; big; small; loud; quiet
Yes I am/Yes you are/No you're not/No I'm not
That way! Wake up! I will eat you up! Help me!

To revise and practise:

Greeting and saying names
Responding to various instructions and questions
Colours and those animal names the children already know

Happy/sad/angry

Performing the actions to 'Have You Seen the Monsters Sleeping?'

Competences:

Can respond to simple instructions appropriately

Can respond to more complex instructions with the help of visual clues

Can engage in simple, rehearsed speech exchange (saying name and greeting)

In final performance

Can repeat the lines clearly

Can perform the appropriate actions and gestures

(Children's names added and removed here as the scheme progresses).

Assessment for Learning Example 2:
The Emperor's New Clothes

This scheme is at the other end of the progression ladder and is aimed at older, more practised language learners within this age range. The principles for assessing children, with the use of the three assessment sheets, remain the same. The list of new vocabulary and lexical chunks the children are intended to learn is not much lengthier than that of the earlier scheme, but the overall language demands are certainly more challenging and include rehearsing grammatical structures, such as the past perfect tense; making more autonomous choices in sentence construction; and learning a rhyme that is far lengthier and more complex than the simple greeting song in the scheme for *Max the Brave*.

As children are exposed to increasing amounts of language learning experiences, an emphasis on competences – on what they are able to do with the language – is likely to become more pronounced. Once again, what the children are expected to be able to do will depend on their previous learning, their ease with the language, their confidence levels and a range of factors that you will need to take into account when deciding on which competences you wish to focus on. Your descriptors need to be precise and observable if you are to make secure judgements. Competences as listed on large-scale assessment maps, such as those provided in the CEFR, cannot simply be grafted on to individual schemes, nor are they intended to be; they should be used as general aims within which you can work out your own specific objectives.

Scheme: *The Emperor's New Clothes*

Specific Language Objectives

(*Secured* or *Developing* or *Emerging* written here)

To listen, understand and respond to:

Put the (crown, slipper, cloak etc.) on my (head, foot, shoulders etc.)
You can't see them
Magic
Minister
Storytelling by the Emperor (teacher in role) and in the whoosh

Vocabulary and lexical chunks to speak and understand:

Use of 'so' as an adjective of degree, as in: so great, so handsome etc.
Items of clothing, such as: crown, scarf, slippers, sunglasses, cloak
Use of past perfect tense: he has put on a scarf, jacket etc.
The (shoes/shirts/socks/coats etc.) are made of (silk, leather, gold, silver,
    diamonds)
Long live the Emperor!
The rhyme: 'The Emperor loves to have new clothes'
The weaver's got …
Pretend/pretending
Fine, wonderful
Look! The Emperor has no (shoes, socks, clothes etc.)

To revisit and practise:

Descriptive adjectives for the Emperor, spoken and written
Items of clothing; colours; parts of the body

Competences:

Can take the lead in a number of language games that have been mod-
    elled by the teacher
Can correct descriptive errors deliberately made by the teacher in role
Can draw a picture accurately following verbal instructions
Can predict what might happen next in the story
Can read lines in the correct sequence in a short performance

(*Children's names added and removed here as the scheme progresses*).

A Simple Assessment Portfolio

Some educators will perhaps see the model I promote here as undemocratically lacking in the participation of the young learners themselves. This concern can be addressed by asking the children to select or create materials to compile a simple assessment portfolio for each scheme of work. It might contain drawings or stick puppets they have made, photographs of themselves in performance and, when they begin to be literate in the language, items of written work. Children can be asked to reflect on where they think they have done particularly well at the end of a unit and a small piece of writing can be included to this effect, scribed in English by yourself or by a teaching assistant if necessary. Such a portfolio will only be of use, however, if it serves to motivate and build up children's confidence as learners. I therefore make no apology for proposing that the creation of an assessment portfolio is of much less significance than is the teacher's professional use of assessment to boost the learning process. I would go so far as to say that such a portfolio would have little chance of boosting learners' self-confidence and motivation unless they felt that it documented good progress in their learning.

Conclusion

I have used the words 'map' and 'mapping' when referring to assessment in ways that will be readily comprehensible to teachers. It is, of course, a metaphor and it is worth considering its limitations. A map provides reference points to help plot a journey but does not constitute the journey itself. 'The map,' writes Helen Nicholson, 'represents knowledge that is official, disciplined and objective.' She then goes on to contrast this metaphor of knowledge as a map with that of knowledge as a *story*: 'The story is associated with everyday moments of creativity, ways of knowing that are practical, embodied and spontaneous.' This, she argues, connects with the concept of 'know how', which manifests itself through 'active, intimate, hands-on participation'.[13]

These two metaphors, of the map and the story as complementary ways of knowing, can be applied to the specific processes of assessment. Although mapping assessment through clearly stated objectives is important in planning for progression and for accountability purposes, it will not provide a proper aid to learning unless the teacher develops the know-how to respond creatively and productively to challenges as they present themselves in the classroom. Both the map and the story need to be in play if assessment is to become a properly effective tool for learning. What matters more than the map is the journey it provides guidance for, and it is in the story of that journey that we find purpose and issues of true human interest.

Assessment is often presented as a dry, objective, scientific process. In the model I argue for in this chapter it is none of those things. In essence it is about active, creative, practical decision-making, about enabling learners to learn more effectively. In order to achieve this, it must be focused and capable of informing your day-to-day teaching in sensible and manageable ways. These are the principles that have shaped this model of assessment as a learning journey, with you, the teacher, and the children in your class as fellow travellers. Bon voyage!

AFTERWORD

This book has been written during lockdown, as the UK, in common with much of the world, reeled under the impact of the Covid-19 pandemic. As I complete it, we have a vaccine, and there is hope of returning to some form of normality in the not-too-distant future, a normality that will see the reopening of cultural venues such as theatres and concert halls, all of which have been closed in the UK for the best part of a year. At regular intervals throughout the pandemic, television and radio reports have featured stories not only about the devastating impact it has had on those who work in the arts but also on the mental health of those who benefit from going to the theatre, singing in choirs, attending dance classes or participating in amateur dramatics. In schools, meanwhile, when they have been open, the classes in drama, dance and singing have been limited or abandoned altogether for fear of spreading the contagion.

A number of creative responses have attempted to re-establish such communal activities online. My local television channel has regularly shown brief features from online choirs and orchestras as well as people following zumba and other popular dance classes in their living rooms. Indeed, the acclaimed children's author Michael Morpurgo recently delivered a very upbeat message on BBC Radio 4, expressing hope for the future in the creative ways that artists and storytellers have found to connect with new audiences through the internet. But no one believes that these new communities are anything other than a substitute rather than a replacement for live participation in close proximity with others, least of all those who regularly join in with them. Whenever interviewed, participants have expressed their longing to return to being able to practise and perform with others in communal spaces rather than through cyberspace.

As young children in the UK have returned to their nursery and primary schools, there has been much talk on two major topics: how these settings need to prioritize children's welfare and mental health and how they must, at the same time, enable them to catch up with their lost learning. These are often presented as oppositional, as though prioritizing the one will inevitably lead to a neglect of the other. Such a vision, as we saw in Chapter 2, is commonly structured into educational debate, pitching the well-being children derive from play against the cognitive demands of academic learning. This book, from the outset, has presented a grounded theoretical argument and numerous practical examples of how such divisive thinking can be countered through teaching approaches that bring together physical and mental activity, aesthetic enjoyment and cognitive challenge, language play and language learning. The pedagogy it promotes sees the social well-being of young children as core to their linguistic development, in both first and additional languages, and has sought to demonstrate how it can be made to work in everyday classrooms.

It has been said that, in order to enjoy working with very young children, we need to reconnect with the child that still exists somewhere within ourselves. The aim of this book would be more accurately expressed as helping teachers of English to connect, or reconnect, with what they share with children that is deeply human, namely, a propensity for play and a need for stories. These not only cross cultural and linguistic boundaries but also, I have suggested, the false boundaries of age that are imposed between the 'playful' world of the young child and the 'workaday' world of the adult teacher. This is not to argue that teaching and learning a foreign language will always be joyful and easy and that performative language teaching will magically transform the classroom into a place of wonder and delight. I have emphasized the skill and preparation that is needed on the part of the teacher to make it work and have refrained from presenting it as a complete curriculum in itself. As a pedagogy integral to a properly balanced language curriculum, however, I suggest that it can serve to promote the well-being of teachers as well as the learning and well-being of young children, something that, in these uncertain times, we need to attend to more than ever.

NOTES

INTRODUCTION

1   See, for example, Jonothan Neelands, *Learning through Imagined Experience: Teaching English in the National Curriculum* (London: Hodder and Stoughton, 1992); Judith Ackroyd, ed., *Literacy Alive! Drama Projects for Literacy Learning* (London: Hodder Education, 2000); Patrice Baldwin, *Teaching Literacy through Drama* (London: Routledge, 2002).

2   Joe Winston, ed., *Second Language Learning through Drama: Practical Techniques and Applications* (London: Routledge, 2012); Joe Winston and Madonna Stinson, eds, *Drama Education and Second Language Learning* (London: Routledge, 2014).

3   See Victoria A. Murphy, *Second Language Learning in the Early School Years: Trends and Contexts* (Oxford: Oxford University Press, 2014). On p. 104 she provides a list of key characteristics of immersion education.

4   Yanling Zhou and Mei Lee Ng, 'English as a Foreign Language (EFL) and English Medium Instruction (EMI) for Three- to Seven-Year-Old Children in East Asian Contexts', in Victoria A. Murphy and Maria Evangelou (eds), *Early Childhood Education in English for Speakers of Other Languages* (London: British Council, 2016), p. 146.

5   Ibid., p. 129.

6   Murphy, *Second Language Learning in the Early School Years*, p. 129.

7   Zhou and Ng, 'English as a Foreign Language', p. 145.

8   Richard Wong Kwok Shing, 'Do Hong Kong Pre-school Teachers of English Engage in Learning and Teaching Activities Conducive to Young Children's Vocabulary Development?', in Murphy and Evangelou, *Early Childhood Education in English*, pp. 195–206.

9   Zhou and Ng, 'English as a Foreign Language', p. 140.

10 Murphy, *Second Language Learning in the Early School Years*, p. 153.

11 Nathan Archer and Beatrice Merrick, *Getting the Balance Right: Quality and Quantity in Early Education and Childcare*, The Sutton Trust and The British Association for Childcare Education, July 2020.

12 Zhou and Ng, 'English as a Foreign Language', p. 142.

13 EFL is the term used by contributors to the edited publication by Murphy and Evangelou, *Early Childhood Education in English*, whereas EYL is used extensively by contributors to Sue Garton and Fiona Copland,

eds, *The Routledge Handbook of Teaching English to Young Learners* (London: Routledge, 2019).

14 See Murphy and Evangelou, *Early Childhood Education in English*.

15 Specifically Murphy, *Second Language Learning in the Early School Years*; Garton and Copland, *The Routledge Handbook of Teaching English*; and also Janice Bland (ed.), *Teaching English to Young Learners: Critical Issues in Language Teaching with 3–12 Year Olds* (London: Bloomsbury, 2015).

CHAPTER ONE

1 These figures were obtained from pp. 162–3 of https://www.oecd-ilibrary.org/docserver/0a156279-en.pdf?expires=1594285320&id=id&accname=guest&checksum=32F8ECDBDE03E7D5CE761970AF56CED1 (accessed July 2020).

2 Victoria A. Murphy and Maria Evangelou, eds, *Early Childhood Education in English for Speakers of Other Languages* (London: British Council, 2016), p. 4. Such figures are only ever approximate. David Crystal estimated them as much higher (2 billion) in 2002. See his *English as a Global Language*, 2nd ed. (Cambridge: Cambridge University Press, 2002).

3 Shelagh Rixon, 'Primary English and Critical Issues: A Worldwide Perspective', in Janice Bland (ed.), *Teaching English to Young Learners: Critical Issues in Language Teaching with 3–12 Year Olds* (London: Bloomsbury, 2015), p. 32.

4 Lixian Jin and Martin Cortazzi, 'Early English Language Learning in East Asia', in Sue Garton and Fiona Copland (eds), *The Routledge Handbook of Teaching English to Young Learners* (London: Routledge, 2019), p. 477.

5 Figures obtained from un.org (accessed November 2020).

6 Victoria A. Murphy, *Second Language Learning in the Early School Years: Trends and Contexts* (Oxford: Oxford University Press, 2014), p. 134.

7 Jin and Cortazzi, 'Early English Language Learning in East Asia', p. 479.

8 Sandie Murao, 'English in Pre-primary: The Challenges of Getting It Right', in Bland, *Teaching English to Young Learners*, p. 53.

9 Cited in Murphy, *Second Language Learning in the Early School Years*, p. 3.

10 Murphy's *Second Language Learning in the Early School Years* is an in-depth study of international research and practice attending to the contexts and different factors that influence the success of early multilingual learning.

11 E. H. Lenneberg, *Biological Foundations of Language* (New York: Wiley, 1967).

12 Tatiana Gordon, *Teaching Young Children a Second Language* (Westport, CT: Praeger, 2007), p. 56.

13 See Rhonda Oliver and Bich Nguyen, *Teaching Young Second Language Learners: Practices in Different Classroom Contexts* (London: Routledge, 2018), p. 3.

14 Ibid., p. 11.

15 Stephen Krashen, *Second Language Acquisition and Second Language Learning* (Oxford: Pergamon, 1981).

16 Murao, 'English in Pre-primary', p. 52.

17 Patton O. Tabors, *One Child, Two Languages: A Guide for Early Childhood Educators of Children Learning English as a Second Language* (Baltimore, MD: Paul H. Brookes, 2008).

18 Murao, 'English in Pre-primary', pp. 55 and 56.

19 Tabors, *One Child, Two Languages*, p. 7.

20 Ibid., pp. 47–51.

21 Ibid., pp. 56–9.

22 Ibid., p. 64.

23 Lilly Wong-Fillmore, 'Individual Differences in Second Language Acquisition', in C. F. Fillmore, D. Kempler and W. S. Wang (eds), *Individual Differences in Language Ability and Language Behaviour* (New York: Academic, 1979), p. 207.

24 Ibid., pp. 208–18.

25 Jenefer Philip and Susan Duchesne, 'When the Gate Opens: The Interaction between Social and Linguistic Goals in Child Second Language Development', in Jenefer Philip, Rhonda Oliver and Alison Mackey (eds), *Second Language Acquisition and the Young Learner: Child's Play?* (Amsterdam: John Benjamins, 2008), pp. 83–103.

26 This point is made by Alison Wray, *Formulaic Language and the Lexicon* (Cambridge: Cambridge University Press, 2002), cited in Philip and Duchesne, 'When the Gate Opens', p. 99.

27 Herbert Puchta, 'Teaching Grammar to Young Learners', in Garton and Copland, *The Routledge Handbook of Teaching English*, p. 204.

28 Ibid., p. 207.

29 Ibid., p. 208.

30 Gordon, *Teaching Young Children a Second Language*, p. 63.

31 Ibid., p. 130.

32 Puchta, 'Teaching Grammar to Young Learners', p. 210.

33 Ibid., p. 214.

34 Gordon, *Teaching Young Children a Second Language*, p. 67.

35 Ibid.

36 Ibid., p. 69.

37 Torill Irene Hestetraeet, 'Vocabulary Teaching for Young Learners', in Garton and Copland, *The Routledge Handbook of Teaching English*, pp. 220–33.

38 Ibid., p. 221. The research is drawn from I. S. Paul Nation, *Learning Vocabulary in Another Language* (Cambridge: Cambridge University Press, 2013).

39 Hestetraeet, 'Vocabulary Teaching for Young Learners', p. 224.

40 Ibid., p. 226.

41 See Tabors, *One Child, Two Languages*, chapter 6.

42 Ibid., p. 99.

43 Ibid., p. 108.

44 Ibid.

45 Ibid., pp. 110–11.

46 Ibid., p. 115.

47 Gordon, *Teaching Young Children a Second Language*, p. 75.

48 Ibid., p. 76.

49 Ibid., p. 78.

50 Ibid., p. 81.

51 See, for example, Yvette Coyle and R. Gomez Gracia, 'Using Songs to Enhance L2 Vocabulary Acquisition in Preschool Children', *ELT Journal* 68, no. 3 (July 2014), pp. 276–85; and Carolyn Graham, *Creating Chants and Songs: Resource Books for Teachers* (Oxford: Oxford University Press, 2006). Graham has a number of videos on YouTube that provide a clear illustration of her great work using jazz chants to teach basic English.

52 Yasemin Kirkgoz, 'Fostering Young Learners' Listening and Speaking Skills', in Garton and Copland, *The Routledge Handbook of Teaching English*, p. 174.

53 Gordon, *Teaching Young Children a Second Language*, p. 86.

54 Ibid., pp. 87–8.

55 Tabors, *One Child, Two Languages*, p. 119.

56 Ibid., p. 121.

57 Gordon, *Teaching Young Children a Second Language*, p. 96.

58 Ibid., p. 99.

59 Ibid., p. 100.

60 Ibid., p. 104.

61 Kirkgoz, 'Fostering Young Learners' Listening'.

62 Murao, 'English in Pre-primary', p. 56.

63 Ibid., p. 62.

64 See Graham *Creating Chants and Songs* and the YouTube videos, referenced in n.51, above.

65 Murao, 'English in Pre-primary', p. 64.

66 Sandie Murao, 'The Potential of Picturebooks with Young Learners', in Bland, *Teaching English to Young Learners*, pp. 199–218.

67 Ibid., p. 204; Annie Kubler, *Head, Shoulders, Knees and Toes* (Swindon: Child's Play, 2001).

68 Murao, 'The Potential of Picturebooks', p. 208; Chris Raschka, *Yo! Yes?* (New York: Scholastic, 1993).

69 Murao, 'The Potential of Picturebooks', p. 208. The quote is from the Council of Europe, *Common European Framework of Reference for*

Languages: Learning, Teaching, Assessment (Cambridge: Cambridge University Press, 2001).

70 Janice Bland, 'Learning through Literature', in Garton and Copland, *The Routledge Handbook of Teaching English*, p. 269.

71 Ibid., p. 272.

72 Janice Bland, 'Grammar Templates for the Future with Poetry for Children', in Bland, *Teaching English to Young Learners*, p. 155.

73 Ibid., p. 156. She acknowledges that the concept of 'overlearning' is taken from Brian Boyd, *On the Origin of Stories: Evolution, Cognition, and Fiction* (Harvard: Harvard University Press, 2009), p. 180.

74 Bland, 'Grammar Templates', p. 163.

75 Bland, 'Learning through Literature', p. 273.

76 Ibid., p. 275.

77 Janice Bland, 'Oral Storytelling in the Primary English Classroom', in Bland, *Teaching English to Young Learners*, p. 190.

78 Janice Bland, 'Drama with Young Learners', in Bland, *Teaching English to Young Learners*, pp. 221–2.

79 Ibid., pp. 219–20.

80 Ibid., p. 223. The reference is to Zoltan Dornyei, 'Creating a Motivating Classroom Environment', in Jim Cummins and Chris Davidson (eds), *International Handbook of English Language Teaching* (New York: Springer, 2007), pp. 721–2.

81 Ibid., p. 220. The reference is to Muriel Saville-Troike, *Introducing Second Language Acquisition* (Cambridge: Cambridge University Press, 2006), p. 82.

82 Bland, 'Drama with Young Learners', p. 223.

83 Ibid., p. 225.

84 Ibid., pp. 233–4.

85 See *The RSC Shakespeare Toolkit for Primary Teachers: An Active Approach to Bringing Shakespeare's Plays to Life in the Classroom* (London: Methuen Drama, 2014), p. 266.

CHAPTER TWO

1 Manfred Schewe, 'Taking Stock and Looking Ahead: Drama Pedagogy as a Gateway to a Performative Teaching and Learning Culture', *Scenario* 7, no. 1 (2013), p. 20.

2 Erika Piazzoli, *Embodying Language in Action: The Artistry of Process Drama in Second Language Education* (London: Palgrave Macmillan, 2018). For a thorough, readable guide to recent studies in performance, see Marvin Carlson, *Performance: A Critical Introduction*, 2nd ed. (New York: Routledge, 2004).

3 See Richard Schechner, *Performance Studies: An Introduction*, 3rd ed. (New York: Routledge, 2013), p. 42, cited in Piazzoli, *Embodying Language in Action*, p. 39.

4 John Austin, *How to Do Things with Words* (Cambridge, MA: Harvard University Press, 1975). The quote is from Carlson, *Performance*, p. 62.

5 Piazzoli, *Embodying Language in Action*, p. 39.

6 Schewe, 'Taking Stock and Looking Ahead', p. 19.

7 Piazzoli, *Embodying Language in Action*, p. 39.

8 See, for example, Nicola Shaughnessy, ed., *Affective Performance and Cognitive Science: Body, Brain and Being* (London: Bloomsbury, 2013).

9 Mark Johnson, *The Meaning of the Body: Aesthetics of Human Understanding* (Chicago: University of Chicago Press, 2008), p. 11.

10 Ibid., p. 2.

11 Piazzoli, *Embodying Language in Action*, p. 28. The quote is from Claire Coleman, 'Precarious Repurposing: Learning Languages through the Seal Wife', *NJ: Drama Australia Journal* 41, no. 1 (2017), p. 32.

12 Ibid., pp. 31–2.

13 I am aware, of course, that children with autism need specific help with such reading of body language. This book does not focus on their specific needs. Teachers looking for specific support for planning activities in this area may well wish to refer to books by Michelle Garcia Winner.

14 Both these examples can be found contextualized in schemes later outlined in this book.

15 John Dewey, *Experience and Education* (first published by Kappa Delta Pi, 1938; New York: Touchstone, 1997), pp. 26–7.

16 John Dewey, *Art as Experience* (New York: Penguin, [1934] 2005).

17 The quote is Dewey's, taken from Matthew DeCoursey, *Embodied Aesthetics in Drama Education: Theatre, Literature and Philosophy* (London: Bloomsbury, 2019), p. 33.

18 Ibid., p. 125.

19 Ibid., p. 131.

20 Pat Broadhead, *Early Years Play and Learning: Developing Skills and Co-operation* (London: Routledge, 2004).

21 Ibid., pp. 35 and 39.

22 Guy Cook, *Language Play, Language Learning* (Oxford: Oxford University Press, 2000).

23 Ibid., p. 201.

24 Mario Herrera and Diane Pinkley, *Backpack Gold, Level 2 Teacher's Book* (Harlow, Essex: Pearson Education, 2010), pp. T33–T44. The story is credited to Pinkley.

25 For the importance of dissonance and harmony in the internal play of the brain, see DeCoursey, *Embodied Aesthetics in Drama Education*, pp. 47–8, where he draws upon Paul Armstrong's *How Literature Plays with the*

Brain: The Neuroscience of Reading and Art (Baltimore: John Hopkins University Press, 2013).

26 See, for example, Flora Annie Steel, 'The Two Sisters: An English Fairy Tale', available on whisperingbooks.com; and Joseph Jacobs, 'The Old Witch', in *English Fairy Tales* (London: Everyman, [1890] 1993), pp. 312–17.

27 Maurice Sendak, *Where the Wild Things Are* (London: Penguin Random House, [1963] 2000).

28 David McKee, *Not Now, Bernard* (London: Red Fox, [1980] 1996).

29 These specific examples are taken from the wonderful retelling by Geraldine McCaughrean and Moira Kemp, *Grandma Chicken Legs* (London: Corgi Books, 2000), which has been a favourite of my granddaughter's since the age of 3.

30 Janice Bland, 'Learning through Literature', in Sue Garton and Fiona Copland (eds), *The Routledge Handbook of Teaching English to Young Learners* (London: Routledge, 2019), p. 270.

31 You can find a range of titles promoting aspects of diversity on the following websites: https://childhood101.com/picture-books-celebrating-who-you-are-individuality; https://www.parentmap.com/article/picture-books-diversity-kids-disability-race-gender; https://bookriot.com/childrens-books-about-diversity.

32 Janet Enever, *Early Language Learning in Europe* (London: British Council, 2011).

33 Fred Inglis and Lesley Aers, *Key Concepts in Education* (London: Sage, 2008), p. 99.

34 Piazzoli, *Embodying Language in Action*, pp. 33–8.

35 Ibid., p. 41. The quote is taken from Michael Fleming, 'Exploring the Concept of Performative Teaching and Learning', in Susanne Even and Manfred Schewe (eds), *Performative Teaching, Learning and Research* (Berlin: Schibri Verlag, 2016), p. 203.

36 Julie Dunn and Susan Wright, 'Signs, Meaning and Embodiment: Learning and Pedagogy in the Early Years', in Michael Fleming, Liora Bresler and John O'Toole (eds), *The Routledge International Handbook of the Arts in Education* (London: Routledge, 2015), p. 224.

37 Ibid., p. 226.

CHAPTER THREE

1 Sarah Hillyard, 'Rhythmic Patterns in Stories and Word Order Production (Adjective+) in Four-Year-Old EFL Learners', in Victoria A. Murphy and Maria Evangelou (eds), *Early Childhood Education in English for Speakers of Other Languages* (London: British Council, 2016), p. 283.

2 Frann Preston-Gannon, *Dinosaur Farm* (London: Pavilion Children's Books, 2013).

3 More examples can be found on subscription at www.activemusicdigital.co.uk.

4 Marcus Pfister, *The Rainbow Fish* (New York: North South Books, 1992); Jarvis, *Mrs Mole, I'm Home!* (London: Walker, 2017).

5 To introduce, for example, Mal Peet, Elspeth Graham and Jez Tuya, *The Treasure of Pirate Frank* (London: Nosy Crow, 2017).

6 More examples can be found in Lucinda Geoghegan, *Singing Games and Rhymes for Early Years* (Glasgow: National Youth Choir of Scotland, 1999); and Cyrilla Rowsell and David Vinden, *The Music Handbook: Teaching Music Skills to Children through Singing: Beginners* (Chigwell, Essex: Jolly Learning, 2008).

7 Robert Roennfeldt, *Tiddalick the Frog Who Caused a Flood: An Adaptation of an Aboriginal Dreamtime Legend* (Victoria: Puffin Books Australia, 1980).

8 Eileen Browne, *Handa's Surprise* (London: Walker, 1994).

9 Marc Martin, *A River* (London: Templar, 2016).

CHAPTER FOUR

1 Ed Vere, *Max the Brave* (London: Puffin, 2014).

2 *The Little Red Hen*, retold by Vera Southgate and illustrated by Stephen Holmes (London: Ladybird Books, 1986).

3 Ed Vere, *Max at Night* (London: Puffin, 2015).

4 Michael Rosen and Helen Oxenbury, *We're Going on a Bear Hunt* (London: Walker Books, 1993).

5 There are many versions of this story, of course. Keep your own retelling focused and simple, emphasizing the repetition.

CHAPTER FIVE

1 Tom MacRae and Elena Odriozola, *The Opposite* (London: Andersen, 2006).

2 See, for example, Susan Young and Joanna Glover, *Music in the Early Years* (London: Falmer, 1998), pp. 100–1.

3 Beatrix Potter, *The Tale of Peter Rabbit* (London: Frederick Warne, [1902] 2002).

4 Jonathan Bate, *English Literature: A Very Short Introduction* (Oxford: Oxford University Press, 2010), p. 3.

5 Ellen Handler Spitz, *Inside Picture Books* (New Haven, CT: Yale University Press, 2000), pp. 146–52.

6 Published by Penguin in 2007.

7 Beatrix Potter, *The Tale of Benjamin Bunny* (London: Frederick Warne, [1904] 2002).

8 John Burningham, *The Shopping Basket* (London: Red Fox, [1980] 2000).

9   Hans Christian Andersen, 'The Emperor's New Clothes', in *Hans Andersen's Fairy Tales*, chosen by Naomi Lewis (London: Puffin, 1981), pp. 35–42.

CHAPTER SIX

1   See Szilvia Papp, 'Assessment of Young English Learners', in Sue Garton and Fiona Copland (eds), *The Routledge Handbook of Teaching English to Young Learners* (London: Routledge, 2019). This chapter, nineteen pages in length, includes five pages of references to one hundred different publications.

2   This point is expounded on at length in Carmen Becker, 'Assessment and Portfolios', in Janice Bland (ed.), *Teaching English to Young Learners: Critical Issues in Language Teaching with 3–12 Year Olds* (London: Bloomsbury, 2015), pp. 261–2; and in Papp, 'Assessment of Young English Learners', pp. 389–91.

3   See Becker, 'Assessment and Portfolios', p. 262, where she references two publications as particularly informative here: Lynne Cameron, *Teaching Languages to Young Learners* (Cambridge: Cambridge University Press, 2002); and Penny McKay, *Assessing Young Language Learners* (Cambridge: Cambridge University Press, 2006).

4   For another perspective on how assessment and evaluation are conceptualized in performative language teaching, see Erika Piazzoli, *Embodying Language in Action: The Artistry of Process Drama in Second Language Education* (London: Palgrave Macmillan, 2018), p. 202.

5   See Papp, 'Assessment of Young English Learners', p. 390.

6   Council of Europe, *Common European Framework of References for Language: Learning, Teaching, Assessment, Companion Volume*, April 2020, updated and made available online (https://www.coe.int/en/web/common-european-framework-reference-languages/reference-level-descriptions).

7   Mario Herrera and Diane Pinkley, *Backpack Gold, Level 2 Teacher's Book* (Harlow, Essex: Pearson Education, 2010), p. T150.

8   Bell Foundation, *EAL Assessment Framework for Schools: Primary*, September 2017, bell-foundation.org.uk.

9   Ibid., p. 5.

10 Council of Europe, *Common European Framework of References for Language*, p. 134.

11 Becker, 'Assessment and Portfolios', pp. 266–75.

12 For those readers who wish also to incorporate assessment in children's social skills and the performing arts, see chapter 6 in *Beginning Drama: 4–11*, 3rd ed. (London: Routledge, 2009), co-authored by myself and Miles Tandy. See also Susan Young and Joanna Glover, *Music in the Early Years* (London: Falmer, 1998), which provides straightforward assessment points at the end of each chapter.

13 Helen Nicholson, *Theatre, Education and Performance: The Map and the Story* (London: Palgrave Macmillan, 2011), p. 7.

INDEX

Note: Endnotes are indicated by the page number followed by "n" and the endnote number e.g., 20n1 refers to endnote 1 on page 20.

www.ingramcontent.com/pod-product-compliance
Ingram Content Group UK Ltd.
Pitfield, Milton Keynes, MK11 3LW, UK
UKHW020700280225
455688UK00004B/193